Smithsonian
American Women

Reach for the stars!
Sally Ride

SMITHSONIAN
AMERICAN
WOMEN

❖

REMARKABLE OBJECTS AND STORIES
OF STRENGTH, INGENUITY, AND VISION
FROM THE NATIONAL COLLECTION

FOREWORD BY Jill Lepore

INTRODUCTION BY Michelle Delaney

EDITED BY Victoria Pope and Christine Schrum

SMITHSONIAN EDITORIAL COMMITTEE Nancy Bercaw, Michelle Delaney,
Lisa Kathleen Graddy, Matthew Shindell,
and Margaret Weitekamp

Smithsonian Books
Washington, DC

CONTENTS

PAGE 2

❖ In this ca. 1980 portrait, Sally K. Ride wears
NASA logo and a Space Shuttle Mission
STS-7 patches. Ride made history on this
space flight, as the first American woman
in space. Ride autographed this print with
an inspirational "Reach for the Stars!"

CHAPTER ONE: 1600–1864

Tradition and Resistance in a Young Nation

CHAPTER TWO: 1865–1920

The Road to Reform

Anacostia Community Museum

Alcione M. Amos, Museum Curator .... AMA

Miriam Doutriaux, Collections Manager .... MD

Jennifer Morris, Archivist .... JM

Archives of American Art

Emily D. Shapiro, Managing Editor, *Archives of American Art Journal* .... EDS

Rihoko Ueno, Archivist .... RU

Arts & Industries Building

Abraham Thomas, Senior Curator .... AT

Asian Pacific American Center

Kālewa Correa, Curator of Hawai'i and the Pacific .... KA

Center for Folklife and Cultural Heritage

Stephanie D. L. Smith, Archives Director .... SS

Cooper Hewitt, Smithsonian Design Museum

Emily M. Orr, Assistant Curator of Modern and Contemporary American Design .... EMO

Freer Gallery of Art and Arthour M. Sackler Gallery

Lisa Fthenakis, Archivist .... AT

Hirshhorn Museum and Sculpture Garden

Sandy Guttman, Curatorial Assistant .... SAG

Evelyn C. Hankins, Senior Curator .... EH

Betsy Johnson, Assistant Curator .... BJ

Anne Reeve, Associate Curator .... AR

National Air and Space Museum

Paul E. Ceruzzi, Curator Emeritus .... PEC

Dorothy S. Cochrane, Curator, General Aviation .... DSC

David H. DeVorkin, Senior Curator, History of Astronomy .... DHD

Valerie Neal, Curator and Chair, Space History Department .... VN

Matthew Shindell, Curator of Planetary Science and Exploration, Space History Department .... MBS

Alex M. Spencer, Curator, Aeronautics Department .... AS

F. Robert van der Linden, Curator of Air Transportation, Aeronautics Department .... FRV

Margaret A. Weitekamp, Curator, Space History Department .... MW

National Museum of African American History and Culture

Aaron Bryant, Curator of Photography .... AEB

Rhea L. Combs, Supervisory Curator of Photography and Film .... RLC

Ariana A. Curtis, Curator of Latinx Studies .... AAC

Mary N. Elliott, Curator of American Slavery .... MNE

Rex M. Ellis, Associate Director Emeritus for Curatorial Affairs .... RE

Paul Gardullo, Supervisory Curator .... PG

Michèle Gates Moresi, Supervisory Curator of Collections .... MGM

Joanne Hyppolite, Supervisory Curator of the African Diaspora .... JH

Loren E. Miller, Curatorial Assistant .... LEM

Elaine Nichols, Senior Curator of Culture .... EN

William S. Pretzer, Senior Curator of History .... WSP

Dwandalyn R. Reece, Curator of Music and the Performing Arts .... DRR

Deborah Tulani Salahu-Din, Museum Specialist, Office of Curatorial Affairs .... DTS

Krewasky A. Salter, Military History Gallery Curator .... KAS

Kevin M. Strait, Curator .... KMS

Damion L. Thomas, Curator of Sports .... DLT

Doretha K. Williams, Program Manager, The Robert F. Smith Fund and Explore Your Family History Center .... DKW

National Museum of American History

Rachel L. Anderson, Research Assistant, Division of Medicine and Science .... RLA

Bethanee Bemis, Museum Specialist, Political History, Division of Political and Military History .... BB

Nancy Bercaw, Curator and Chair, Division of Political and Military History .... NB

Hanna BredenbeckCorp, Project Assistant, Division of Cultural and Community Life .... HB

Judy M. Chelnick, Curator, Medical History, Division of Medicine and Science .... JMC

Kenneth Cohen, Edward and Helen Hintz Secretarial Scholar and Curator, American Culture and Politics, Divisions of Cultural and Community Life, Political and Military History .... KC

Nancy E. Davis, Curator Emeritus, Costume History, Division of Cultural and Community Life .... NED

Virginia Eisemon, Volunteer, Textiles Collection, Division of Cultural and Community Life .... VE

Kristen M. Frederick-Frost, Curator, Modern Science History, Division of Medicine and Science .... KFF

Kathleen Golden, Curator, Military History, Division of Political and Military History .... KAG

Lisa Kathleen Graddy, Curator, Political History, Division of Political and Military History .... LKG

Connie Holland, Project Assistant, Office of Curatorial Affairs .... CH

Eric W. Jentsch, Lead Curator, Entertainment and Sports, Division of Cultural and Community Life .... EWJ

E. Claire Jerry, Lead Curator, Political History, Division of Political and Military History .... ECJ

Paula J. Johnson, Curator, Food History, Division of Work and Industry .... PJJ

Stacey Kluck, Chair, Division of Cultural and Community Life .... SK

Peter Liebhold, Curator, Manufacturing and Working Class History, Division of Work and Industry .... PL

Sara Murphy, Museum Specialist, Political History, Division of Political and Military History .... SM

Shelley K. Nickles, Curator, Social and Cultural History, Division of Cultural and Community Life .... SKN

Katherine Ott, Curator, Medical History, Division of Medicine and Science .... KO

Jane Rogers, Curator, Sports History, Division of Cultural and Community Life .... JR

Harry R. Rubenstein, Curator Emeritus, Political History, Division of Political and Military History .... HRR

Fath Davis Ruffins, Curator, African American History and Culture, Division of Cultural and Community Life .... FDR

Noriko Sanefuji, Museum Specialist, Asian Pacific American History, Division of Cultural and Community Life .... NS

Debbie Schaefer-Jacobs, Curator, Education History, Division of Cultural and Community Life .... DSJ

Madelyn Shaw, Curator, Textile History, Division of Cultural and Community Life .... MCS

Barbara Clark Smith, Curator, Political History, Division of Political and Military History .... BCS

Carlene E. Stephens, Curator, Science and Technology History, Division of Work and Industry .... CES

Miranda Summers Lowe, Curator, Modern Military History, Division of Political and Military History .... MSL

John Troutman, Curator, American Music History, Division of Cultural and Community Life .... JT

L. Stephen Velasquez, Curator, Latinx History and Culture, Division of Cultural and Community Life .... LSV

Deborah Jean Warner, Curator, Science and Technology History, Division of Medicine and Science .... DJW

Mallory Warner, Museum Specialist, Division of Medicine and Science .... MW

Timothy K. Winkle, Curator, Community Organization History, Division of Cultural and Community Life .... TKW

Tsione Wolde-Michael, Jefferson Fellow, Division of Political and Military History .... TWM

William H. Yeingst, Curator Emeritus, Domestic Life History, Division of Cultural and Community Life .... WHY

National Museum of the American Indian

Cécile R. Ganteaume, Curator, Museum Research and Scholarship .... CRG

Rachel Menyuk, Processing Archivist .... RM

Rebecca Head Trautmann, Assistant Curator of Contemporary Art .... RHT

National Museum of Natural History

Adrienne L. Kaeppler, Curator of Oceanic Ethnology, Department of Anthropology .... ALK

National Portrait Gallery

Robyn Asleson, Curator, Prints and Drawings Department .... RA

Taína B. Caragol, Curator of Painting and Sculpture and Latinx Art and History .... TC

Brandon B. Fortune, Chief Curator .... BBF

Kate Clarke Lemay, Historian .... KCL

Dorothy Moss, Curator of Painting and Sculpture .... DM

Ann M. Shumard, Senior Curator of Photographs .... AMS

National Postal Museum

Lynn Heidelbaugh, Curator of Postal Operations .... LH

Daniel A. Piazza, Chief Curator of Philately .... DP

Office of the Provost and Under Secretary for Museums, Education, and Research

Jennifer A. Schneider, Program Manager, American Women's History Initiative .... JAS

Smithsonian American Art Museum

Saisha Grayson, Curator of Time-Based Media .... SG

Melissa Ho, Curator of Twentieth-Century Art .... MH

Karen Lemmey, Curator of Sculpture .... KL

Crawford Alexander Mann III, Curator of Prints and Drawing .... CAM

Virginia M. Mecklenburg, Chief Curator .... VMM

E. Carmen Ramos, Deputy Chief Curator and Curator of Latinx Art .... ECR

Leslie Umberger, Curator of Folk and Self-Taught Art .... LU

Smithsonian Gardens

Joyce Connolly, Museum Specialist, Collections Management and Education Department .... JMC

Kelly A. Crawford, Museum Specialist, Collections Management and Education Department .... KAC

Smithsonian Institution Archives

Pamela M. Henson, Historian, Institutional History Division .... PMH

Marcel Chotkowski LaFollette, Research Associate .... MCL

Thanks to Smithsonian staff and volunteers for their support:

Mark Avino, Erin Beasley, Cathy Carver, Alicia Cutler, Sam Dargan, Sunae Park Evans, Katherine Fogden, Debbie Hashim, Janice Hussain, Kate Igoe, Stephanie Kurasz, Manda Kowalczyk, Bill Lommel, Eric Long, Julia Murphy, Jaclyn Nash, Vanessa Pares, Dane Penland, Douglas Remley, Erin Rushing, Erik Satrum, Riche Sorensen, Nathan Sowry, Richard Strauss, Benjamin G. Sullivan, Hugh Talman, Leslie J. Ureña.

A very special thank you to Lori Yarrish, the late director of the Anacostia Community Museum, for her steadfast support of this project.

❖ Among the most poignant objects in the collections are artist and activist Faith Ringgold's narrative quilts, which include *Faith Ringgold Self-Portrait* (1998). Gorgeously stitched and meticulously hand painted, these works share memories of Ringgold's Harlem childhood and the lives of the women around her. As Ringgold has explained, "I began making quilts . . . to tell my story."

BECAUSE OF HER STORY

◐ Smithsonian

A T THE SMITHSONIAN INSTITUTION, the centennial of women's suffrage brings a sense of renewed commitment. For too long and still too often, women's stories have remained unheard and undervalued. Encouragingly, recent storytelling, whether about the excellence of female athletes, the achievements of women scientists, or the excitement surrounding the increasing number of female elected representatives, offers a welcome corrective.

As women's voices gain prominence at the national level, the work of providing context, exploring women's history, and understanding that history as *American* history is more vital than ever.

The Smithsonian is uniquely positioned to do this work. Through our museums, libraries, and research and education centers, the institution offers enormous depth of collections and expertise. These resources allow us to explore the richness of the American past and deepen our understanding of the present. At the same time, such an endeavor requires us to examine overlooked chapters in our own history, especially the many achievements and experiences of American women.

This is where the Smithsonian American Women's History Initiative, *Because of Her Story*, comes in. The initiative seeks to understand the ways in which women's stories, experiences, creativity, and labor have shaped and continue to shape this institution and this country. Marshaling resources from every corner of the Smithsonian, the initiative educates and inspires audiences across the country and the world.

Like the American Women's History Initiative, *Smithsonian American Women* illuminates a wide-ranging and complex set of stories, weaving together collections and expertise across the Smithsonian. This project has required collaborative work from staff across many different fields. It has strengthened connections throughout the institution and brought us closer to our goal of being "One Smithsonian" to amplify the power of the stories we tell. As codirectors of the initiative, we have been privileged to witness these collaborations in action—sewing colorful and diverse pieces into one expressive fabric.

From a nineteenth-century telescope to Amelia Earhart's flight suit, every object in this book tells a story. You'll find stories of innovation, creativity, and persistence. Tales of ordinary and extraordinary women, as diverse and multifaceted as the American experience. *Smithsonian American Women* illuminates and amplifies our country's history, giving voice to women across disciplines and decades to present a picture of what it means to be American. We hope you find it as inspirational as we do. ■

John Davis
Provost and Under Secretary for Museums, Education, and Research
Co-chair, Smithsonian American Women's History Initiative

Stephanie Stebich
The Margaret and Terry Stent Director, Smithsonian American Art Museum
Co-chair, Smithsonian American Women's History Initiative

A FEW YEARS BACK, I spent a cloudy spring morning in a public elementary school in my city, a city of families from all over the world. I walked past the playground, its swings and benches the colors of penny candy—Twizzlers, Starbursts, Life Savers—and into a building just as brightly lit, its hallways covered with murals, its stairwells decorated with tiles pressed with tiny handprints. I was there to visit a kindergarten classroom, a fleet of four- and five-year-olds who were studying the American Revolution.

Each kid had picked someone to study. Most of them couldn't write yet, or at least not more than a handful of letters or words, but they'd made portraits of their subjects, crayon on oak tag, and they'd learned little stories, and I'd come to hear them. We sat in a circle, criss-cross applesauce–style. When I'd asked the names of the people they'd picked, they shouted out, all in a tumble: "Benjamin Franklin!" "George Washington!" "Patrick Henry!" "Sam Adams!"

"Anyone here studying a woman?" Silence. "Why not?" I asked. And then a very little, very smart girl wearing a Spiderman T-shirt, the cornrows in her hair tipped with polka-dotted pink and purple beads, called out, "Because there were no women then!"

I would like to think that a book like *Smithsonian American Women* might not be necessary any more. Aren't women everywhere? And aren't these books old-fashioned? After all, American women, mainly white women, have been putting together books like this since at least 1850, when Sarah Josepha Hale, editor of *Godey's Lady's Book*, published her thousand-page *Woman's Record: Or, Sketches of All Distinguished Women, from the Beginning Till A.D. 1850.*But that little girl is a good reminder that this book is necessary, really necessary. Because that four-year-old girl, looking around, in her classroom, at the posters on the walls, in the picture books in her school library, she just didn't see any women (nor, for that matter, any people of color except for Martin Luther King Jr.). So, making a perfectly reasonable deduction from the available evidence, she decided that there must not have been any.

For a very long time, from the start, museums have been collecting objects like the amazing, beautiful, compelling, and even distressing things you'll see in this book. The stuff of women's daily lives, the relics of their political campaigns, the remains of their suffering, the products of their invention. Quilts, banners, looms, telescopes. But these objects haven't often been displayed, or interpreted, or, to be honest, they haven't usually even been catalogued under women's names (things made or owned by women were often listed under the names of their husbands who, until the reform of marriage laws, essentially owned them). There has also never been, in the world of historical museums, a revolution like the revolution waged by the Guerilla Girls in the world of art museums. Beginning in 1985, the Guerilla Girls, a New York–based feminist collective, began holding events and making art to protest the exclusion of art by women from museum walls. They plastered all over the city posters of sculptures of naked women wearing gorilla masks and added text that read, "Do women have to be naked to get into the Met Museum?" They made sassy, hot-pink, brilliantly biting handwritten

Dearest Art Collector,
It has come to our
attention that your
collection, like most,
does not contain
enough art by women.
We know that you
feel terrible about this
and will rectify the
situation immediately.
All our love,
Guerrilla Girls

BOX 1056 COOPER STA., NY NY 10276

Dearest Art Collector (from *Portfolio Compleat: 1985–2012*), Guerrilla Girls, 1986

postcards that read, "Dear Art Collector, It has come to our attention that your collection, like most, does not contain enough art by women. We know that you feel terrible about this and will rectify the situation immediately. All our love, Guerilla Girls." I know a four-year-old girl who would have really loved that.

Dear Smithsonian Museum Curators, It has come to our attention that you are publishing a book of objects in your collections that chronicle the lives of American women, the lives of all sorts of American women. This is a good idea. Thank you, Jill Lepore. ■

JILL LEPORE IS THE KEMPER PROFESSOR OF AMERICAN HISTORY AT HARVARD. HER MANY BOOKS INCLUDE THESE TRUTHS: A HISTORY OF THE UNITED STATES.

"From the Smithsonian's earliest years, women have influenced the growth of the national collections to the 158 million objects we house today. From anthropological artifacts to American art to the First Ladies Collection, women have pushed the Smithsonian to represent a broader array of human experience." —**Pam Henson**, historian, Smithsonian Institution Archives

AS THE NATION CELEBRATES the one hundredth anniversary of the ratification of the Nineteenth Amendment, which gave voting rights to many, but not all, women, American women's history has achieved a new order of importance at the Smithsonian. Our curators are committed to acquiring, displaying, and interpreting objects that tell the stories of women—women of all races and gender expressions—many of whose achievements were hidden or underappreciated in the past. Reflecting the spirit of the new American Women's History Initiative, this volume charts rich territory in exploring diverse women's lives through the myriad collections of the Smithsonian. It gathers together one hundred scholars from sixteen Smithsonian museums, libraries, archives, and research centers to interpret the individual objects, collections, and stories of unique holdings of the institution that bring to life the remarkable and varied experiences of women.

When we came together to work on a book to commemorate the centennial of US women's suffrage, we quickly realized that we wanted this volume to cover more than amendments and laws. Like the second-wave feminists who popularized the expression, we believe the personal is political. We wanted this book to reflect the millions of individual choices, actions, and emotions that women experience every day—and that influence, and are influenced by, the world in which they live. As Smithsonian scholars met and discussed collections across the institution, the book's themes quickly emerged: women's rites of passage; their roles as trailblazers, activists, and professionals in the workplace; and their significant responsibilities at home and in their communities, representing agency over self-care and self-expression. *Smithsonian American Women* presents a broad look at the diverse experiences of American women and at the politics of, and challenges to, equality.

MICHELLE DELANEY IS SENIOR PROGRAM OFFICER FOR HISTORY AND CULTURE, SMITHSONIAN INSTITUTION.

❖ Sarah Hewitt (1859–1930) and Eleanor Hewitt (1864–1924) were strong, independent sisters who grew up wealthy in New York City during the Victorian era. The granddaughters of industrialist Peter Cooper, they embraced their grandfather's support of philanthropy, education, craftsmanship, and technology. The sisters longed to create a free museum to display their various collections of textiles, etchings, engravings, furniture, books, and plaster casts purchased from New York dealers and artists and during travels to Paris, London, Vienna, and Russia, and in 1897, they succeeded, opening the Cooper Union Museum. When World War I slowed international travel, the sisters crossed the United States instead and continued their collecting. In 1967, the Smithsonian purchased their collection and preserved it in New York City's Carnegie Mansion, where it has remained intact. In 2014, the museum was renamed the Cooper Hewitt, Smithsonian Design Museum. Today, it remains focused on the intersection of art and science, innovation, and creativity.

PAGE 13

❖ American portrait photographer Gertrude Käsebier (1852–1934) was best known for her painterly platinum images of New York City society, her fellow artists, and her children. This portrait of Zitkala-Ša (1876–1938) is one in a series of photographs taken at Käsebier's Fifth Avenue studio in 1898, in which the Yankton Sioux woman of Indian and white ancestry wore Native American dress and Western clothing. Born on the Pine Ridge Reservation in South Dakota, Zitkala-Ša was educated at reservation schools, the Carlisle Indian School in Pennsylvania, Earlham College in Indiana, and the Boston Conservatory of Music. Also known as Red Bird and Gertrude Simmons Bonnin, Zitkala-Ša became an accomplished author, musician, composer, and dedicated worker for the reform of Indian policies in the United States. A significant collection of Käsebier's photographs, including Zitkala-Ša's portraits, was donated to the Smithsonian in 1969 by Mina Turner, the photographer's granddaughter, and is now housed in the National Museum of American History's Photographic History Collection.

From Helen Keller's "touch watch" and Oprah Winfrey's iconic on-set couch to Maria Mitchell's telescope and Georgia O'Keeffe's *Manhattan* abstract painting, the objects selected for this book represent the current Smithsonian collections for art, history and culture, and science. Curators and archivists suggested more than two thousand objects for this volume. We have whittled down to 300 pieces to present and illuminate both individual and collective history and the strength, ingenuity, and vision of American women. New insights from the curators' research are represented in chapters incorporating a chronological history of women's impact on society from precolonial times to the present in America, with major contributions from the collections of the National Museum of American History, National Museum of African American History and Culture, National Portrait Gallery, and National Air and Space Museum.

We are seeking to restore a history too frequently ignored. Curatorial research and collecting efforts have expanded greatly in the past century. Examples of the slow change to hire female staff and to collect specific items related to American women's history are documented in Smithsonian archives. In 1918, the Smithsonian was offered a portrait of Susan B. Anthony for the history collections. The curator, Theodore Belote, politely declined, indicating the painting might be more appropriate for the national portrait collection in the future. One year later, in June 1919, the female leaders of the National American Woman Suffrage Association (NAWSA) succeeded with the passage of the Nineteenth Amendment to the Constitution by both houses of Congress. With characteristic tenacity, Helen Gardner, vice president of NAWSA, approached the Smithsonian again for the donation of the Anthony portrait and additional objects related to the American woman suffrage movement. This time, Head Curator William Henry Holmes accepted the gift, declaring, "There can be no question of the historical importance of the movement initiated by Miss Anthony and now carried out to a successful ending." The institution started the long path to cultural change.

The Smithsonian has been fortunate to have extraordinary women in science, art, and history and culture within its walls as well. Nonetheless, records show that for decades in the late nineteenth and early twentieth centuries, many women at the Smithsonian were volunteers or received little compensation compared with their male colleagues. Mary Jane Rathbun, copyist in the marine invertebrate collection, and botanist Agnes Chase forged long and distinguished tenures at the institution. They opened new career opportunities for generations of scientists, including such contemporary women as astrophysicist Margaret Geller of the Smithsonian Astrophysical Observatory. The Cooper Hewitt, Smithsonian Design Museum, located in New York City, was founded by sisters Eleanor and Sarah Hewitt, who used ingenuity and entrepreneurial savvy to amass a varied collection of American and international furniture, textiles, ceramics, and much more. At the National Museum of American History, curator emerita Bernice Johnson Reagon documented many aspects of African American music and hosted the Smithsonian Folkways/National Public Radio series *Wade in the Water: African American Sacred Music Traditions*.

As we collaborated to produce this volume, many of the Smithsonian scholars learned new things about the history of their predecessors and collecting over time for the US National Museum and the growing institution. One key objective of the project was to recover the histories of women of color in order to consider a broader understanding of women in America. The institution's expanded efforts to collect and interpret a more inclusive American history continues into the twenty-first century. With the establishment of the National Museum of the American Indian in 1989, the Smithsonian Latino Center and Asian Pacific American Program in 1997, and the National Museum of African American History and Culture in 2003, the Smithsonian became both more inclusive and more diverse. Recent collecting efforts reflect a keen desire on the part of curators to look closely at the contributions of women of color, including photographs of Sylvia Rivera, a Latina whose important LGBTQ+ activist work in the history of New York gay and transgender communities is now documented in the national collections. Many families and communities helped the Smithsonian to create a more comprehensive history by donating materials belonging to women who excelled in their fields despite the many obstacles placed in their way.

Scholars at the National Museum of the American Indian interpret the lives and material culture of women who worked both within and outside their respective Native communities. Curator Cécile Ganteaume points

❖ Gertrude French Howalt (1897–1994) wore this yeoman (F)—the letter *F* suffix indicated her status as female—uniform during her service in World War I. The Naval Reserve Act of 1916 established the right for the enlistment of qualified "persons," which made it possible for women to join the Naval Coast Defense Reserve on the home front and perform needed tasks as telegraphers, translators, clerks, stenographers, mess attendants, ship camouflage designers, and recruiting agents. Twelve thousand women enlisted in the navy and served the nation during the war, but all were discharged in peacetime by July 1919. Some women veterans were eventually hired by the federal civil service. Howalt's Norfolk-style yeoman's uniform included a jacket in navy blue with gold buttons, an A-line skirt, and a wide-brimmed sailor-style blue felt hat. Today, the uniform is part of a significant collection of women's World War I military uniforms in the Armed Forces History Collection of the National Museum of American History.

❖ This 2005 Marian Anderson thirty-seven-cent stamp is part of the Black Heritage Series collection. The stamp features an Albert Slark oil painting, which was inspired by an original photograph taken in Stockholm, Sweden, during Anderson's 1934 international concert tour. America's foremost opera singer from the 1930s to the 1960s, Anderson faced racial discrimination and a struggle for success in a nation of inequality. In 1939, when denied the opportunity to perform in Constitution Hall in Washington, Anderson (1897–1933) famously held an Easter Sunday concert on the steps of the city's Lincoln Memorial; President Franklin Roosevelt arranged for the event at the urging of supporters Eleanor Roosevelt and Secretary of the Interior Harold Ickes. The award-winning Anderson was talented in a range of musical styles, including opera, traditional American songs, and African American spirituals. Materials and clothing from her long career have been collected across the Smithsonian, including at the National Museum of African American History and Culture, the National Museum of American History, the National Portrait Gallery, and the Anacostia Community Museum. This original stamp art is part of the collection of the National Postal Museum.

BLACK HERITAGE
USA 37
Marian Anderson
2005

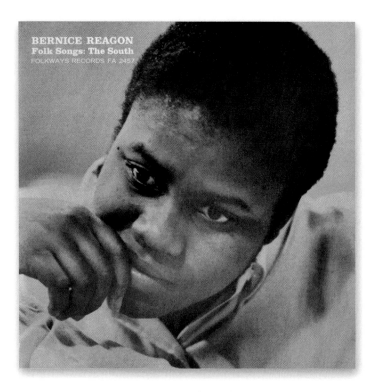

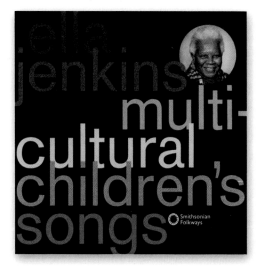

❖ Smithsonian Folkways artists Bernice Johnson Reagon, Hazel Dickens, Alice Gerrard, Barbara Dane, and Ella Jenkins are all pioneering American musicians and sociopolitical advocates. Bernice Johnson Reagon's profound contributions began as a founding member of the Student Nonviolent Coordinating Committee (SNCC) Freedom Singers, which traveled nationally in the 1960s to raise money for civil rights causes. Later, Reagon joined the Smithsonian as a curator and scholar at the National Museum of American History. Hazel Dickens (1935–2011) and Alice Gerrard broke ground by establishing the first female bluegrass duo. During their career together, they released two full-length albums on Folkways Records: *Won't You Come and Sing for Me?* (1965) and *Who's that Knocking?* (1973). In 1996, these albums were combined and released together as *Pioneering Women of Bluegrass*. Barbara Dane's album, *When We Make It Through*, is a rousing tribute to working-class women and men. It was released in 1982 on Paredon Records, a label that Dane cofounded with Irwin Silber in 1969 and operated until donating it to the Smithsonian in 1991. Ella Jenkins has achieved a six-decade career in children's music. As a GRAMMY Award winner and National Endowment for the Arts National Heritage Fellow, she has dozens of albums on Smithsonian Folkways Recordings. The Center for Folklife and Cultural Heritage holds the archives of Smithsonian Folkways and is committed to keeping the commercial collection available to the public in perpetuity, including the work of these five premier women folk artists.

out that "Native American women either worked in very traditional ways within their own communities to confront and deal with contemporary situations or embraced making a mark within mainstream society and taking on Western roles to meet their needs." Objects selected from that museum for this book represent Native American women in a wide range of roles, from traditional basket weavers to university-trained professionals, including anthropologists. The museum will open the National Native American Veterans Memorial in 2020 and continues to acquire collections and stories of Native American women in the military.

The National Museum of African American History and Culture has become a repository for biographical materials and objects of noteworthy black women, in slavery and freedom from precolonial to modern day. Founding director Lonnie G. Bunch III, now the secretary of the Smithsonian, quickly hired a strong and energetic curatorial team, including many female scholars, to build the newest Smithsonian collection. Sometimes objects and images did not exist, so words were all that could be collected from the personal narratives of African American women. But extensive community research and sheer determination helped curators locate thousands of items representing African American women living in every region of our nation. From the letters and papers of New York and California–based architect Norma Sklarek to luminous works by expressionist painter and arts educator Alma Thomas, the museum's large holdings of art, fashion, and photography represent the creativity, passion, and entrepreneurship of African American women successful in their professions.

But *Smithsonian American Women* does more than highlight unique achievements; it also seeks to explore women's everyday realities. Thanks to the medicine and health collections at the National Museum of American History, objects related to female reproductive health—including early sanitary napkins made from moss—are part of this book's narrative. Military collections across Smithsonian museums incorporate the uniforms and equipment used by women who have served the country, from the Civil War to the present, with great honor but little recognition.

As the Smithsonian Institution commemorates the ratification of the Nineteenth Amendment in 1920, we remember that the fight for women's voting rights did not end then. In 1924, the Indian Citizenship Act was passed in the United States, but racist policies and obstructive practices in some states still prevent many Native American women from voting in regular elections. Only in 1952, with the passage of the McCarran-Walter Act, were the race restrictions of the Naturalization Act of 1790 repealed, thereby granting voting rights and citizenship to Japanese Americans, including women. Although the Voting Rights Act of 1965 prohibited racial discrimination in voting across the nation, the civil rights movement still needed to advocate for practical access to the ballot for African American women and men in many communities. And battles over voter registration laws and voter suppression continue to affect women's access to the franchise to this day.

Self-expression, activism, and the freedom and right to work and to live an equal existence—these themes are all reflected in the struggles and triumphs of the women in these pages. The diversity preserved within the Smithsonian's national collections of art, history and culture, and science document not only some of the most compelling and complex stories of American women but also their lasting impact on a nation. Through exhibitions and educational programs, we are able to focus our attention on American women throughout time, bringing them from the sidelines of history to the foreground.

These powerful stories demonstrate that it was through women's active struggle to participate in, and contribute to, the life of this nation that they saw their rights expanded; it was by dint of their ambition and entrepreneurship that they gained footholds in the American economy; it was their hard-fought campaigns for the Nineteenth Amendment and public office that brought them into the halls of state and federal government; it was their contributions to the arts that garnered the United States one of the most creative and dynamic art communities in the world; and it was because of their dedication to health, family, community life, and national defense that they connected the domestic to the civic in an ever-evolving and developing country. Women continue to innovate despite being under very real constraints. The Smithsonian remains committed to collecting and sharing these diverse women's stories and voices, even as we continue to reexamine and reinterpret what is already within the collections. ∎

CHAPTER ONE

1600-1864

Tradition and Resistance in a Young Nation

COLONIAL NORTH AMERICA was an assortment of cultures without a shared idea of what it meant to be a woman; women defined their place and the source of their power quite differently depending on circumstance. As peoples from Europe, Africa, and the Americas sought to conquer or free themselves, some women took advantage of this chaos. In the 1600s, English Puritan Anne Hutchison defied male authority and claimed spiritual leadership. In the 1700s, Elizabeth Freeman, an enslaved woman, used the courts to sue for her freedom and won, setting a precedent for the abolition of slavery.

The formation of the United States provided women with a common language of liberty, even as their experiences remained different from men, and from one another. In 1832, Maria Stewart, an African American journalist, was the first American woman to speak in public linking abolition to women's rights. In 1848, women gathered in Seneca Falls, New York, to demand equal rights—consciously building on Iroquois concepts of womanhood to claim power in community decision making. In the arts, the celebrated, gender-bending actress Charlotte Cushman played Hamlet and new male roles.

Their actions reverberate today as women continue to use art, politics, culture, work, religion, and innovation to express and debate their understandings of American belonging. ■

Seneca woman's outfit
(ca. 1830–70), Tonawanda
Reservation, New York

PREVIOUS SPREAD

Seneca Finery

This calico dress, decorated with 216 etched-silver brooches, glass beads, and silk ribbon, belonged to Gagwi ya ta, or Charlotte Sundown (1853–1911), a member of the Beaver Clan of the Tonawanda Band of Seneca Indians. In the mid-nineteenth century, a treaty signed by the Seneca Nation called for the sale of Tonawanda land in western New York and the adoption of a new form of government. In opposition, Tonawanda seceded from the Seneca Nation.

Born seven years after that separation, Gagwi ya ta steadfastly maintained Seneca dressmaking traditions. This outfit, complete with leggings and beaded slippers, included hide, porcupine quill, and sinew as decorative elements. The abundance of silver brooches on it signifies it was worn on special occasions. Although Gagwi ya ta was not a clan mother, her dress was typical of those worn by clan mothers, who wielded significant authority at Tonawanda council meetings. Gagwi ya ta died in 1911, during a flu epidemic. —CRG

Pocahontas is born in what is now Virginia. As the daughter of a Native American chief, she acts as a peacemaker between her Powhatan tribe and English colonists.

The first enslaved African women arrive in Jamestown.

The Salem witch trials disproportionately affect the women of Salem, Massachusetts. The town is irrevocably changed as accusations of witchcraft being practiced spread.

The American Revolutionary War begins, ending in 1783.

Abigail Adams writes her "remember the ladies" letter to her husband, Congressman John Adams, urging him to address women in the "code of laws" that might accompany any declaration of independence.

Martha Washington becomes the first first lady of the United States.

Sacagawea, along with her infant son, joins Lewis and Clark on their expedition to the Pacific Ocean.

Sojourner Truth, having escaped to freedom with her infant daughter in 1826, wins a legal battle against a white man to secure freedom for her son.

Oberlin College becomes the first United States college to admit women as well as men for a baccalaureate, and the first to enroll both black and white students.

Led by Elizabeth Cady Stanton, women gather at the Seneca Falls Convention and craft the Declaration of Sentiments.

The American Civil War begins.

As a strategic move in the Civil War, President Abraham Lincoln issues the Emancipation Proclamation, freeing all enslaved people in the Confederate States of America.

Harriet Tubman leads the Combahee River Raid, ultimately freeing over seven hundred enslaved men, women, and children.

Sampler, embroidered by Abigail Adams, silk cross-stitch embroidery on linen foundation, 1789

Silhouette of Martha Washington, unidentified artist, nineteenth century

Sacajawea dollar coin, United States Mint, 2000

Matte collodion photograph of Harriet Tubman, Harvey B. Lindsley, ca. 1871–76

The Proclamation of Emancipation, by the President of the United States, to take effect January 1st, 1863, written by

Invoking Earth Mother

A COMPLEX AGRICULTURAL SOCIETY flourished from 900 to 1600 CE in what is now known as the southeastern United States. The people who lived in the region, the Mississippians, crafted sculptural clay effigy bottles like this one in reverence of the divine feminine.

These Native American societies built large towns all along the Mississippi River valley and its vast surrounding area. Their great, open plazas featured flat-topped earthen mounds on which stood temples and leaders' residences. For hundreds of years, women supported these major population centers by cultivating extensive maize, bean, and squash crops in large communal tracts and smaller family plots. Not just farmers, Mississippian women also owned, distributed, stored, and exchanged their bounty to feed and support their communities.

> **Made by Native American women, these female effigy bottles invoke the spiritual power of the supreme female deity, Earth Mother.**

Unlike patriarchal communities, the extended families in these societies organized themselves into clans based on their kinship to specific women, or clan mothers, to whom each member could trace his or her ancestry. While both clan and town membership were key to a Mississippian's sense of identity, a clan—and its maternal lineage—transcended town boundaries. As such, women were the center of clan identity and also played a key role in Mississippian religious ceremonies related to childbirth and death.

Much of Mississippian visual culture seems to revolve around male imagery and, more specifically, around warriors and their prowess. But the designs and figurative imagery found on objects like engraved shell cups, gorgets (ornamental collars), and embossed copper depict the place of humans in the cosmos and their relationships with the deities who inhabit both the underworld and the upper world.

Mississippians sculpted effigy figures from stone and clay in pairs, often portraying both a male and female to symbolize ancestral forms. However, especially after 1250, they also created sculptural clay vessels showing women on their own. These effigies typically represented Earth Mother, a feminine deity of the utmost importance in Mississippian thought. In the oral tradition of Mississippian descendants, Earth Mother (also known as Corn Mother) is believed to be responsible for gifting humankind with agricultural plants, most notably maize, beans, and squash. She is also closely associated with fertility, rebirth, and renewal.

This particular effigy bottle represents a woman with her hands resting on her knees. Although her chest is clearly defined, she is humpbacked, with a dramatically pronounced spine and protruding vertebrae that seem to signify advanced age (roughly half of all Mississippian female effigy bottles represent humpbacked women, whereas others sit erect, conveying youth). As in similar vessels made around this time, the woman here has her legs bent underneath her. The hairstyles on these effigies vary regionally; this figure, from northeast Arkansas, has an especially elaborate hair design that suggests social or religious significance.

Made by Mississippian women in the realm of the living, and around whom extended kin networks revolved, these sculptural clay effigy bottles acknowledge both the divine feminine and women's intimate association with its power. ■ —CRG

For more than two hundred years, in the 1400s and 1500s, women sculpted these female effigy bottles within present-day southeast Missouri, middle Tennessee, and northeast Arkansas.

MATOAKA ALS REBECCA FILIA POTENTISS PRINC POWHATANI IMP VIRGINIÆ

Ætatis suæ 21. Aᵒ
1616.

Matoaks als Rebecka daughter to the mighty Prince
Powhatan Emperour of Attanoughskomouck als virginia
converted and baptized in the Christian faith, and
wife to the worḷḷ Mᵣ Joh Rolff.

Si: Pass: sculp: Compton Holland excud:

This 1618 engraving of twenty-one-year-old Pocahontas is the only portrait of the famed
"Indian Princess" known to be made during her lifetime.

The True Story of Pocahontas

❖ HER INDIAN IDENTITY WAS ERASED AND REINVENTED

POCAHONTAS (CA. 1596–1617) may well be the most famous Native American in history, but the facts of her life remain uncertain. She left behind no letters or diaries to document her circumstances. Rather, Englishmen with commercial, religious, and personal motives wrote (and rewrote) her life story, portraying her as an assimilated, English-speaking Christian. Generations of playwrights, novelists, and historians followed, imaginatively romanticizing Pocahontas as a peacemaking Indian princess eager to abandon her Native identity.

The earliest published account of Pocahontas appeared in 1608, written by John Smith soon after his arrival in the New World to establish the colony of Jamestown on behalf of the Virginia Company of London. Smith's supposed courtship of Pocahontas was a fiction invented in the eighteenth century, but he clearly found the young girl charming. Introduced as the favorite daughter of Powhatan, chief of the Algonquian-speaking tribes of the Chesapeake region, Pocahontas was not yet in her teens, but she negotiated with the English as her father's emissary. According to Smith, her "feature, countenance & proportion, much exceedeth any of the rest of his people," and "for wit, and spirit, [she is] the Nonpareil of his Country." Pocahontas made quite a different impression on another English settler, William Strachey, in 1610. Recalling her frequent appearances at the English fort to turn cartwheels, naked, with the young boys, he dismissed her as "a well featured, but wanton yong girle."

Aware of Powhatan's attachment to his daughter, a British naval officer kidnapped Pocahontas in 1612 and ransomed her for corn, weapons, and English prisoners. She remained in captivity in 1614, when tobacco farmer John Rolfe wrote that he had fallen hopelessly in love and wished to marry her, having become "so intangled, and inthralled in so intricate a laborinth, that I was even aweared to unwind my self thereout." Rolfe resolved his inner turmoil over marrying an "unbeleeving creature" by vowing to ensure Pocahontas's conversion to Christianity. She was duly baptized and christened Rebecca, and she gave birth to a son, Thomas, following her marriage to Rolfe in April 1614.

The Virginia Company viewed Pocahontas as a success story—proof that America's Indians could live in harmony with white settlers. Hoping to attract investments for their colonial enterprise, the firm brought Pocahontas to England in June 1616. This engraving by the Flemish artist Simon de Passe was probably made as part of the publicity campaign. It erases Pocahontas's Indian identity and reinvents her as an English gentlewoman, tightly encased in damask and lace. Latin and English inscriptions emphasize her noble birth, stating that "Matoaks" (her Indian name), also known as Rebecca, was "daughter to the mighty Prince Powhatan Emperour of . . . Virginia." Her religious and marital states were also advertised: "converted and baptized in the Christian faith, and wife to the worthy Mr. John Rolff."

While in England, Pocahontas attended elegant entertainments and had an audience with the bishop of London, who reportedly "entertained her with festival state and pompe, beyond . . . his hospitalitie afforded to other Ladies." She met the king and attended a masquerade ball where Ben Jonson's *The Vision of Delight* was performed. When the time came to return to America, writers commented on her reluctance to go—echoing prior claims of her preference to remain with her captors rather than return home to her father.

In the end, a fatal illness settled the question. She died in England in March 1617 at the age of twenty-one and was buried at Gravesend. Pocahontas lived little more than two decades but has endured as a national myth for more than four centuries. It remains a question how much of herself she would recognize in the legendary figure we know. ■ —*RA*

Charles Willson Peale's 1769 portrait of Anne Green is extremely rare for eighteenth century America, in that it highlights her vocation and intellectual accomplishments.

Printer, Publisher, Wife

❖ **WHEN HER HUSBAND DIED, ANNE GREEN CONTINUED HIS LEGACY— AND THEN SOME**

I N ADDITION TO CARING for her fourteen children, Anne Green (1720–75) worked along-side her husband, Jonas, running the *Maryland Gazette*, the leading newspaper in Annapolis, Maryland. When she was forty-seven, her husband died and she took over as manager of his printing shop and as the newspaper's editor. Under her supervision, the business thrived, and she gained a reputation for fair-minded coverage of opinions and events leading up to the American Revolution. She also became the official printer of documents for the colony of Maryland. One of only a handful of women printers and newspaper owners during the colonial period, she ran the newspaper for eight years.

In this portrait, among the first that the artist and fellow Annapolis resident Charles Willson Peale painted after returning in 1769 from a study trip to London, Green is depicted not as her obituary recorded (a mother and wife of "a mild and benevolent Disposition . . . an Example of her Sex"), but instead as a professional printer, with a copy of the *Maryland Gazette* in her hand. ■ —*BBF*

This silk banner, hand embroidered in chenille thread, displayed a figure of Liberty, and was probably carried at a public celebration or political parade in the 1790s.

Goddess, Citizen, Muse

Rare and fragile today, this embroidered banner representing "Liberty" dates to the 1790s, when it was probably carried in a Philadelphia parade. The female figure wears a classical toga, carries a pole topped with a "freedom cap" (an international symbol of liberation), offers drink to an eagle (symbol of the new United States), and stands atop the broken chains of monarchy. Although civic life was largely reserved for men, female figures often appeared as idealized goddesses and muses in civic art and statuary.

Yet it was actual women, with fine embroidery skills, who surely stitched this banner. Excluded from the vote in every state except New Jersey, women found other outlets for expressing patriotic or partisan views. In the 1790s, they attended and supported public parades, although they rarely marched in them. They challenged long-standing hierarchies, including the subordination of women. And they later directed their energies to female education as a means to transform their sex from idealized goddesses to human women with real interests and political views. ■ —BCS

A Mirror to Social Change

Today kitchens are often described as the "heart of the home," the hub of family life and social interaction. Over the generations, they have been the site of many different activities and emotional associations. In early America, cooking responsibilities fell to women, but maintaining the hearth for daily meals demanded the labor of both sexes. Women's lives centered on the kitchen, and prosperous families relegated the drudgery to female servants or enslaved workers. As cooking methods and equipment evolved from the open hearth to cast-iron coal stoves to shiny electric ranges, industrialization removed men's work from the home while kitchens remained a "woman's place." For some women, time spent in the kitchen could be a huge constraint and the root of conflict; for others, it was a source of pride, authority, creativity, and even income. A few women were able to gain public recognition by professionalizing their kitchen skills.

But in 1963, the same year Julia Child launched her pathbreaking career as a chef and television host, Betty Friedan published her feminist manifesto critiquing society's dominant image of women as happy homemakers. For Friedan and others, the kitchen was symbolic of the ways in which household work constrained women's ambitions beyond the domestic and rendered them invisible in a male-dominated society. The questions of who presides over the kitchen and what she or he is doing there remain powerful indicators of social values.

The Smithsonian's collections of kitchen-related artifacts document not only the extraordinary women whose achievements we celebrate but also the everyday work and lives of the women left out of history books. Their stories can be found in cook pots, recipes, and memories.

The national collections of these artifacts at the National Museum of American History owe their foundation to Edna Greenwood, who in 1951 donated more than two thousand early New England kitchen utensils, household objects, and a colonial-era house complete with a kitchen hearth, all of which she had diligently amassed over decades. At a time when historical scholarship and curatorial work were viewed as men's work, Greenwood's donation channeled her ambition into actions that would safeguard knowledge of this often unnoticed labor.

From toasters to tortilla presses, curators have expanded Smithsonian collections in recent decades to explore how women of different eras and diverse class, race, ethnic, and regional backgrounds used their kitchens. For many women working in low-paying jobs, and for women of color who faced prejudice outside their homes, their kitchens could be a safe haven.

Research on widow and custodian Mary Scott's kitchen revealed that this "unobtrusive" grandmother held three generations together during World War II. She cooked meals using scarce resources when her familial role became a wartime obligation. Other artifacts document how women with limited means turned kitchen knowledge into entrepreneurial opportunities, whether immigrant women selling homemade tortillas or single mothers pitching Tupperware to eke out a living. Across generations and within communities, kitchens tell diverse stories. ■ —SKN

KITCHEN STORIES

Opposite: The kitchen of this house from Ipswich, Massachusetts, now in the Smithsonian, holds the stories of many women who cooked first on its hearth, then on a coal-and-wood range. To re-create how renter Mary Scott used the kitchen during World War II (shown here), curators drew from her diary, photos, and her grandson's memories of helping her can vegetables from her victory garden. —SKN

EARLY AMERICAN TOASTER

Above: This wrought-iron toaster (ca. 1750–1800) is one of more than two thousand early American kitchen utensils and other objects collector Edna Greenwood donated to the Smithsonian in 1951. By saving the specialized tools found in many early American kitchens, Greenwood helped curators highlight the skills of women who cooked on fireplace hearths and the value of their work to history. —SKN

JULIA'S KITCHEN

When chef and television host Julia Child (1912–2004) donated her home kitchen to the National Museum of American History in 2001, Smithsonian staff spent many hours in Cambridge, Massachusetts, learning the kitchen's history from America's beloved cooking teacher, author, and television personality. In the ensuing months, they documented and moved all twelve hundred parts and pieces to the museum. These included her six-burner Garland range, a table made in Norway, a giant mortar and pestle purchased in 1948 at a Paris flea market, a shelf's worth of cookbooks she actually used, her cabinetry and wall art, and hundreds of tools and gadgets.

Julia's arrangement of her kitchen reflected her preference for keeping the proper tools at hand: pots and pans within arm's reach of the range, cutting boards and knives near the sink for easy cleanup. The Smithsonian team faithfully re-created it when they rebuilt the kitchen inside the museum. Visiting on her ninetieth birthday in 2002, Child exclaimed, "It makes me feel like turning something on and starting to cook!" —PJJ

MARTHA ROSLER

Not all women saw culinary work as a path to empowerment or wanted to celebrate being constrained by unending, unpaid kitchen duty. Artist Martha Rosler's influential 1975 video, *Semiotics of the Kitchen*, parodies Julia Child's television show, which presumed a female audience able to devote ample hours and resources to each meal. Facing the camera in a cramped kitchen, Rosler holds up, names, and then vigorously demonstrates a series of cooking utensils. While her deadpan expression never changes, her gestures become more violent, suggesting suppressed rage at the confining expectations of society. With her tongue firmly in cheek, Rosler also evokes the basics of semiotic theory—that, as individuals acquire language, they learn how society is organized and their place in it—as a way of condemning the stereotyping of women. —*SG*

LEAH CHASE

"We changed the world over a bowl of gumbo" is how Chef Leah Chase (1923–2019) recalled the strategy sessions led by civil rights leaders at Dooky Chase's restaurant. *Driven* is how the Queen of Creole cuisine described herself. It's the kind of drive that compelled her to eschew the factory jobs left to Creole girls for restaurant work in New Orleans's French Quarter. The same drive led her to transform Dooky Chase's, a sandwich shop opened by her plucky mother-in-law in the early 1940s, into a fine-dining establishment with crisp, white tablecloths and signature African American art. Up to her ninth decade, Chase was often in the restaurant's kitchen well ahead of the rest of the staff, or presiding over the meals of visiting American presidents.

Diners at Dooky Chase's have included not only residents of Tremé, the historic African American community where it is located, but also jazz greats, famous authors, countless other celebrities, and legions of visiting tourists. —*JH*

Leah Chase often donned a red chef's jacket (left) while serving up Creole cuisine in her family's restaurant. In 2012, Gustave Blache III painted this portrait of Chase cutting squash.

New Mexican artist Pedro Antonio Fresquís likely relied on prints of Catholic saints as inspiration for his *retablos* (devotional works), which reveal the Virgin's deep roots in the southwestern United States. This piece was created ca. 1780–1830.

Patroness of the Americas

❖ FROM MEXICAN ICON TO SYMBOL OF CHICANX IDENTITY AND FEMALE EMPOWERMENT

Lovingly known as the patroness of Mexico and the Americas, the Virgin of Guadalupe has long been a revered symbol in both Mexico and the United States. While her history and image are inextricably linked to the European colonization of the New World, she remains a powerful, far-reaching icon of Chicanx identity, from the devotional to the political.

Legend holds that in 1531, ten years after the Spanish conquest, the Virgin miraculously appeared to a converted Indigenous peasant named Juan Diego just outside Mexico City. The Virgin spoke to Diego in Nahuatl —the language of the Aztecs—and requested that the local Bishop build a chapel in her honor in Tepeyac, an Indigenous pilgrimage site dedicated to the female deity Tonantzin. The Bishop heeded Diego's call, but only after Diego revealed the Virgin's image emblazoned on his *tilma* (cloak).

Devotion to the Virgin spread as the Spanish crown sought to evangelize Native populations by linking Christian icons to Native ones in the Viceroyalty of New Spain and elsewhere. The people of the Americas fervently followed local venerations of the Virgin Mary, especially during times of crisis. Mexican-born elites in the eighteenth century deployed her likeness and symbolism as an American virgin to distinquish themselves from the ruling class of Spaniards. In 1810, when Father Miguel Hidalgo y Costilla initiated a revolution against the Spanish Empire, he strategically deployed the image of the Virgin of Guadalupe as an emblem of an insurgent Mexican nation.

By the eighteenth century, the cult of the Virgin of Guadalupe had reached the remote northern frontier of New Mexico, where *santero* (creator of saint images) Pedro Antonio Fresquís (1749–1831) was born. Fresquís's humble *retablo* (devotional painting), which you see here, was created between 1780 and 1830 and largely follows conventional representations of the Virgin of Guadalupe and other Immaculate Conception depictions. Surrounded by a radiant sunburst, the crowned Virgin stands demurely, eyes downcast and hands clasped, on top of a crescent moon held up by an angel. The first native-born *santero* in New Mexico, Fresquís surrounded his elegant Virgin with decorative patterns within and along the border of this shaped wooden panel, which is a recurring design feature in his work. His use of simplified forms, humble materials, and local pigments reveals a distinctive New Mexican folk style born of geographic isolation from Mexico City. Under Spanish colonialism, friars and bishops had rejected local *santeros'* works as crude art forms. But New Mexicans embraced them. Used in home altars, *retablos* like this one spoke to the intimate bond between the Virgin and her followers.

With the start of the Mexican Revolution in 1910, people across all social strata galvanized around the Virgin as rebel leaders Emiliano Zapata and Pancho Villa invoked her image in their quest for social and agrarian reforms. In the United Sates, the Chicano civil rights movement of the 1960s and 1970s thrust the Virgin into public spaces once again. Alongside the black-eagle emblem of the United Farm Workers, Cesar Chavez led marches and pilgrimages under the banner of the Virgin of Guadalupe.

Chicanx artists widely deployed her image in posters, public murals, low riders, and paintings as a way to contest assimilation, affirm Mexican culture in the United States, and broadcast a collective Chicanx identity. Chicana artists like Patssi Valdez, Yolanda López, Ester Hernández, and Alma López questioned her portrayal as passive and submissive in both Catholic and Mexican culture. Their work, born out of the intersection of the civil rights, feminist, and LGBTQ+ movements, radically reimagined the Virgin of Guadalupe as a self-determined figure relevant to contemporary women's lives. ■ —ECR

Porcupine quillwork is a form of embroidery indigenous to North America. It was often employed by Native American women to express cosmological beliefs.

The Art of Cradleboards

❖ CARRYING ANISHINAABE CHILDREN IN SYMBOLIC DECORATION

THIS RARE, late-eighteenth-century quilled panel was made by an Anishinaabe woman for her infant child. Part of a cradleboard used to transport a swaddled baby, it is embroidered with black, white, and red porcupine quills, and is further decorated with brass cones and glass beads, both trade items, and red-dyed deer hair. While the incorporation of manufactured items clearly indicates Anishinaabe interaction with Europeans who were long trading in the region, the five animal patterns worked into the quilled panel likely represent underwater panthers, powerful spiritual beings who inhabited the underworld. Anishinaabe women excelled in quillwork, a couched embroidery technique, and (not unlike English ecclesiastical embroidered textiles) their iconography often expressed their understanding of the cosmos and its life-giving powers.

The panel was acquired between 1792 and 1794 by Andrew Foster, a young lieutenant in the British Army, at what was then the westernmost outpost of the British Empire, Fort Michilimackinac. Located on the northern edge of Lake Michigan, the fort was a strategic hub for both Indigenous peoples—the Anishinaabe, Wendat, and Dakota—who lived, hunted, and traded in the region, and colonial powers—the English, French, and Americans—who vied for domination of the area through warfare and diplomacy.

The exchange of valued gifts, both practical (such as food) and symbolic (such as silver or quilled objects), was an important aspect of Anishinaabe-British diplomacy. Although it is impossible to know exactly how Lieutenant Foster acquired this quilled panel, it is likely he was offered it as a diplomatic present along with other items he is known to have received. Such a gift would have signified that the region Foster had entered was a vibrant nexus of Indigenous life controlled by the Anishinaabe. It was, in other words, a physical world of forests, rivers, lakes, and trails, and a spiritual world animated by powerful cosmological beings who inhabited not only the earth but also the sky and the deepest bodies of water. Anishinaabe women made their spiritual environment visible—and mindful—for their British allies, as well as for themselves, through this profoundly meaningful form of visual expression. ■ —CRG

As she recorded at the bottom of this sampler, young Betsy Bucklin completed her work in September 1781, just weeks before the decisive Battle of Yorktown.

Schoolgirl Patriot

SUPPORTING REVOLUTION WITH NEEDLE AND THREAD

Betsy Bucklin (1768–99) was thirteen years old when she stitched this patriotic verse into her schoolgirl sampler. It evokes America's zeal to fight the British, and then celebrates female support for the Revolution: "Women would scorn / To be defyd if led by / WASHINGTON."

We don't know whether Betsy or her teacher wrote the verse, but it illustrated her family's pro-independence fervor. Her father, Daniel, commanded the Rhode Island privateer *Montgomery*, and Betsy may well have been in the crowds that cheered George Washington as he rode into Providence on March 13, 1781, after visiting his French ally, General Rochambeau, in Newport.

Embroidering a sampler was a female rite of passage in the eighteenth and nineteenth centuries. It also spoke to a girl's future domestic role. Most girls learned to do "plain sewing" as soon as they were old enough to hold a needle; a sampler displayed more refined skills. Betsy's ornamental handiwork shows that her family had the money and social position to pay for special lessons and purchase expensive silk threads. ∎ —MCS

Phillis Wheatley

"Should you, my lord, while you peruse my song,
Wonder from whence my love of Freedom sprung,

. . .

I, young in life, by seeming cruel fate
Was snatch'd from Afric's fancy'd happy seat:
What pangs excruciating must molest,
What sorrows labour in my parent's breast?
Steel'd was that soul and by no misery mov'd
That from a father seiz'd his babe belov'd:
Such, such my case. And can I then but pray
Others may never feel tyrannic sway?"

—Letter from Phillis Wheatley to the Right Honourable William, Earl of Dartmouth, published in 1773

PHILLIS WHEATLEY (1753–84) became a household name after she published *Poems on Various Subjects, Religious and Moral* in 1773. As a young girl, she was kidnapped in Senegal, sold into slavery, shipped to Boston, and purchased in 1761 by the Wheatley family. As an enslaved young woman who had mastered classical English, Latin, and Greek, she was held up as a symbol by international antislavery advocates.

Wheatley's strength of character is reflected in her work and in her ability to navigate in a society that both enslaved and celebrated her. At face value, her poems are straightforward reflections on virtue. Closer attention to the text, however, reveals a more trenchant layer of meaning in which she allies herself with those who had power over her while cleverly exposing critical views of society. Once free, Wheatley and her husband, John Peters, faced persistent poverty despite their talents. ■ —*NB AND TSW*

POEMS

ON

VARIOUS SUBJECTS,

RELIGIOUS AND MORAL;

BY

PHILLIS WHEATLEY,

NEGRO SERVANT to Mr. JOHN WHEATLEY,
of BOSTON, in NEW ENGLAND.

LONDON:
Printed for A. BELL, Bookseller, Aldgate; and sold by
Messrs. COX and BERRY, King-Street, BOSTON.
MDCCLXXIII.

Published according to Act of Parliament, Sept. 1. 1773 by Arch.d Bell,
Bookseller N.º 8 near the Saracens Head Aldgate.

Phillis Wheatley published *Poems on Various Subjects* while enslaved. Dependent on the family who owned her for support and access to publishers, she was reluctant to write directly about slavery. Instead, she used her skills as a poet to subtly weave a vision of freedom through her works.

Opposite: The sculptor and printmaker Elizabeth Catlett (1915–2012) returned to the subject of Phillis Wheatley several times in her exploration of black women. "In *Phyllis Wheatley*," Catlett explained, "I proved intellectual equality in the midst of slavery."

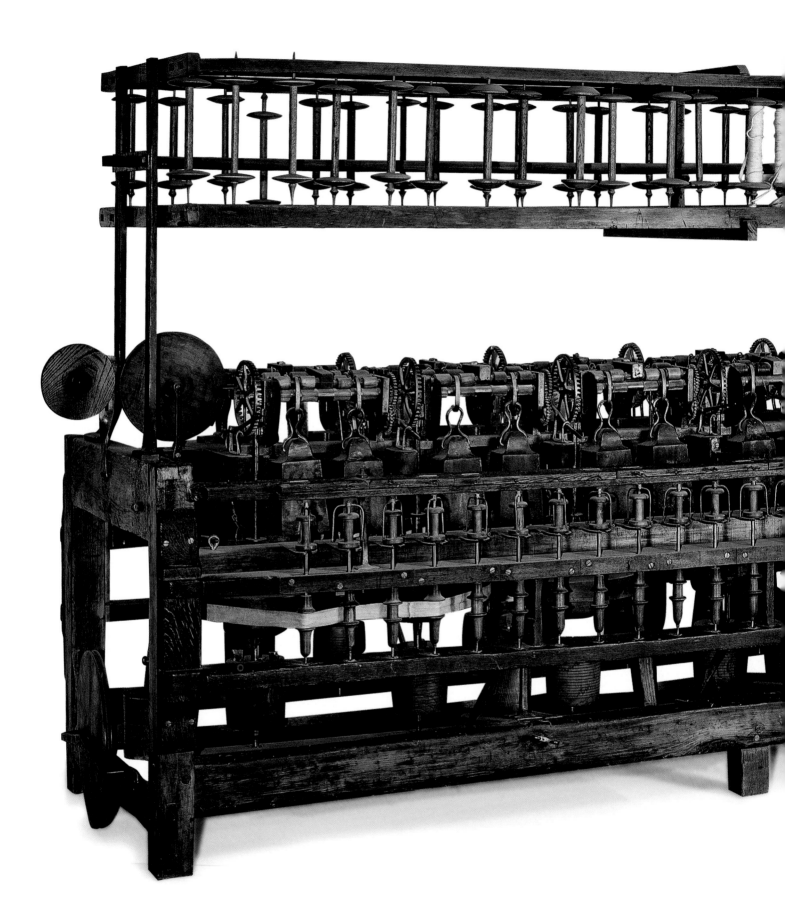

The Slater Mill workers, many of them women and girls, spun thread with specialized machines like this forty-eight-spindle frame, built in 1790 by Samuel Slater. Local weavers used the thread to make fabric.

Uncertain Opportunity at Work

❖ **NEW TECHNOLOGY AND THE RISE OF WOMEN'S FACTORY LABOR**

T HE ORIGINS OF US textile factories revolve around a saga of innovation, opportunity, and exploitation. In the mid-1700s, the British government safeguarded their dominance in mechanized textile production by banning the export of textile machinery and prohibiting skilled workers to emigrate. Things changed in 1789 when British opportunist Samuel Slater (1768–1835) snuck into the United States with industrial secrets. Backed by a wealthy merchant, Slater and his skilled American mechanics built machines like this spinning frame and established the nation's first water-powered cotton mill in Pawtucket, Rhode Island. Emulating the British labor system, Slater hired families—including children as young as seven—to toil long hours at the dangerous machines and do menial work.

Challenged by a glut of British imports, Pawtucket mill owners quickly moved to mechanize the remaining steps of cotton production between 1814 and 1824. The increased speed of operations, however, made it difficult for children to keep up; young unmarried women were increasingly hired to operate the machines. On May 24, 1824, the mill owners decided to reduce their costs by running the mills one hour longer each day and cutting the pay of the weavers by 25 percent. They claimed the women weavers earned two dollars a week above their board, which was "generally considered to be extravagant wages for young women."

Outraged, the workers responded by embarking upon one of the earliest factory strikes in US history. The protestors, including women, paraded through the streets in front of the owners' sumptuous houses. After a week, the two sides reached a compromise and the mills reopened. With opportunities for unskilled people few, the drudgery and rigor of industrial work became an acceptable way of life. ■ —PL

The Cruel Fate of the Fancy Girls

❖ ENSLAVED GIRLS AND WOMEN SOLD FOR SEXUAL SERVICES

There's no question that this bill of sale for a teenager named Polly is proof of a shameful chapter in this nation's history. But what does it tell us of the life of a young woman, sixteen years old, bought and sold as property, based on her race, gender, and appearance? The receipt does not provide details of what lay ahead for the teenager—the likelihood of forced domestic and sexual servitude. Nor does it account for the loss of her childhood, her chastity, her loved ones, and so much more.

Although we do not know what became of Polly, the document helps us to consider the "fancy girl" trade, in which enslaved girls and women were "fancied" or desired by slaveholding men and commodified and sold as property for the sole purpose of sexual services. It ran parallel to the domestic slave trade during the height of the ante-

---

"One Negro girl named Polly, aged about sixteen years, yellow complexion and black Eyes."

---

bellum period, and one of the leading market sites was New Orleans, where women of mixed-race descent were purchased for their appearance, particularly their fair skin and fine hair. While women of fair complexion were most often part of the market, all enslaved women were subject to being placed in the fancy girl trade. By law, the status of enslaved mothers determined the status of their children; mothers gave birth to daughters potentially subject to the trade. They were often valued at higher rates than the most prized male field hands. Women and girls considered more refined and presentable were purchased to serve as concubines of the slaveholders; others were forced into prostitution.

Enslaved women and girls were subject to sexual violation at any given moment, including publicly while under inspection on the auction block. An observer of the trade noted what he saw at the auction of a young woman named Mary. He states, "Her eyes are large, soft, and languishing. She seeks in vain to hide the streaming tears with her small and delicate hands." He further observes, "In the Slave States, she is openly sold, as though she were nothing more than a 'beautiful mare' or a 'splendid cow'!"

Once sold to a slaveholder, the girls and women were also exposed to further violation by any man who had access to them, including the overseer, relatives of the slaveholder, and business acquaintances. Narratives of formerly enslaved women provide some insight into the deep emotional toll of sexual abuse and slavery. In *Incidents in the Life of a Slave Girl*, Harriet Jacobs writes, "Soon she will learn to tremble when she hears her master's footfall. She will be compelled to realize that she is no longer a child. If God has bestowed beauty upon her, it will prove her greatest curse." Jacobs further explains the additional fear of wrath from the slave-owning mistress, who was aware of her husband's sexually abusive behavior and the expected role of the fancy girl.

The experience of enslaved girls and women sold as fancy girls is the embodiment of the traumatic confluence of race, gender, commodification, violence, and sexual abuse. Many African American women fought against such treatment. Some endured the pain and sorrow, as they tried to hold on to their humanity and survive.

The bill of sale does not tell the story of Polly. But behind its hard language of transaction lies an American tale of trauma inflicted on enslaved African American women—a tale never to be forgotten. ■ —*MNE*

Know all Men by these presents.
That I Martin Bridgeman of Jackson County
in the Territory of Arkansas for and in
consideration of the sum of Six Hundred Dollars
lawful money of the United States of America
to me in hand paid the receipt whereof is hereby
Acknowledged, have this day granted bargained
and Sold. and by these presents doth grant
bargain and sell unto Wm H Wood of Jackson
County in said Territory. his heirs and assigns
One Negro Girl named Polly aged about
Sixteen years, yellow complection and
black Eyes, to have & to hold the said Negro
Girl unto the sd H Wood his heirs and assigns
for ever, And further that I warrant and
Shall defend the right and title to said
Negro against all costs Suits or Suits at
law, or in Equity that may have been or
may hereafter be commenced by any person
or persons whatsoever — In witness whereof
I have hereunto set my hand and seal
this twenty third day of December One
Thousand Eight Hundred and Thirty five

Witness   his
                    Martin Bridgeman   (Seal)
Thomas R Pell   mark

John Nall

The State of Texas
County of Montgomery   Before me H. B
Boston Clerk, of the county Court, in & for said county

This 1835 bill of sale underscores the physical and psychological toll on the fancy girls. And yet a number of them fought back using self-defense, the courts, and written accounts.

Sojourner Truth: Image as Activism

❖ A GALVANIZER WHO USED SELF-PORTRAITS TO FIGHT FOR EQUAL RIGHTS

SOJOURNER TRUTH (ca. 1797–1883) understood the power of photography. In the image to the right, her body is taut with strength and her eyes shine with resolve. Standing nearly six feet tall, this pioneer for social justice for women and racial equality shrewdly used the new technology of photography and its relatively inexpensive cabinet cards to support her activism. "I Sell the Shadow to Support the Substance" was the message written under many of the reproductions that she sold at her public appearances in the mid-1800s. She demonstrated agency over her image at a time when women and blacks were not fully valued or appreciated. Through photography, she secured her place in history when she might have otherwise been overlooked.

A moving speaker, Truth traveled the country from the mid-1840s until her death in 1883, advocating for equal rights. She paid for the first printing of her *Narrative of Sojourner Truth* (written with friends) by selling her photographs at rallies and advertising them in antislavery publications. She also purchased a home in Battle Creek, Michigan, with the proceeds from these sales and her speaking engagements.

Sojourner Truth was born Isabella Baumfree around 1797 in upstate New York. Dutch was her first language, and she never learned to read or write in English. Separated from her parents around the age of thirteen and sold several times afterward, a field accident removed part of her index finger on her right hand, leaving it badly mangled. This disfigurement is visible in several of the portraits that she would later sell. Truth escaped slavery in 1826 around the age of thirty. After a religious conversion at forty-six, she changed her name to one she felt better reflected her life's purpose.

The great black statesman Frederick Douglass dismissed her as "uncultured" because of her illiteracy, but her supporters knew better. Truth believed that although she could not read a book, she could read people. Her empathy, coupled with her religious convictions, gave her a dynamism that would capture the public imagination well beyond her lifetime, continuing to inspire others to help to end racial and gender oppression. ■ —*RLC*

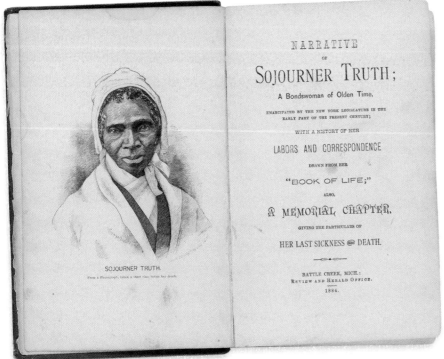

NARRATIVE
OF
SOJOURNER TRUTH;

A Bondswoman of Olden Time,

EMANCIPATED BY THE NEW YORK LEGISLATURE IN THE
EARLY PART OF THE PRESENT CENTURY;

WITH A HISTORY OF HER

LABORS AND CORRESPONDENCE

DRAWN FROM HER

"BOOK OF LIFE;"

ALSO,

A MEMORIAL CHAPTER,

GIVING THE PARTICULARS OF

HER LAST SICKNESS AND DEATH.

BATTLE CREEK, MICH.:
REVIEW AND HERALD OFFICE.
1884.

SOJOURNER TRUTH.
From a Photograph, taken a short time before her death.

Sojourner Truth's copyrighting of this 1864 photograph and her use of the first person in its caption (not visible) suggest she realized the material value of her image.

Opposite: *Narrative of Sojourner Truth* (1874) featured one of Truth's most reproduced images as the frontispiece.

This image of Lucretia Mott enjoyed wide circulation in 1853 when it was reproduced as a handsome lithographic print suitable for framing.

Lucretia Mott. Phil a. '86 1851.

"I Am No Advocate of Passivity"

❖ CHAMPION OF RACIAL AND GENDER EQUALITY

THE PICTURE OF PROPRIETY in her modest bonnet and shawl, Lucretia Mott (1793–1880) could easily be mistaken for a quiet Quaker matron. She was, in fact, a fearless and outspoken activist whose commitment to ending slavery and securing rights for women became the defining features of her life. Labeled a "firebrand" by the more conservative members of her Quaker faith, Mott vigorously defended her stance, declaring, "I am no advocate of passivity. I have no idea . . . of submitting tamely to injustice inflicted either on me or on the slave."

Calling for "the overthrow of the outrageous system of American slavery," Mott helped to found the Philadelphia Female Anti-Slavery Society in 1833. When she and her cohort of American women delegates were barred from participating in the World's Anti-Slavery Convention in London in 1840 because of their sex, her advocacy for women's rights strengthened. In July 1848, Mott joined Elizabeth Cady Stanton in organizing the convention at Seneca Falls, New York, that galvanized the American women's suffrage movement. ■ —*AMS*

Abolitionist Joanna L. Howard used this silver-plated tea set—an 1858 gift from an unnamed friend—to host civil rights discussions in the safety of her home.

Tea as Abolitionist Activism

❖ A FAMILY HEIRLOOM AND POWERFUL EMBLEM OF SOCIAL JUSTICE

JOANNA L. TURPIN HOWARD (1825–72) used this silver-plated tea set for more than socializing. An African American abolitionist, educational activist, and mother, Howard served tea in her Boston home to many antislavery organizers, black and white, including Lydia Maria Child and Frederick Douglass. Together they debated political strategies and helped form the antislavery movement. Male abolitionists met in many public spaces, but women activists were much more likely to gather in homes and churches to work for equality.

Howard (née Turpin) lived with her husband, Edwin Frederick Howard, and their three children in Boston's fashionable West End. The Howards were prominent black organizers in the Bostonian African American community. In New England during the 1800s, evening and afternoon teas were popular social affairs among the middle and upper classes, and the Howards used them to affect change. Their home provided a safer space for abolitionists to meet without the threat of violence than could occur at public events.

In addition to Howard's abolitionist work, she aided her husband in his barbering and catering businesses and educated all of her children—including the two girls. She was also instrumental in efforts that eventually succeeded in desegregating Boston public schools.

The Howards' commitment to education and service was later reflected in the careers of their children. Their oldest daughter, Adeline Turpin Howard, worked in several freedmen's schools after the Civil War. She later became principal of the Wormley School for African Americans in Washington, DC. Her younger sister, Joan Imogene Howard, was the first African American graduate of the Girls' High and Normal School in Boston. She earned two master's degrees and taught for years in the New York City public schools for colored children. In 1900, she became a principal. She also served on the Board of Managers for New York State for the Columbian Exposition. The Howards' son, Edwin Clarence Turpin Howard, spent five years researching hospitals in Liberia and in Europe. When Harvard Medical School opened their previously segregated admissions policies, he entered and in 1869 became the first African American graduate. He later moved to Philadelphia and became a prominent throat specialist, remaining active in local and national medical societies. The success of Joanna Howard's children is a testament to the strong values and broad worldviews she served along with her tea. ■ —FDR

During her Diamond Jubilee year in 1897, Queen Victoria gave this silk, lace, and linen shawl to Harriet Tubman in recognition of the freedom fighter's courage and heroism.

Opposite: This carte de visite of Harriet Tubman, taken ca. 1868 when she was around forty years old, is the earliest known image of the freedom fighter.

A Woman Called Moses

❖ HARRIET TUBMAN'S EXTRAORDINARY RESOLVE IN FIGHTING FOR EQUALITY

A CONDUCTOR ON THE Underground Railroad; a spy, scout, and nurse for the Union army; the leader of a successful military raid; a freedom fighter committed to justice and equality—Harriet Tubman lived a life of great consequence.

Araminta "Minty" Ross (ca. 1820–1913) was born in Dorchester County, Maryland, to enslaved parents, Ben Ross and Harriet Green. By law, the status of African American children followed that of their mother, thus Araminta and her eight siblings were all born enslaved. She served as a field hand, and over the years various slaveholders leased her for labor. Like many enslaved women, she was subjected to brute cruelty and sexual violation. But she never accepted the yoke of bondage and, as a young girl, even attempted to escape her owner. In 1844, Araminta Ross married John Tubman, a free black man. She took his last name and changed her first name to Harriet, after her beloved mother.

In 1849, Tubman was bound for the auction block to pay off the debts of her deceased slaveholder. She took her destiny into her own hands and, with the help of an intricate network that included free and enslaved African Americans, fled to Philadelphia. A decade later, Tubman shared these thoughts with her biographer, Ednah Dow Cheney: "God's time is always near. He set the North Star in the heavens; He gave me the strength in my limbs; He meant I should be free." Living as a freewoman, Tubman never forgot her family and was determined to liberate them one day.

A woman of faith, Tubman faced down her fears and returned to the South as part of the Underground Railroad network. With each mission, Tubman knew the risks and prepared herself for what lay ahead. She traveled back to Maryland at least ten times and freed more than seventy enslaved African Americans, including many family members. Those working around her began calling her Moses, after the prophet who had led his people to freedom. Her greatest sorrow was her inability to free one of her two sisters, who died before Tubman could rescue her.

Harriet Tubman was not only determined to free enslaved African Americans but also to abolish the system of slavery. In June 1863, while serving as a Union army spy, she displayed great heroism by leading a raid up the Combahee River in South Carolina, a unique role for a woman to have played in a military operation. Her successful effort helped free seven hundred enslaved African Americans. In her later years, this woman of conviction served those in need, from orphans to the elderly, and took up the cause of women's rights. It is a measure of her devotion that despite her meager means and chronic health problems, she never stopped fighting for others. ■ —MNE

Stirring the National Conscience

❖ HARRIET BEECHER STOWE TURNED PUBLIC OPINION AGAINST SLAVERY

NEW YORK ARTIST Alanson Fisher (1811–96) painted this portrait of Harriet Beecher Stowe in 1853, when the writer was already celebrated far and wide for *Uncle Tom's Cabin*, the abolitionist novel that jolted many Americans into a condemnation of slavery. The painting had been commissioned by theater impresario Alexander Purdy for a stage adaptation at the National Theater in New York. "According to the picture the distinguished writer is quite a good-looking woman, apparently about forty-five years of age," the *New York Evening Post* reported. Stowe described herself around the same time as "a little bit of a woman—somewhat more than forty, about as thin and dry as a pinch of snuff; never very much to look at in my best days, and looking like a used up article now." We see her as a thoughtful person of middle age, with an

---

Stowe's *Uncle Tom's Cabin* was an overnight sensation, selling three hundred thousand copies in its first year of publication.

---

inscrutable, quiet demeanor despite her fame and influence as a writer.

A year earlier, at the age of forty-one, Stowe (1811–96) achieved instant celebrity. *Uncle Tom's Cabin* was an overnight sensation, selling three hundred thousand copies in its first year of publication. It would become the most read book, next to the Bible, in mid-nineteenth-century America. But it also drew violent criticism from the proslavery South and from some Northerners who questioned the novel's portrayals as unrealistically brutal.

But for many of the book's readers, Stowe's depiction of slavery was revelatory. The inhuman treatment of African Americans is made plain in a saga of danger, cruelty, and redemption, set in motion when a Kentucky family decides to sell two of its enslaved men. One of them, the kind and selfless Uncle Tom, shows forbearance in the face of every outrage. "My object will be to hold up in the most lifelike and graphic manner possible slavery, its reverses, changes." Stowe wrote in 1851.

Stowe was brought up in a family of New England intellectuals and Calvinist ministers. From an early age, her writing drew praise, and she began a literary career in her twenties. In 1832, she married Calvin Ellis Stowe, a seminary professor. While bearing seven children and managing the household, she continued to write essays for *Godey's Lady's Book* and other journals, often to make ends meet for her family.

Raised with antislavery views, Stowe was deeply affected by the passage of the Fugitive Slave Law in 1850, which mandated the capture and return of runaway slaves to their owners. As a consequence, the North was no longer a safe haven, as all states and all Americans were required to follow this federal law. Abolitionists feared that slavery could conceivably spread throughout the country—a concern that may have contributed to Stowe's decision to write her book. And she was no doubt encouraged by a letter from her sister-in-law urging her to depict "what an accursed thing slavery is."

Ultimately her novel was profoundly changed in subsequent theatrical renditions, which often added minstrel acts and songs, subverting its original radical message of social reform and distorting the characters, especially Uncle Tom, who became an overdrawn caricature of servility. But the book and its tenacious author indisputably changed hearts and minds at a time of great danger and fury in a divided country. ■ —BBF

Women of the Battlefield

❖ **THE CIVIL WAR'S "DAUGHTERS OF THE REGIMENT"**

This uniform belonged to a vivandière attached to a Zouave unit of the Union army in the American Civil War. Vivandières were women who followed the army to provide support for the troops. They served with the French military during the Napoleonic Wars of the early nineteenth century, assisting the sutlers who sold food, drink, and other goods to combatants. Later they began to assume other duties, including caring for ill and wounded soldiers. During the Crimean War (1853–56), American military officers observing the fighting noticed vivandières administering to the soldiers in the French camps. The idea was transported to the United States, where vivandières figured in camp life on both sides of the Civil War.

Vivandières were commonly referred to as "daughters of the regiment" during the Civil War. (They were often the wives of soldiers or daughters of officers.) They served to comfort and support the men and were considered part of the unit. Some of the women were even awarded medals for their bravery on the battlefield.

Because the vivandières were not officially sanctioned, their uniforms were not subject to regulations. Each uniform had three essential pieces—a jacket, skirt, and trousers—but the trim and material were up to the individual. The skirt was knee-length, worn over long trousers, and the jacket was short and formfitting. Jaunty hats and sometimes aprons completed the ensemble. Among the most colorfully attired vivandières were those attached to Zouave units, American soldiers inspired by the uniform and tactics of the Zouaves in the French Army. Their uniforms matched the regiment's colors and its distinctive blousy trousers.

Although vivandières were prevalent in the early years of the Civil War, their numbers declined as the conflict became protracted. Many decamped and did not return. ■ —*KAG*

This uniform (1861–65) of the female vivandière is reminiscent of those worn by Union Zouave troops during the Civil War. The term *vivandière*, derived from French and Latin, means "hospitality giver."

In this portrait ca. 1866–67, Mary Walker wears the sort of unrestricted clothing she believed was most healthy.

Above: This inscription was written in the Bible given to Mary by the chaplain of Richmond's Castle Thunder Confederate prison when she was held on spying charges there.

Freethinking Mary

A LIFE OF ACTIVISM AND STRONG VIEWS

B ORN INTO A WORLD with clearly defined gender roles, Mary Walker (1832–1919) defied them all. One of America's first female physicians, she believed that restrictive clothing such as the corset encumbered healthful movement. She wore and advocated for "reform dress"—a shortened dress and pants as shown in the above photo. Eventually she abandoned the skirt altogether, although she was physically attacked and arrested for wearing pants in public.

Strong abolitionist beliefs led her to volunteer as a doctor during the Civil War. Told that as a woman she could serve only as a nurse, Walker persisted until, in 1863, she became the sole female surgeon in the US Army. In 1864, she was captured for spying, held in a Confederate prison, and released three months later. The following year she was awarded a Congressional Medal of Honor, the only woman ever to receive one.

In 1917, the army revoked Walker's Congressional Medal of Honor because she hadn't served in direct combat. Walker refused to return the medal, continuing to wear it proudly until her death two years later. ■ —BB

Reaching Out for the Stars

❖ **ASTRONOMER MARIA MITCHELL MENTORED WOMEN IN SCIENCE**

M ARIA MITCHELL (1818–89) was already famous when she began teaching at Vassar College in 1865. She was America's first female astronomer—indeed, its first woman scientist of note. Matthew Vassar, the founder of the college, was so pleased by her recruitment that he personally took charge of buying the Henry Fitz telescope that would have pride of place at the college observatory.

Mitchell was a Quaker from Nantucket whose family encouraged her interest in astronomy. While still a girl, she helped her father, an avid public school teacher, observe a solar eclipse and rate the chronometers used by sailors to determine their longitudes at sea. In her late twenties, she worked as a librarian in the local athenaeum, handling astronomical calculations for the US Coast Survey and the US Nautical Almanac. On October 1, 1847, while observing the skies with her father's telescope, she spotted a comet not seen before. As news of this discovery spread throughout the scientific community, Mitchell received a gold medal from the king of Denmark, thus becoming one of the first Americans to win any medal for science.

Mitchell's move to Poughkeepsie, New York, to become the professor of astronomy at the newly opened Vassar College—the first school offering women resources comparable to those at the leading colleges for men—would represent a considerable step forward in the education of women in science. At the college observatory, Mitchell had charge of a large refracting telescope and other instruments. During her years at Vassar, she mentored many young women who would embrace science as a future vocation. ∎ —*DJW*

Above: The Vassar College telescope was made by Henry Fitz, America's first successful commercial telescope maker. With a thirteen-inch diameter objective lens and a clock-driven equatorial mount, it was one of the largest telescopes in the country in the 1860s.

Opposite: Maria Mitchell and an unnamed male assistant with the Vassar College telescope, ca. 1878

Challenging Convention

W HEN CHARLOTTE CUSHMAN (1816–76) first wore this costume in 1857 for the role of Cardinal Thomas Wolsey in Shakespeare's *Henry VIII*, she challenged a conventional boundary for women. That she was applauded for it in an age renowned for its confining expectations of proper women speaks volumes about Cushman's personality. "[She] is the only living actress who could undertake such a character with success," a reviewer noted.

Playing Wolsey broke with a century of theatrical precedent. Women (including Cushman) had long played tragic male characters such as Romeo and Hamlet, donning tights that exposed legs normally concealed under dresses. By choosing to portray Henry VIII's ambitious and machinating chief minister, Cushman not only broadened the scope of characters available to women but also picked one whose loose-fitting robes put the emphasis on her acting rather than her body.

In an unusual move for a young woman, Cushman became a teenage performer to support her family. As an adult, she funded and lived in a community of what she and her friends called "jolly female bachelors." All the romantic relationships documented in her personal papers were with women.

At a time before such words as lesbian, queer, and transgender came into use, most Americans thought that not having relationships with men made Cushman chaste and pure. Cushman herself strove to confirm this view and ordered her partners and lovers to burn her letters to preserve her public image. But in the decades after her death in 1876, as homosexuality among women became more recognized—and ridiculed—she fell out of public favor and was largely forgotten. Only in recent years has her story been recovered by scholars and activists, who see Cushman as an early advocate for a woman's right to be whoever she wants to be—on and off the stage. ■ —*KC*

Made in London and accentuated with an apron of seventeenth-century Milanese lace, this ca. 1857 ensemble projected Wolsey's wealth and power while concealing Cushman's body and focusing attention on her acting.

Alberta Elizabeth Lewis wore this gown at her christening in the Washington, DC, Fifteenth Street Presbyterian Church, where her father was an elder and Keckly a member.

Gown Made with Love

❖ **A GODMOTHER RESPONDS IN THE WAY SHE KNOWS BEST**

ONLY A PRECISE AND highly skilled seamstress could have fashioned this cotton christening gown. Its creator, Elizabeth Keckly (1818–1907), was both. Handmade lace trims the sleeves and hem, four rows of gathering ribbon provide detail to the back waist, and twenty narrow pleats adorn the gown's full skirt.

Keckly arrived in Washington, DC, in 1860, having purchased her own freedom after thirty-seven years of enslavement (as well as that of her son) using the proceeds from her dressmaking. Poor but determined to get work in her profession, she found lodgings with Virginia and Walker Lewis, a well-established African American couple in the city. When the Lewis's daughter Alberta Elizabeth was born in June 1863, the parents named Keckly her godmother and, in a further sign of closeness, gave their daughter Keckly's name. Alberta's christening gown was likely made in Keckly's shop on Twelfth Street NW, on the same street as the Lewis's residence.

By the time of Alberta Elizabeth's birth, Keckly had built a flourishing business. Her beautifully draped gowns had caught the attention of Washington's society women, and when President Lincoln and his wife arrived in the capital in 1861, one of her clients introduced her to the first lady. For the next four years, Keckly sewed numerous dresses for Mary Todd Lincoln. Lonely, isolated, and temperamental, Mary Lincoln shared many confidences with Keckly, whose patience and sympathy often diffused tense moments in the White House during the tumultuous years of the American Civil War.

On the night of Lincoln's assassination, Keckly and the Lewises walked to the White House to offer comfort and help. Keckly stayed on and became the first lady's stalwart companion. Yet her long association with Mary Lincoln would end unceremoniously. In 1868, Keckly wrote her autobiography. Mary Lincoln wrongly perceived it as a tell-all and rejected her faithful friend. The two never reconciled. In 1907, Keckly died in the Washington, DC, Home for Destitute Colored Women, a charity she had helped found. ■ —*NED*

CHAPTER TWO

1865-1920

The Road to Reform

B Y THE END OF THE Civil War, more than two million African American women and girls celebrated their emancipation from slavery. Extending the cause of freedom, many joined their sisters, black and white, in the longstanding fight for women's rights. Alliances frayed when the United States granted African American men, but not women, the right to vote in 1870. Deeply embittered, some powerful white women argued that, unlike them, people of color did not deserve the vote. This exposed a common racism and created deep divisions among suffragists.

Yet rights were defined in many ways. On the Great Plains, as the US Army forced Native Americans from their land, activists like Sarah Winnemucca and Susette La Flesche condemned this travesty of justice. In the cities, labor and suffrage movements intertwined as immigrant women and girls sought redress for harrowing working conditions and successfully attained a reduced fifty-two-hour workweek.

When World War I broke out, women were accepted into limited military service for the first time. Still working for voting rights, suffragists pressed on. When the Nineteenth Amendment was ratified on August 18, 1920, women could no longer be barred from voting because of their sex. However, other discriminatory restrictions remained in place. ■

This watch was a gift to Helen Keller from John Hitz, superintendent of a center for deafness research in Washington, DC.

PREVIOUS SPREAD

Reaching through Darkness

Her hands, Helen Keller once wrote, were the means to "reach through isolation and darkness." She even kept track of time with her hands, with this Swiss watch as her prized ally for noting the passing hours. Deaf and blind from the age of nineteen months, Keller (1880–1958) received the watch as a gift when she was a teen. She used it throughout her remarkable career as a writer and human rights crusader.

Designed to tell time in the dark by touch, the watch features a case studded with pins that correspond to the hours, one through twelve, on the dial. On the case back, a revolving hand stops at a point that corresponds to the hour and minute. With the hand and pins as locators, Keller could feel the time. She lost the watch in New York City in 1952, but it was eventually found in a pawnbroker's shop and returned. —CES

1860 — The American Civil War ends with the surrender of the Confederate States of America. The Thirteenth Amendment is passed abolishing slavery.

1865 — Wyoming Territory grants women twenty-one or older the right to vote and hold office.

The Fifteenth Amendment is passed, granting African American men the right to vote.

1870 — Victoria Claflin Woodhull is the first woman US presidential candidate, nominated by the National Radical Reformers, a third-party ticket.

1875 — Susan B. Anthony casts a ballot to test whether the Fourteenth Amendment would be interpreted broadly to include women.

1880 — Ida B. Wells-Barnett publishes a pamphlet titled *Southern Horrors: Lynch Law in All Its Phases,* a compilation of her speeches against lynching.

1885 — Queen Liliʻuokalani is overthrown by a U.S.–backed coup; the Kingdom of Hawaiʻi becomes a de facto territory of the United States in 1898.

1890 — The girls' basketball team of Montana's Fort Shaw Indian Boarding School is the world basketball champions at the World's Fair in Saint Louis.

Margaret Sanger and others establish the first contraception clinic in the United States, in Brooklyn, New York. In 1942, this clinic becomes Planned Parenthood.

1895 —

1900 — Jeannette Rankin of Montana becomes the first woman elected to the US House of Representatives.

The United States enters World War I.

1905 — The Eighteenth Amendment is ratified. In January, and Prohibition, which bans the production, transportation, and sale of alcoholic beverages, goes into effect nationwide.

1910 —

The Nineteenth Amendment is ratified. It declares that "The right of citizens of the United States to vote shall not be denied or abridged by the United States or by any State on account of sex."

1915 —

Bessie Coleman becomes both the first African American woman and the first woman of Native American descent to earn a pilot's license.

1920 —

Red silk shawl, worn by Susan B. Anthony, ca. 1870-1906

Engraving of Queen Liliʻuokalani, August Weger, ca. 1870–90

Button with "Votes for Women" slogan, ca. 1912–14

Margaret Higgins Sanger, Ira L. Hill, 1917

Bessie Coleman, unidentified photographer, ca. 1923

Teaching the Solar System

❖ ELLEN HARDING BAKER DESIGNED A LIFE
AROUND SCIENCE AND FAMILY

To create this remarkable quilt, Ellen Harding Baker (1847–1886) combined three acceptable activities for women in the nineteenth century: quilt making, the study of astronomy, and teaching. Its depiction of the solar system was unusual enough to merit a mention in the *New York Times* (September 22, 1883). An Iowa newspaper wrote that Baker had finished a quilt with the "the solar system worked in completely and accurately. The lady went to Chicago to view the comet and sun spots through the telescope [so] that she might be very accurate. Then she devised a lecture in astronomy from it."

Baker started the wool-appliqué quilt in 1876, but it took her seven years to complete it, perhaps because she was also raising a large family. Included in its design are the appliquéd inscription "Solar System" and the embroidered inscriptions "E. H. Baker" and "A. D. 1876." The lining is a red cotton-and-wool fabric and the filling is cotton fiber. Her inspiration may have come from illustrations of the solar system found in several astronomy textbooks from the 1860s, as well as from her own viewing of the skies at the original Dearborn Observatory in Chicago. The quilt depicts the orbits of planets and shows Halley's Comet, rendered in a plume of silver-toned silk threads.

Baker used the quilt as a visual aid for lectures she gave on astronomy in the Iowa towns of West Branch, Moscow, and Lone Tree. Although we cannot be sure what caused Baker to add the study and teaching of astronomy to her domestic duties, her choice followed a path blazed by the famed astronomer Maria Mitchell (see page 56). Through her intricately stitched creation, Baker blended home and career at a time when few women had both. ■ *—VE AND MCS*

Ellen Harding Baker needed seven years to complete the solar system quilt (1876–83), a wool-fabric appliqué embellished with wool braid and wool and silk embroidery.

The Death of Cleopatra

❖ **EDMONIA LEWIS'S MASTERWORK WAS ALMOST LOST TO HISTORY**

MANY NINETEENTH-CENTURY artists depicted the powerful Egyptian queen Cleopatra, usually showing her as a voluptuous, brooding, and menacing figure. By contrast, this marble sculpture by Edmonia Lewis (ca. 1844–1907) portrays the Egyptian ruler in her last moments, still gripping the poisonous snake she used to commit suicide rather than surrender to Roman forces, serenely enthroned and effecting decisive control over her fate.

Lewis made this sculpture for the 1876 Philadelphia Centennial International Exhibition. Although some critics recoiled at its forthright depiction of death, the work was so widely acclaimed that Lewis shipped it to the 1878 Chicago Interstate Industrial Exposition. Afterward, it was lost to art lovers for nearly a century, suffering various absurd placements—in a saloon, on the grave of a racehorse named Cleopatra, and on a golf course—before ending up in suburban Chicago's Forest Park Historical Society. In 1994, the sculpture was conserved and donated to the Smithsonian, which holds the largest collection of Lewis's work.

Lewis made this sculpture in Rome, where she had moved in 1866, drawn to its vibrant art colony and compelled by a yearning to "find a social atmosphere where I was not constantly reminded of my color." Her parents—a black father, possibly from Haiti, and an Anishinaabe Indian mother—died when she was a child, leaving Lewis to be raised by maternal aunts and a half-brother who paid for her education at Oberlin College. Frederick Douglass introduced her to the abolitionist community in Boston, where she earned enough money sculpting portraits to move to Europe permanently. Historians only recently discovered that Lewis died in 1907 and was buried in London. Although much of her biography remains unknown, her extraordinary accomplishments continue to draw admiration. ■ —KL

The Death of Cleopatra (1876) weighs nearly three thousand pounds and was Edmonia Lewis's largest and most important work.

When married in this highly fashionable wedding dress in 1881, Susette La Flesche, born Inshata-Theumba (Bright Eyes), was well on her way to becoming a prominent Native American activist.

A Marriage of Minds

❖ **THE UNION OF TWO CRUSADERS FOR NATIVE RIGHTS**

WHEN SUSETTE LA FLESCHE (1854–1903), a well-established crusader for Native American causes, married Thomas Tibbles in 1881, she wore this then-fashionable two-piece woolen wedding dress, exquisitely trimmed with silk, satin, and lace.

La Flesche was born Inshata-Theumba (Bright Eyes) on the Omaha Reservation, the same year the United States established both it and the Nebraska Territory. Her father, a respected tribal leader, raised her and her siblings in the Omaha tradition. But he also sent them to the reservation's mission school, believing that additional exposure to American culture and the English language would be in their best interest. After attending the Elizabeth School for Young Ladies in New Jersey, La Flesche returned to the Omaha Reservation as a teacher.

In 1877, she witnessed the forced removal of the Ponca from their homelands in Nebraska to Indian Territory (present-day Oklahoma), which shook her to her core. The following year she went with her father to Indian Territory to visit the Ponca. Their misery sparked her decision to fight for Indian rights. Her future husband, Tibbles, a reporter for the *Omaha Herald*, shared her outrage.

When in 1879 the Ponca chief, Standing Bear, was imprisoned for leaving Indian Territory without the permission of the US government, La Flesche joined a campaign to fight for his release, which included a petition arguing for the right of the Ponca to remain in their homeland. According to the *New York Herald*, the petition was "one of the most extraordinary statements ever published in America." The trial that ensued led not only to the release of Standing Bear from prison but also to one of the country's major civil rights decisions—that "an Indian is a person within the meaning of the law of the United States" and has the right to legal redress before the courts. After the trial, La Flesche continued her activism against the forced removal of Native peoples from their homelands and for Indian civil liberties, including their right to become US citizens. ■ —*CRG*

Making the Case for Suffrage

❖ **A TRAVELING PODIUM, MAKESHIFT NEWSSTAND, AND ROLLING BILLBOARD**

THE STRUGGLE TO WIN voting rights for women developed over years of partnership as well as fracture, with rivalries, conflicting priorities, disagreements over tactics, and tensions caused by prejudices related to race and class.

Yet women fighting for change found allies in their quest for greater equality. By the mid-nineteenth century, women across the country were forming suffrage associations and reaching for voting rights, hoping that the ballot would be a powerful weapon in the fight for civil and cultural equality.

When abolitionists and early suffrage leaders Elizabeth Cady Stanton, Susan B. Anthony, and Lucy Stone strongly disagreed over how to respond to the exclusion of women from post–Civil War voting rights amendments, they founded rival organizations with different strategies. Stanton and Anthony blended suffrage with controversial reforms in women's rights, including changes in divorce law, and advocated a constitutional amendment enfranchising women. Stone focused on organizing statewide campaigns to win the vote. They would ultimately merge their associations, and some of their tactics.

In the 1870s, Stone began using an unpainted wagon as a podium at speaking engagements and to distribute her newspaper, *Woman's Journal*. In 1913, suffragist and labor activist Elisabeth Freeman took it on a well-publicized trip from New York to Boston, hauling a hurdy-gurdy organ to draw crowds. It was still used for suffrage publicity, but by then the wagon had been painted. It made the trip to Boston covered in slogans advertising *Woman's Journal* and calling for equal pay, just labor laws, and the vote for women of all classes. ■ —*LKG*

First used in the 1870s, this suffrage wagon was last used, as indicated by its painted slogans, in 1917 or 1918. It was brought out of retirement in 1943, the twenty-third anniversary of the ratification of the Nineteenth Amendment, to be used at the dedication of the Women's Rights Collection at Radcliffe College.

The Story of Suffrage

❖ SHAPING HISTORY WITH A CAREFULLY CURATED DONATION

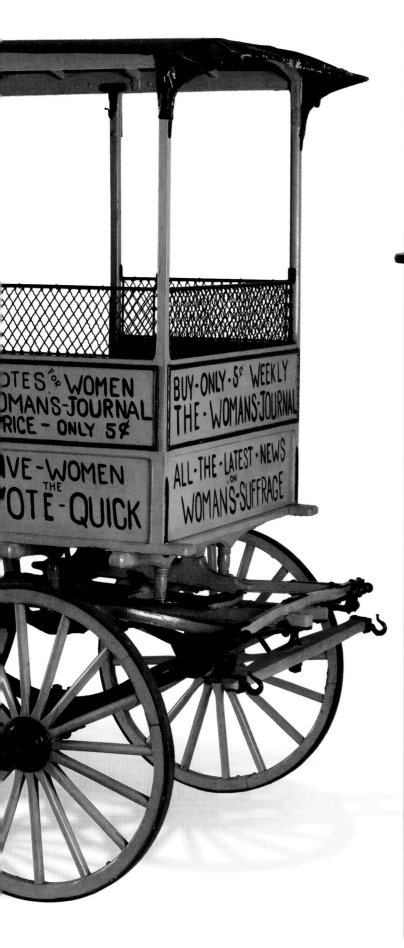

Declaration of Sentiments table, 1848

S HORTLY AFTER the woman suffrage amendment was passed by Congress in 1919 and sent to the states for ratification, leaders of the National American Woman Suffrage Association (NAWSA) approached the Smithsonian. To ensure that the suffrage story, "the greatest bloodless revolution ever known," would be represented at the institution, they donated memorabilia of suffragist leader Susan B. Anthony and this mahogany table on which Elizabeth Cady Stanton drafted the Declaration of Sentiments. Presented at an 1848 women's rights convention in Seneca Falls, New York, the groundbreaking document recounted the many curbs to women's freedoms. Anthony's niece Lucy called the display at the Smithsonian "the crowning glory to everything."

NAWSA's version of suffrage history shaped the traditional account long taught in schools—that heroic, unified women won the vote. The Smithsonian is now reinterpreting and expanding its one-hundred-year-old collection to move beyond this traditional story and tell a more diverse and complex history of the US suffrage movement. ∎ —*LKG*

Solving Mail Mysteries

❖ WOMEN MAKING A MARK IN THE POSTAL SERVICE

WHEN WE PUT SOMETHING in the mail, we expect it to be delivered. Since the founding of the United States, the mail that went unclaimed at local post offices, bore insufficient postage, or lost momentum due to incomplete, illegible, or missing addresses was forwarded to the specialists in "dead letters" at the Post Office Department. The Dead Letter Office clerks used analytical reasoning, languages, and geography to "blind read," or deduce, the correct addresses and send the mail on its way.

The Dead Letter Office hired its first women in 1862. Men were fighting in the Civil War, and the Post Office Department was flooded with mail. Three years later, the Dead Letter Office employed thirty-eight "ladies," who outnumbered their seven male counterparts. But the women each earned only $600 annually—$300 less than their male coworkers. Several female employees signed a petition requesting a raise; their pay increase was granted in a subsequent congressional appropriation, along with a title change to "clerks." Still, the women's salaries remained lower than the men's, and their offices and entrances were separate. Although both offices were visible to tourists visiting the nation's capital and were written about in the popular press, the conspicuous presence of these white, middle-class women working in a federal agency challenged nineteenth-century norms.

This "Blind Reading" scrapbook preserves a proud selection of the clerks' accomplishments in just a two-year period. Each of the twenty-one carefully mounted envelopes bears the following marking: "Deficiency in Address Supplied at Dead Letter Office." Like answers to a puzzle, the solutions are written on the backs of the pages, denoting successful delivery. The elegant handwriting and construction of this unsigned volume are identical to those in an album in the United States Postal Service's collection attributed to Clara M. Richter (ca. 1845–99). Shortly after the Civil War, the unmarried German immigrant joined the staff at the Washington, DC, headquarters of the post office. During her thirty-plus years of public service, Richter became chief of the Dead Letter Office's foreign mail, reviving letters from the dead and helping make international communications more reliable. ■ —LH

Renowned Native American basket maker Elizabeth Hickox learned to craft these baskets (ca. 1920) from her mother. She later passed the knowledge along to her daughter.

Art Bearing Witness

❖ **SURVIVING MASS GENOCIDE, PRESERVING THE HISTORY OF THE WIYOT PEOPLE**

On THE NIGHT OF February 26, 1860, off the coast of what is now Eureka, California, the townspeople of Humboldt County murdered approximately two hundred Native American men, women, and children as they slept. A Wiyot woman named Polly Steve was one of the few to survive the racially motivated Indian Island Massacre. Twelve years later, she gave birth to a daughter who would preserve the cultural heritage of her people through baskets like these.

Elizabeth Hickox (1872–1947) was one of the finest American Indian basket makers of her time and remains renowned among collectors of Indigenous art. From her mother, she learned the craft of twining and of decorating baskets with traditional designs using spruce root, bear grass, dyed porcupine quills, and maidenhair fern. Hickox was noted for both her exquisite execution and the innovative shapes of her baskets and lids. Her intricate, elegantly crafted baskets belie not just the horrors of her mother's history but also the violence against her people.

The Indian Island Massacre was among many incidents in one of the darkest chapters in California and US history: the mass slaughter of American Indians in California between 1848 and 1860. This killing spree has been described as the worst atrocity that Americans have never heard of. With the 1848 discovery of gold in Northern California, hundreds of thousands of immigrants flooded into the region. No other Indigenous territory in what is now the United States was inundated with Euro-Americans as rapidly. The Wiyots, and other Native Americans who inhabited Northern California, were ill-equipped to cope with the sudden flood of immigrants. An estimated one hundred thousand Native Americans died during the first two years of the gold rush.

Hickox's mother was left for dead at Indian Island. That she survived and taught her daughter basket weaving, an art form at which Native American women of present-day California excelled, speaks most profoundly to the senselessness of the massacres. Today, the Wiyot people number approximately six hundred. New generations continue working to perpetuate their cultural traditions. ■ —*CRG*

Living Together, Working Together

❖ PURSUING SUCCESSFUL CAREERS IN THE ARTS
WHILE LIVING A COMMUNAL LIFE

In 1902, artists Violet Oakley (1874–1961), Elizabeth Shippen Green (1871–1954), and Jessie Willcox Smith (1862–1949) leased a sprawling country estate outside Villanova, Pennsylvania. This property, previously known as the Red Rose Inn, would serve as their home and studio for the next four years. Called the Red Rose Girls in the popular press, these longtime friends from art school in Philadelphia established a cooperative living arrangement to support one another financially, emotionally, and professionally.

The unmarried artists' respectability was safeguarded by the sheltered gentility of country living. Green and

Left: Green, Oakley, Smith, and Cozens re-create the composition of Oakley's poster for a 1902 exhibition at the Plastic Club, a women's arts organization. Each artist holds a long-stemmed rose while Cozens lifts a watering can.

Above: Oakley's sketches (1918) of Pennsylvania's founder, William Penn, for her murals at the Pennsylvania State Capitol. Penn's ideals held her interest for years to come.

Right: A devoted pacifist, Oakley painted this mural entitled *International Understanding and Unity* during World War I, ca. 1917.

Smith worked as successful illustrators; Oakley became recognized as one of the best allegorical mural painters in America.

Crucial to this unconventional family structure was Henrietta Cozens (1862–1949), who maintained their household and the property's extensive gardens while the others pursued art. As friend and fellow artist Anna Lea Merritt archly noted in a 1900 article, "The chief obstacle to a woman's success is that she can never have a wife."

Commercial illustration offered women a socially acceptable and economically lucrative field of artistic endeavor.

Given the majority female readership of American magazines in the early twentieth century, Green's and Smith's commissions were largely geared toward domestic subjects. Oakley likewise began her career illustrating books and women's magazines, but a stained-glass window commission for All Angels' Church in New York City led to a job painting fifteen murals for the governor's Grand Executive Reception Room at the Pennsylvania State Capitol building, the largest US mural program awarded to a woman to that time. Excelling in a field dominated by men, Oakley also designed panels for the building's senate and supreme court chambers. ■ —EDS

The Powerful Pen of Ida B. Wells

❖ **A LIFETIME CONFRONTING RACIAL VIOLENCE THROUGH JOURNALISM**

Early one morning in 1898 in Lake City, South Carolina, town postmaster Frank Baker and his family were awakened by a raging fire engulfing the building that doubled as their home and the post office. The blaze had been deliberately set by a lynching party of more than three hundred local whites who resented the African American man's appointment as postmaster. As the family ran for the door to escape, the mob fired on them, killing Baker and his infant child, Julia.

When the news of these premeditated murders was reported, one of the first to respond was activist, journalist, women's rights advocate, and author Ida B. Wells (1862–1931). A meticulous investigator and tireless crusader against a rising epidemic of racial violence across the South, Wells had penned the influential pamphlet,

---

"The more I studied the situation, the more I was convinced that the Southerner had never gotten over his resentment that the Negro was no longer his plaything."

Southern Horrors, in 1892. Now, in the wake of the Baker killings, she authored a petition addressed to President William McKinley, asking for his aid in stemming lynching, torture, and murder aimed at the African American community. "Nowhere in the civilized world save the United States of America do men, possessing all civil and political power, go out in bands of 50 and 5,000 to hunt down, shoot, hang or burn to death a single individual, unarmed and absolutely powerless," the petition declared.

The McKinley administration ordered a comprehensive investigation of the Baker affair. A federal grand jury was convened, but the all-white jury failed to reach a decision, resulting in a mistrial.

Wells was born in Holly Springs, Mississippi, into an enslaved family. She was only sixteen when both of her parents died of yellow fever in 1878. She attended Shaw University in Raleigh, North Carolina, the first historically black college or university founded in the South, but was expelled because of "confrontational behavior." She eventually made her home in Chicago, where she lived with her husband, Ferdinand L. Barnett, and their four children.

Ridiculed by many for her uncompromising opinions, Wells was willing to confront all segments of society regardless of station or rank. Her exposés on lynching got her driven out of Memphis, where she lived as a newspaper editor. Her reporting was blunt and unambiguous. Writing in her autobiography about the fiendish cruelty of the "lowest element of the white South," she concluded, "The more I studied the situation, the more I was convinced that the Southerner had never gotten over his resentment that the Negro was no longer his plaything, his servant, his source of income."

Wells was also a tireless worker for women's rights and is credited with integrating the suffrage movement in America. In a 1913 march in Washington, DC, she refused to leave the Illinois delegation and walk with other African American women in the rear of a parade—a request made by the organizers to appease southern white delegates. "I am not taking this stand because I personally wish for recognition," she said. "I am doing it for the future benefit of my whole race." ■ —*RE AND AMS*

1893

MISS GARRITY.
PHOTOGRAPHER.

CHICAGO.

This albumen silver print of Ida B. Wells was taken by Sallie E. Garrity, a photographer who earned national recognition in the 1890s as one of the few women to achieve success in the field of commercial photography. Garrity is believed to have photographed Wells at the time of the 1893 World's Columbian Exposition in Chicago. The Exposition drew protests from both Ida B. Wells and

Critics praised Cassatt's experimental, loose brushwork and her ability to capture the personality and emotions of young children, both evident in this painting, *The Caress* (1902).

Painter of Maternity

❖ **THE ONLY AMERICAN ARTIST TO EXHIBIT WITH THE IMPRESSIONISTS IN PARIS**

IN 1904, MARY CASSATT's oil painting, *The Caress*, won prizes in two prestigious shows of contemporary American art. For the accomplished sixty-year-old, such public acclaim was overdue. Yet Cassatt (1844–1926) politely refused to accept them. "No jury, no medals, no awards," she wrote, expressing a desire for self-determination that defined both her career and her artistic style.

Although Cassatt's parents discouraged her early art studies, their wealth facilitated her training in Philadelphia and Europe. The artist settled in Paris in 1874 and soon began exhibiting with Edgar Degas, Claude Monet, and other Impressionist painters. For her pictures of women and children, she usually hired models, creating modern-day Madonna-and-child motifs, but the "painter of maternity" remained unmarried and childless.

Success allowed Cassatt to reject prizes and reproach her elite patrons for giving insufficient support to emerging artists, especially women. Nonetheless, she respected the public role of museums, and when *The Caress* entered the Smithsonian's collection, she sent its donor, William T. Evans, a personal letter of thanks. ■ —*CAM*

Occupational portraits were wildly popular in the nineteenth century. Workers expressed pride in their trade through their clothing and tools. However, photographs of professional black women, like this tintype from the 1890s, were rare.

Vital Midwives

MERGING MODERN MEDICINE AND WEST AFRICAN TRADITIONS

Curators at the National Museum of African American History and Culture purchased this tintype at auction in 2014 because it provided rare visual evidence of a nineteenth-century black woman as a medical professional. Additional research uncovered a possible identification: Sarah Loguen Fraser (1863-1933), an African American female doctor—one of only about 115 in the nation in the 1890s. Loguen Fraser educated black midwives to integrate modern medical knowledge into their traditional routines.

Until the early twentieth century, midwives, not male doctors, assisted at most births in the United States. In the North, most were immigrant European women; in the South, African American women assisted at both black and white births. These black midwives saw their work as a sacred duty that sustained intergenerational gender and community cohesion by employing time-honored practices derived from West African traditions.

Although the white medical establishment began a campaign to replace midwifery in the late nineteenth century, African American midwives still delivered as many as half of the black babies born in some southern states in the 1950s. ■ —*WSP*

Hawai'i's Queen Lili'uokalani

"I, LILI'UOKALANI OF HAWAI'I . . . do hereby protest against the ratification of a certain treaty, which . . . has been signed at Washington . . . purporting to cede those Islands to the territory and dominion of the United States. I declare such a treaty to be an act of wrong toward the native and part-native people of Hawai'i, an invasion of the rights of the ruling chiefs, in violation of international rights both toward my people and toward friendly nations with whom they have made treaties, the perpetuation of the fraud whereby the constitutional government was overthrown, and, finally, an act of gross injustice to me."

—EXERPTED FROM A LETTER TO PRESIDENT MCKINLEY PROTESTING THE ANNEXATION OF HAWAI'I, 1897

Lydia Lili'u Loloku Waiania Kamaka'eha (1838–1917), better known as Queen Lili'uokalani, was the Hawaiian Kingdom's only reigning queen and last monarch before the overthrow of the sovereign state. Queen Lili'uokalani presided over the Hawaiian Kingdom during a time of great economic growth. By 1890, twenty-one international treaties and more than eighty embassies around the world recognized the Hawaiian archipelago. Additionally, Hawai'i and its multiethnic society enjoyed universal suffrage in 1840 (a full 120 years before the United States), universal health care, state neutrality (1855), and a 95 percent literacy rate, the second highest in the world. Deceit and treachery also marked the queen's tenure: on January 17, 1893, the queen was forcefully removed in a coup de main supported by American troops and warships under the direction of John L. Stevens, US minister to the Hawaiian Kingdom. The United States argued that it needed Hawaiian ports to fight the Spanish-American War deeper in the Pacific, which the Hawaiian Kingdom's neutral status prevented. Despite years of unsuccessful appeals to international states and the United States government, Lili'uokalani was confined at home in Honolulu until her death in 1917. While not an American woman, Queen Lili'uokalani marks a significant voice in the framework of American imperialism. A force to be reckoned with, she protected her country, citizens, and role as sovereign until her passing. ■ —KC

Queen Lili'uokalani's cabinet card (above) dates from 1891, the year she assumed the throne. This autographed copy of *Hawaii's Story by Hawaii's Queen Liliuokalani* (opposite) is held in the Smithsonian's Joseph F. Cullman Library, which features a collection of rare books in anthropology and the natural sciences. The queen's memoir tells her story from childhood to coronation, the overthrow of the Hawaiian monarchy, her imprisonment in the palace, and her forced abdication. Dated February 3, 1898, this book was one of the first copies the queen distributed. —ALK

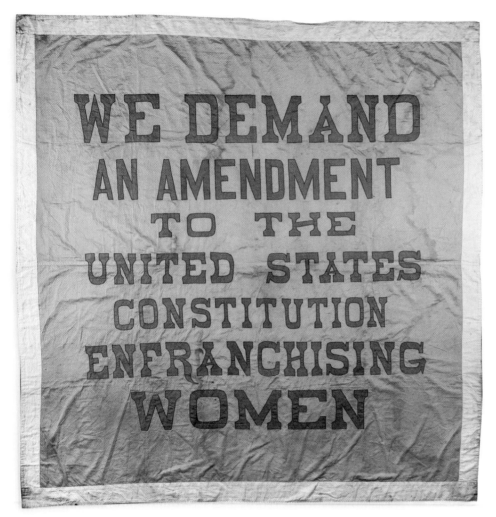

The letters on the "Great Demand" banner (1916–17) were made using a stencil. They were basted in place and then finished with a sewing machine.

Great Demand Banner

❖ "THE RIGHT OF CITIZENS OF THE UNITED STATES TO VOTE SHALL NOT BE DENIED OR ABRIDGED BY THE UNITED STATES OR BY ANY STATE ON ACCOUNT OF SEX."

MARIE GILMER LOUTHAN (1891–1954) confidently carried this silk banner proclaiming the "Great Demand"—woman suffrage by constitutional amendment—in the streets of the nation's capital. It was a particularly gutsy thing for her to do, as she explained to her son, Martin, when he was growing up in Oklahoma: While her husband was deployed in World War I, she stayed in Washington, DC, with her in-laws. Her father-in-law, Martin B. Louthan, was the captain of the Capitol police force, and in 1917, he arrested suffragists protesting at the US Capitol.

Marie's son and grandchildren donated her banner to the Smithsonian in 2009. Another nearly identical copy modeled on the "Great Demand" float from the National Woman's Party (NWP) 1913 suffrage parade now hangs in the NWP's Capitol Hill headquarters and museum.

Ratification of the "Great Demand"—the Nineteenth Amendment—was both a victory and a first step. In many states, women, especially women of color, fought to overcome the same discrimination in voting as their male counterparts. ■ —LKG

Coming Out Swinging

The symbols on this wooden hatchet (ca. 1904)—the turtle, bluebird, rooster, and swallow—all hold significant meaning within the temperance and prohibition community.

THE EXCESSIVE CONSUMPTION of alcohol was widespread in the nineteenth century but not frequently discussed. Alcoholism wreaked havoc on families and communities. Father John Ireland, the archbishop of Saint Paul, Minnesota, stated in a sermon that "The American saloon is the mortal enemy of the family, piety, the maternal and intellectual well-being of the people."

Over the winter of 1873–74, women across the Midwest spontaneously formed coalitions to stop the sale of liquor in saloons. They felt that as protectors of the home, women needed to take action against alcohol. From this loosely organized movement, the Women's Christian Temperance Union (WCTU) was formed. The WCTU strove to abolish the liquor trade, reduce consumption of alcohol, and secure pledges of abstinence.

Initially, the crusades against the saloons were peaceful. The protestors, led by clergy and women volunteers, would sing hymns and say prayers at saloons. Although Carry A. Nation is most frequently associated with her use of a hatchet, she was not the first in the movement to do so. In 1873 at the courthouse in Washington, Ohio, women celebrated the closing of two saloons with songs and prayers, but then, according to contemporary accounts, "axes were placed in the hands of the women who had suffered most, and swinging through the air, they came down with ringing blows, bursting in the heads of the casks, and flooding the gutters of the street."

As the movement grew, the group also began to address causes such as prison reform, an eight-hour workday, and facilities for orphans and kindergartens. The vast number of women involved forced local and state governments to address their concerns. By doing so, they placed themselves in a position of political power and forced changes in their communities and in the nation. ■ —*SM*

A Lifetime Lifting Black Lives

❖ **ACTIVIST AND WRITER MARY CHURCH TERRELL LED THE CHARGE FOR DESEGREGATION**

POISED PROUDLY at the intersection of race, gender, and class, Mary Church Terrell (1863–1954) served as one of the women who ushered in the national black women's club movement of the late nineteenth century. In this photograph, taken around 1910 at the Scurlock Studio in Washington, DC, Terrell strikes a serious and thoughtful pose. As one of the founders of the National Association of Colored Women's Clubs (NACWC) in 1896, Terrell and her colleagues advocated for black women and their efforts toward realizing racial justice and equality for African Americans. Using the motto Lifting as We Climb, black club women sought to redefine the role of middle-class black women.

In the decades after the Civil War, as Jim Crow laws enforced racial segregation and broad political support for white supremacy flourished, African Americans persevered by building their own educational systems, businesses, and racial justice initiatives. Black women formed literary clubs, racial uplift groups, and social services at settlement houses as a response to attacks on their womanhood and race.

Through her writings and activism, Terrell demonstrated the central role of African American women in their mighty struggle to achieve equality. "We refer to the fact that this is an association of colored women, because our peculiar status in this country seems to demand that we stand by ourselves," Terrell said in her inaugural address as NACWC's first president in 1897.

In forming the NACWC, Terrell and her fellow activists saw the need for a national organization to provide a network of women-led initiatives, among them voting rights and racial justice. Terrell made her mark as a civil rights leader; most notably, she was among the principals in the 1953 Supreme Court case that desegregated restaurants and stores in Washington, DC.

Grandson Ray Langston and his wife, Jean, became the keepers of Terrell's legacy in 1989, maintaining the summer home and personal belongings of the activist and those of her husband, Robert Terrell, in Highland Beach, Maryland. Langston recalls spending many summer days at Highland Beach, the vacation shorefront secured in 1893 for black residents through the efforts and foresight of Charles Douglass, son of the preeminent black social reformer Frederick Douglass. Women summered there with their children; husbands came on the weekends. But Langston's grandmother insisted that he join her on the picket lines at the Hecht Company, a prominent department store in downtown Washington, DC, before going to the beach.

The extensive Terrell collection donated to the Smithsonian features such items as opera glasses and playing cards (inscribed with her initials), which relate to her class and lifestyle. Other objects, such as her driver's license, are emblematic of women's increasing mobility and independence. Still other materials speak to her engagement in politics, among them letters indicating her role in the Republican Party between 1916 and 1920. Included as well are letters and samples of her published work. This trove of materials presents the full story of a prominent family while also casting a light on the social activism of the politically engaged upper-class African American community. ■ —*MGM AND DKW*

This NAACP convention delegate's badge (opposite) was worn by Mamie Williams, who, along with several other politically active members of the NACWC, organized the National Republican League of Colored Women in 1924. Addison N. Scurlock made this gelatin silver print portrait of Terrell around 1910. Terrell sent it to the *Chicago Defender* newspaper, which featured her column, Up to Date, from 1927 to 1929.

Union banner made shortly after Local 17 of the ILGWU was founded in 1905. Embroidered on red silk are two clasped hands, the traditional emblem of organized labor.

Courageous and Defiant

❖ **OUT FROM THE TENEMENTS AND INTO THE STREETS**

Members of the International Ladies' Garment Workers' Union (ILGWU) Local 17 proudly displayed this banner in their New York office and defiantly marched behind it on picket lines.

In the first decade of the twentieth century, young Jewish and Italian women fueled a heroic labor revolt in New York City's garment sweatshops and factories. These recent immigrants—tired of long hours, low wages, and irregular employment—undertook the 1909 shirtwaist makers' "uprising of 20,000" and the 1910 cloak makers' strike, which together forced changes in the cutthroat garment industry and helped build the fledging ILGWU into a major labor organization.

With the aid of the Women's Trade Union League, strikers found allies in the growing women's movement across economic class lines that included New York socialites, leading suffragists, and progressives. Their collective activism would inspire and be repeated as union women organized to improve working conditions and demand greater equality for women throughout society. These victories created a foundation for progressive political organizations and an expansion of women's rights for generations who followed. ■ —*HRR*

Bordered with gold fringe, this royal-purple silk banner proudly proclaims the presence of politically active black women in Oklahoma.

A Banner for Change

❖ **ORGANIZING FOR PROTECTION AND EDUCATION IN TWENTIETH-CENTURY OKLAHOMA**

THIS STRIKING BANNER was created circa 1924 by the Oklahoma Federation of Colored Women's Clubs (originally the Oklahoma Federation of Negro Women's Clubs), which was founded in 1910 as an organization of societal reform and community service. Reflecting the rise of Race Women in the Central Plains, as well as the migrations of black people to the West, the federation's founding was flanked by the arrival of statehood in 1907 and the steady climb in violence by white supremacists and others who profited from the destruction of the growing, prosperous black communities, epitomized by the vicious massacre of African Americans in Tulsa in 1921. Because of increasing racism and violence in the region, the organization made the protection and education of African American children and young black women a priority. The federation successfully received funding and support from the state legislature to create a "Negro Girls' Training School."

In addition to schools, Oklahoma clubwomen were integral in securing funding for the building of libraries, including the Excelsior Library in Guthrie, a library in Muskogee, and the Genevieve M. Weaver Library in Ponca City. ■ —DKW

The White House, Their Way

For more than one hundred years, *The First Ladies* exhibition in the National Museum of American History has been one of the Smithsonian's most popular collections. It is also the Smithsonian's first exhibition by, for, and about women.

The collection's origins were serendipitous. Cassie Mason Myers Julian-James, a Washington society figure and frequent donor to the Smithsonian, told some members of the staff about her family's project to create a small collection of women's fashion. The museum urged Julian-James to exhibit the collection at the museum; she readily agreed. Assuming the position of volunteer curator, Julian-James expanded the idea into a larger exhibition of historic American clothing. She formed a partnership with Rose Gouverneur Hoes, the great-granddaughter of President James Monroe, and the two developed a special feature for the new costume collection: separate cases highlighting the "costumes of the ladies of the White House." Within two years, they had assembled a collection of fifteen gowns contributed by the friends and families of former first ladies, and the collection opened to the public in 1914.

Women crowded the new exhibition, and soon it became one of the museum's most visited attractions. Museums had routinely offered the relics of notable men as inspiration for the public, but not those of women. Now first ladies were included alongside George Washington and Ulysses S. Grant as American role models and historical figures. Ball gowns as well as uniforms told the story. Exhibition labels included brief identifications, but no biographical information about the women or detailed descriptions of the dresses. A more exhaustive exhibition catalog written by Hoes was available for purchase, a source of income for the cash-strapped volunteer.

Over the years, the exhibition became more elaborate. In 1964, more lifelike, gowned mannequins were displayed in large period spaces modeled after rooms in the White House, with architectural elements salvaged from President Harry Truman's recent renovation, heightening the feeling of authenticity. Many visitors loved this beautiful display. Some focused on the material culture. Some didn't want the first ladies "politicized" in any way. But for others, simply seeing women represented in the museum was no longer enough. They wanted to hear about the contributions made by the first ladies and the roles they played in the White House and the presidency—to see them as actors in their own right. In response, curators worked to blend the display of traditional dresses with objects that reflect the first ladies in full, adding and reinterpreting objects to show the range of their interests and obligations. For example, state gifts illustrate their ceremonial and diplomatic roles; posters and programs attest to the causes they have supported. Objects as varied as calling cards and campaign buttons document their social and political activities. Unwittingly, Hoes and Julian-James paved the way for this new interpretation by defining first ladies not by their marital status but by their work. The exhibition's founders would be pleased but not surprised by its enduring popularity. ■ —*LKG*

BEYOND BALLROOMS

Helen Taft (1861–1943) was an early supporter of the First Ladies Collection, contributing the white chiffon and silver gown (right) she wore to her husband's 1909 inauguration. Her gift established a precedent for future first ladies; each one since who has attended an inaugural ball has donated the gown she wore. Inaugural gowns mark the first lady's public debut in her new role, while other clothing in the collection can illustrate her participation in state dinners, public appearances, and everyday life. Mary Lincoln's purple-velvet day dress (top right), made by Elizabeth Keckly gives us an opening to consider Lincoln's relationship with her African American dressmaker and confidante and to highlight Keckly's social activism. Melania Trump's off-the-shoulder couture gown (bottom right) reflects a fashion sense honed during her career as a successful model.

Left: Helen Taft's inaugural gown, 1909

Above: Mary Lincoln's velvet day dress, 1861–62

Right: Melania Trump's inaugural gown, 2017

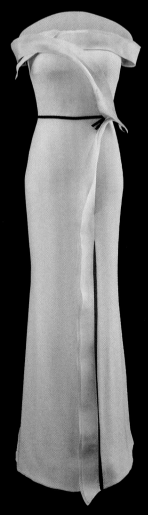

Candidates' wives made their first campaign appearances in the late 1800s, greeting delegations of supporters at their homes. Buttons and ribbons trace their emergence as full-fledged campaigners. In 1960, Pat Nixon (1912–93) became the first candidate's wife to "run" for first lady when the Republican National Committee Women's Division proclaimed the initial week in October "Pat for First Lady" week.

MICHELLE OBAMA'S PRUNING SHEARS

First ladies have championed causes and used their position to raise issue of concern with the president and the public. Several modern first ladies have launched their own programs from their East Wing offices. Michelle Obama's *Let's Move!* initiative, which combated childhood obesity and promoted health and good nutrition, included the cultivation of a widely publicized White House vegetable garden.

ADVERTISING CARDS

When Frances Folsom (1864–1947) married President Grover Cleveland in 1886, she became the nation's youngest first lady and a media sensation. Starstruck Americans purchased photographs and souvenirs of Mrs. Cleveland and copied her hairstyle and wardrobe. Manufacturers capitalized on her popularity, using her image to advertise products she had never endorsed.

DOVES OF PEACE

This brooch, designed by famed French designer René Lalique (1860–1945), was presented to Edith Wilson (1872–1961) in 1919, when she traveled to Paris after World War I for the signing of the Treaty of Versailles. Wilson was the first first lady to travel abroad as part of a presidential diplomatic trip.

NANCY REAGAN'S STATE CHINA

China, invitations, and menus illustrate White House receptions and state dinners, each one an opportunity for the first lady to build America's international relationships. Nancy Reagan (1921–2016) practiced this "soft diplomacy" at fifty-five state dinners and developed a warm relationship with Soviet general secretary Mikhail Gorbachev during a 1987 Washington summit.

BARBARA BUSH'S DESERT CAMOUFLAGE

As first ladies have become more familiar public figures, they have been able to inject candor and humor into the presidency, as well as express compassion and concern for Americans. Barbara Bush (1925–2018) excelled in this role. In 1990, she donned camouflage to join the president in a Thanksgiving visit to American troops stationed in Saudi Arabia, continuing a tradition of concern for the country's service personnel that began with Martha Washington.

This Navy nursing cape was worn in World War I by Sara Cox, a career military nurse who served with the precursor to the Army Nurse Corps in the Spanish-American War before joining the navy. She is buried in Arlington National Cemetery.

Opposite: During World War I, many women risked their lives to care for troops and took on active roles, as depicted in this poster seeking contributions for war relief efforts.

In Service and at the Ready

❖ WORLD WAR I NAVY NURSES SERVED WITHOUT COMMISSIONED RANK

ORLD WAR I PROVIDED American women with a new opportunity to serve their country. It was the first major armed conflict in which the US military accepted both men and women. Although women were still denied the right to vote, the government allowed them to serve in limited roles, ranging from dietitian to telephone operator. But the majority of female service members—more than twenty-three thousand over the course of the war—were nurses.

This indoor uniform, meant to be worn on duty in a hospital ward, belonged to Sara Cox (1883–1943), a US Navy nurse. She enrolled with the navy in 1908 as one of the original Navy Nurse Corps nurses, a group known as the "Sacred Twenty." During the war, she was stationed as a chief nurse at a naval hospital in Washington, DC.

Navy nurses wore the same style of starched dress and cap as civilian nurses. For nurses overseas, however, the dresses did not always hold up well in the cold, muddy reality of treating severe, often heavily infected war wounds in field hospitals. In a letter home, one nurse remarked on the absurdity of wearing a pinned-on nursing cap while moving in and out of low-entranced hospital tents.

Cox's cape was the most iconic part of her uniform. The image of a nurse, cape blowing in the wind or flung over a shoulder to show off the lining, was a mainstay of recruitment posters. The navy wool garments with red linings became symbols of patriotism and sacrifice.

A careful observer will note a missing element of Cox's uniform: a sign of rank. The government refused to grant American military nurses permanent commissioned rank and its accompanying benefits until after World War II.

Although regulations required that capes be returned after the war, many seem to have gone home with the nurses. When donating hers to the Smithsonian in the 1920s, Cox may have found it difficult to part with. In preparation for a 2017 exhibit case, "Modern Medicine and the Great War," costume conservator Sunae Park Evans discovered that a perfect triangle of its red lining had been removed. Perhaps Cox wanted one last tangible souvenir of her time in service to her country. ■ —MW

Hold up your end!
WAR FUND WEEK
One Hundred Million Dollars

Marriage by Matchmaker

❖ **JAPANESE WOMEN JOINING HUSBANDS, SIGHT UNSEEN, IN HAWAI'I AND ON THE WEST COAST**

I N JULY 1913, seventeen-year-old Tei Shida (1892–1989) left her home in Fukushima, Japan, and traveled thousands of miles away to Hawai'i to marry a man she hardly knew. Her future husband was a successful Japanese immigrant and pineapple grower who lived on a plantation high in the mountains. Museum records give only his last name, Saito. Shown at right is the traditional dress of a *montsuki* (formal family crest kimono) with a gold-brocade obi (sash), which Tei Shida would have worn for her wedding and on special occasions.

Tei Shida Saito was one of an estimated twenty thousand Japanese "picture brides" whose families betrothed them to Japanese, Korean, and Okinawan immigrant men living in Hawai'i and on the West Coast between 1908 and 1924. A family member or a friend served as a go-between following the Japanese practice of *omiai* (matchmaking). Frequently the couple would know each other only through an exchange of photos and family information. It was common for men to send old or retouched photos, sometimes of themselves dressed in borrowed suits to feign more affluence than they had. The average age of the brides ranged from sixteen to twenty; their husbands tended to be much older. Although the women were seeking greater personal and economic opportunities through these marriages, they frequently faced harsh conditions. Like many other picture brides, Tei Shida Saito found her new life difficult. She struggled with the loneliness of a hardscrabble life on an isolated plantation. ■ —*NS*

Tei Shida wore traditional clothing for both her graduation photograph (above left) in 1913 and her wedding a year later to a Hawaiian pineapple grower. Her marriage kimono (above right) would have also been worn at other ceremonial occasions.

Left to right: Psychologist Helen Lois Koch; biologist Caroline Elizabeth Whitney; physiologist Charlotte Haywood; biochemist Lois Phoebe MacKay

Lens and Microscope

❖ **PIONEERING WOMEN SCIENTISTS CAPTURED ON FILM**

TRADITIONAL STUDIO PORTRAITS of women scientists from the early twentieth century offer few clues to their subjects' occupations or intellectual achievements. Fortunately for historians, a skilled amateur photographer, Julian Papin Scott (1877–1961), captured a more fulsome cultural view. His photographs showed women at work, in offices and laboratories, peering through microscopes, focused intently on their research.

Excluded from military service during World War I because of a hearing impairment, Scott volunteered to assist a medical researcher who traveled to laboratories around the United States. That circumstance enabled him to photograph thousands of scientists during the 1910s and 1920s.

Reflecting the demographics of science at the time, the majority of Scott's subjects were male, but a collection at the Smithsonian Institution Archives preserves his photographs of more than sixty women, such as those shown above. Psychologist Helen Lois Koch (1895–1977) first taught at the University of Texas but returned in 1929 to the University of Chicago, where she had earned her PhD. A professor of child psychology, Koch researched sibling and twin relationships and helped train teachers for war nurseries in the 1940s. Charlotte Haywood (1897–1971) also returned to her alma mater, Mount Holyoke College, after completing her PhD at the University of Pennsylvania. Haywood taught physiology for thirty-four years, eventually becoming chair of the department, and studied sea urchins, toadfish, and other marine creatures every summer at the Woods Hole Oceanographic Institution. Caroline Elizabeth Whitney (1899–1928) was among the first female graduates of Washington University Medical School. She had just been appointed to a faculty position in pathology at Washington University when she died suddenly from tuberculosis. Lois Phoebe Lockard (1898–1978) had two degrees from Vassar College when she accepted a graduate fellowship in biochemistry in 1922, earning her PhD from Stanford University in 1926. By then she had married another medical researcher, Eaton M. MacKay, and the couple began a long-term scientific collaboration investigating renal hypertrophy (kidney enlargement) and related metabolic disorders.

Each female scientist photographed by Scott had already earned several graduate degrees, often as one of the few women in her field. Most were just embarking on careers combining research and teaching. Although their interests, personal lives, and academic paths varied, these women shared a common dedication to science and an ability to succeed in disciplines hitherto dominated by men. ■ —*MCL*

Above: Madam C. J. Walker's Wonderful Hair Grower was Walker's first hair-care invention.

Right: Walker established approximately two hundred schools nationwide; graduates received rings like this one from a Washington, DC, program.

Opposite: In 1917, Walker agents attending their first national convention in Philadelphia received this badge. Walker used the convention, themed *Women's Duty to Women*, to financially reward agents for their dedication and to remind them of their obligation to protest injustices.

Madam C. J. Walker: Meaningful Beauty

❖ HELPING AFRICAN AMERICAN WOMEN DISCOVER PROSPERITY AND RESPECT

AFRICAN AMERICAN women have often used grooming and dress as defenses against racial and economic injustices. They deliberately created a "look" that informed the world they were a persons of business and substance, even when they lacked financial means. It helped preserve their sense of worth in a society that devalued them because of race, gender, and class. During the post-slavery era, many black women sought beauty routines to advance that goal and thus turned to Madam C. J. Walker products.

Born Sarah Breedlove (1867–1919) on a Delta, Louisiana, plantation, Walker became a successful entrepreneur who helped to shape the images and identities of African American women during the early to mid-twentieth century. She was born into extreme poverty and had to work low-paying jobs as a sharecropper, laundress, and cook. She was orphaned by age seven, married by fourteen, and widowed by twenty. But she persevered and became a wealthy businesswoman, generous philanthropist, and a recognized change agent on issues of race. "I am not satisfied in making money for myself," she said. "I endeavor to provide employment for hundreds of women of my race."

Walker built her beauty empire after the Civil War, when the country was experiencing a social, racial, and political transformation, which included a growth in cities and more working women. However, legal and de facto segregation severely limited economic choices for African American women mostly to field work or domestic service.

NATIONAL CONVENTION OF MADAM C.J. WALKER'S AGENTS

Walker was able to forge a different path, first selling Annie Malone's Poro beauty products and then developing, manufacturing, and selling her own hair products. She created new opportunities for black women, offering formal training and education to those wanting to become beauticians, salon owners, and Walker sales agents. She also hired teachers and trainers for more than two hundred Walker schools across the nation.

Effective marketing was critical to her success. Company advertisements routinely connected good grooming with success. In one such ad, "Amazing Progress of Colored Race," she identified key black leaders whose "Good Looks, Neatness / Were Very Important Essentials / in the Success of these People."

Walker's generous philanthropy to various African American civic, social, and political organizations enhanced her success and recognition, and on a broader scale, it helped create change in America. In addition to providing financial support to the NAACP, the Tuskegee Institute, and the black YWCA, she also spoke out for fair treatment of black soldiers and helped to transform discriminating and restrictive policies and practices in America.

When Walker died in 1919 at the age of fifty-one, she had created sustainable opportunities for African American women to become independent entrepreneurs and established an international legacy as a pioneer of the modern beauty industry. ■ —*EN*

Dedicated, Dutiful and Diverse

❖ JULIETTE GORDON LOW ENVISIONED A BROAD-BASED GIRL SCOUT MOVEMENT

EARLY IN 1912, Juliette Gordon Low (1860–1927) returned to Savannah, Georgia, from Britain with a mission. Excitedly, she phoned her friend Nina Anderson Pape, a progressive local educator. "I've got something for the girls of Savannah, and all America, and all the world," she reported, "and we're going to start it tonight!" That "something" was the establishment of the Girl Scouts.

Juliette "Daisy" Gordon was born at the onset of the Civil War to a prosperous Savannah family and grew to be an active and headstrong young woman with a keen sense of duty. She wed wealthy Englishman William Mackay Low, but their unhappy marriage ended with his death in

1905, amid divorce proceedings. Always conflicted about her status as a "woman of ease," Low looked for a call to service and found it in scouting. In 1911, she met Sir Robert Baden-Powell, the founder of the Boy Scouts in Britain, and his sister Agnes, who had recently launched the Girl Guides. With Baden-Powell's encouragement, Low journeyed back to America to do the same.

By 1913, Low had expanded her organization onto the national stage. She established a headquarters in Washington, DC, and published *How Girls Can Help Their Country*, the US version of the scout handbook. She backed a change in uniforms from the blue of the Girl Guides to a more military khaki like the uniform at right, which belonged to Dorothy Emmert (1905–93), a Girl Scout from Hutchinson, Kansas, during World War I.

Low insisted her girls be "scouts" rather than "guides" and resisted pressure from critics who insisted that girls' use of the word *scout* trivialized and "sissified" the term. Her vision was to develop the potential of all girls through a mix of skills building, character development, healthy fun, and service. From the beginning, membership included girls from different religious, ethnic, and social backgrounds, as well as girls with disabilities. (Low herself was severely hearing impaired for much of her life.)

In the run-up to World War I, membership boomed, especially as more women and girls saw scouting as a way to help the war effort. By war's end, Girl Scout membership had soared to about forty thousand and kept growing, aided through the high-profile involvement of first ladies Edith Wilson and Lou Hoover. Today there are more than 2.5 million Girl Scouts in the US and in nearly ninety other countries, and more than 50 million women have participated in Juliette Gordon Low's vision. ■ —*TKW*

Opposite: Juliette Gordon Low sat for this portrait by Edward Hughes in 1887, soon after her marriage into British society. Years later, her vision for a Girl Scout uniform, like this one from 1918, was inspired not by frills but by practical military khaki of the period.

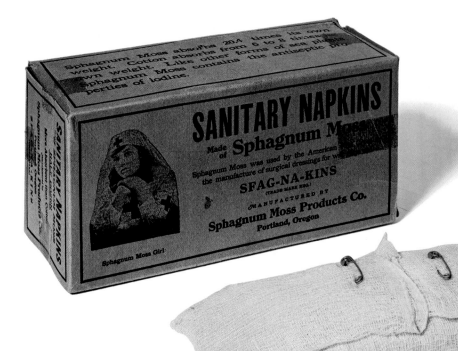

Sfag-Na-Kins packaging used scientific-sounding claims to tout the efficiency and medical value of sphagnum moss as a sanitary napkin, countering consumer hesitation to purchase a disposable product.

Changing Menstrual Culture

❖ AN UNUSUAL SANITARY NAPKIN MADE ITS DEBUT IN THE WAKE OF WORLD WAR I

BEFORE THE AVAILABILITY of mass-marketed sanitary napkins, women created their own menstrual supplies, sewing or folding rags into washable, reusable napkins. But World War I changed America's menstrual culture.

Battlefield medicine, with its increased emphasis on sanitary practices and sterile materials, reinforced the nation's growing awareness of the relationship between cleanliness and good health. It helped to inspire a burgeoning market for sanitary and disposable products of all kinds.

On June 2, 1918, the *Oregon Daily Journal* announced that great quantities of sphagnum moss had been brought to Portland's Red Cross surgical dressings workroom. With cotton supplies running low, Allied armies needed a substitute for cotton dressings. Sphagnum moss, growing abundantly in Pacific coast bogs, proved to have the necessary absorbent and antiseptic properties. The town rallied its women to process the moss and pack it into surgical dressings.

For months, newspapers around the country would feature photographs of women sorting, cleaning, and drying heaps of the moss before folding it into precisely sized surgical dressings. By the time the war ended, the American Red Cross had produced hundreds of thousands of the sphagnum pads; Allied organizations had produced many millions.

In 1919, the Sphagnum Moss Products Company announced it would pioneer the production of a new kind of sanitary menstrual napkin: Sfag-Na-Kins. Although advertised as "a new discovery," in design, material, and application Sfag-Na-Kins were nearly identical to the soldiers' dressings. The product's box reminded female consumers that the mildly antiseptic moss pads had excelled at soaking up many a soldier's blood, while the imagery of the Red Cross–capped "Sphagnum Moss Girl" suggested the health expertise and practicality of the World War I nurse or volunteer.

Production of moss for wartime surgical dressings had relied on the labor of thousands of volunteers, and without that unpaid workforce, the moss proved an inefficient material for both surgical dressings and sanitary napkins. Despite sphagnum moss fervor during the war, Sfag-Na-Kins soon disappeared from the commercial market. ∎ —RLA

The hands and dial of this Waterbury Turnout alarm clock (1918–20) featured luminescent radium paint that glows in the dark. A number of young women who painted the dials fell victim to radiation poisoning.

Radium Risks Exposed

❖ **YOUNG WOMEN FACTORY WORKERS CAUGHT UNAWARE**

RADIUM-BASED LUMINESCENT paint made this circa 1920 alarm clock glow in the dark. It also made many of the young women who painted the dials fatally ill. Their detailed work required a precisely tipped paintbrush, which they were instructed to draw into a fine point with their lips. The dial painters did not know the risks of ingesting radium because there was a delay between their exposure and symptoms.

The awakening of America to radium hazards was in part due to the struggles of these women to seek redress. Lawsuits filed in New Jersey, Connecticut, and Illinois during the mid-1920s and 1930s raised awareness of the plight of the "radium girls" and the need for labor safety.

Exposure limits for dial painters were recommended in 1941. Just as World War I popularized luminescent paint for watch dials, compasses, and gun sights, World War II required tools for soldiers to tell time, find their way, and locate their enemies in the dark. The breath and bones of dial painters provided data used to determine how long workers could be exposed to radiation and how much radium was deemed injurious. The document establishing limits states that "before an individual is employed he shall be informed in detail of all known dangers involved." We, not just he, are all informed today because of she. ■ —*KFF*

Flying Firsts in Triumph

❖ TWO SPIRITED WOMEN—ONE BLACK,
ONE WHITE—CHANGED AVIATION HISTORY

" I JUST WANTED TO BE FIRST ... that's all," Harriet Quimby (1875–1912) explained after becoming the first American woman, and the thirty-seventh person in the world, to receive a pilot license in August 1911. Bessie Coleman (1896–1926) didn't want to be a manicurist or a wife (though she was already both). She wanted to "amount to something." These two spirited women changed the twentieth-century social order when they became flying firsts in the fledgling world of aviation.

Already a popular theater critic and globe-trotting writer-photographer for *Leslie's Illustrated Weekly*, Quimby started flying lessons after witnessing the exhilarating 1910 International Aviation Meet at Belmont Park on New York's Long Island. Immediately on earning her license

Left: Bessie Coleman enjoyed strong support from the African American press in her fight for racial and gender equality. When rejecting a movie role that required her to play an ignorant woman wearing tattered clothing, she said, "No Uncle Tom stuff for me."

Right: Harriet Quimby designed her own practical yet stunning purple satin flying suit, complete with a stylish hood and culottes that converted to a skirt, cognizant of the need to clamber in and out of a cockpit in view of the public and the press.

Below: The post office authorized experimental airmail flights at the 1912 Boston Aviation Meet, but they ended up being cancelled. Some mail was marked with the postal slogan anyway. —DP

at thirty-five, she joined the Moisant flying team for exhibition shows in Mexico, becoming the first woman to fly there. After purchasing a Blériot XI monoplane—a distinct design departure from the biplanes of the day—she flew it solo twenty-two miles from Dover, England, to Hardelot, France, on the morning of April 16, 1912, becoming the first woman to fly a plane over the English Channel. She returned in triumph to the United States, eager to pursue and write about her new avocation. But she met with disaster in July, when she and a passenger were thrown to their deaths from her fragile plane over Boston Harbor.

Twenty-seven-year-old Bessie Coleman, whose father was American Indian, was at a personal crossroads in segregated Chicago when she was challenged about her future by her brother, a World War I veteran who taunted her with stories of French women flyers. She sassed back, "That's it. . . . You just called it for me!" But black men were not welcome in aviation, let alone black women. Unfazed, Bessie learned French and earned her pilot license in France—the first for an African American woman. She learned aerobatics, performed for thousands of people, and lectured too, all in pursuit of opening an instruction school for African Americans. "We must have aviators," she said, "if we are to keep up with the times." But in a scenario eerily similar to Quimby's fate, she too fell out of her plane, a Curtiss Jenny, while flying over Jacksonville, Florida, in 1926. Following her untimely death, the African American aviation community embraced her name and mission, establishing flying clubs in her name. ■ —DSC

CHAPTER THREE

1921–1948

The Rise of the Modern Woman

THE FREE-SPIRITED WOMAN of the 1920s shattered the Victorian model of respectable womanhood. Amelia Earhart, the first female aviator to fly solo across the Atlantic, epitomized that declaration of independence. With her iconic bomber jacket and short, tousled hair, she telegraphed a glamorous image of rugged self-reliance. This expression of freedom rippled across the country as women moved to northern cities to find work and escape racial segregation laws.

These doors slammed shut during the Great Depression as local laws blocked women from "taking jobs away" from men. Thousands of women were unemployed, and Mexican American women were rounded up and deported. Fed up with segregation and racism, accomplished women of color such as Josephine Baker pursued successful careers in Europe. At the same time, in America, the Daughters of the American Revolution barred celebrated contralto Marian Anderson from performing at Constitution Hall. After protest from the NAACP, President and Mrs. Roosevelt intervened, and Anderson held a concert on the steps of the Lincoln Memorial.

With America's entrance into World War II, the job market opened up; millions of white, married women joined the paid workforce. For many, it was their first taste of financial independence. At war's end, however, they were pressured to leave those jobs to make way for male veterans. ■

PREVIOUS SPREAD

Marian Anderson

Philadelphia-born Marian Anderson (1897–1993) was one of the twentieth century's greatest classical vocalists. When the all-white Daughters of the American Revolution refused to allow her to perform at Constitution Hall, the NAACP mounted a campaign that resulted in Secretary of the Interior Harold Ickes arranging for Anderson to give a public concert on the steps of the Lincoln Memorial on Easter Sunday, April 3, 1939. Attended by 75,000 people, the concert proved to be one of the most important public events in the struggle for civil rights, and a monumental moment in Anderson's long, illustrious career. Her excellence as a vocalist, along with the grace and dignity she exuded as a citizen of the world, showed how artists could be instruments of social change. —DRR

Anderson wore a version of this tailored orange shantung jacket and black velvet skirt at her Lincoln Memorial concert in 1939. The jacket's original fabric was replaced in 1993, but the trim and buttons are from the original.

1920

Alice Paul first proposes the Equal Rights Amendment.

Native Americans are granted the right to US citizenship by the Snyder Act of 1924.

The Great Depression begins with the stock market crash in October.

1925

The Dust Bowl begins, exacerbating the financial crisis begun in the Great Depression.

Hattie Wyatt Caraway of Arkansas becomes the first woman elected to the US Senate.

Amelia Earhart becomes the first woman to complete a nonstop transatlantic flight solo. She had crossed the Atlantic four years earlier as a passenger.

1930

Frances Perkins becomes the first woman member of a presidential cabinet, serving as Franklin Delano Roosevelt's secretary of labor.

Mary McLeod Bethune is appointed director of the Division of Negro Affairs of the National Youth Administration, becoming the first black woman administrator in the federal government.

1935

Zora Neale Hurston publishes *Their Eyes Were Watching God*, which she wrote while doing anthropological fieldwork in Haiti.

Billie Holiday records "Strange Fruit" on the Commodore label after Capitol, her usual record label, refuses to issue a song about lynching. It eventually sells one million copies.

1940

The United States enters World War II after the attack on Pearl Harbor.

Chicago Cubs owner Philip Wrigley organizes the All-American Girls Baseball League.

1945

World War II ends; millions of women lose their war work jobs when servicemen return.

Former First Lady Eleanor Roosevelt becomes the chair of the United Nations Commission on Human Rights, which would publish the UN Declaration of Human Rights in December 1948.

1950

Hattie W. Caraway postage stamp, 2001

Portrait of Mary McLeod Bethune, Scurlock Studio, ca. 1930–40

Signed first edition of Their Eyes Were Watching God *by Zora Neale Hurston, 1937*

Shellac record of "Strange Fruit," recorded by Billie Holiday and Her Orchestra, 1939

South Bend Blue Sox Baseball Dress, worn by Besty Jochum, ca. 1943–48

Pioneering a Shifting Landscape

❖ **ANNETTE HOYT FLANDERS FLOURISHED IN A MALE-DOMINATED FIELD**

THE "FRENCH GARDENS" at Sunken Orchard, created on the vast McCann estate on Long Island, left nothing to chance. The series of formal gardens incorporated a wide grass allée, expanses of lawn, and symmetrical pathways, evoking an atmosphere of carefully groomed grandeur. Its formal knot garden, planted with white flowers and boxwood hedges, was positioned close to the music room of "The Playhouse," so the pattern of its plantings could be viewed from above. A model of precision and grace, it is little wonder that the Architectural League of New York awarded the 1932 Gold Medal in Landscape Architecture to its designer, landscape architect Annette Hoyt Flanders (1887–1946).

However deserving Flanders was of this honor, it was nonetheless a signal achievement for a woman to win

---

"It is folly to take it up as a part-time interest for it demands so much energy and time," Annette Hoyt Flanders told her students.

---

the award. Although women were entering the field of landscape architecture, they were still a minority in the profession overall. When Flanders would eventually establish her own firm, she would hire graduates of the Lowthorpe School of Landscape Architecture for Women and the Cambridge School of Architecture and Landscape Architecture. These schools, founded in 1901 and 1915, respectively, educated many women because existing programs, including the distinguished Harvard School of Landscape Architecture, did not admit women. With degrees in hand, opportunities for apprenticeships were

critical for new graduates to gain the skills and necessary experience to launch their own careers. Successful women landscape architects like Flanders, who mentored and hired other women, enabled a generation of women to break barriers in a largely male-dominated field.

Many of Flanders's early designs were in keeping with the prevailing transitional style, which melded aspects of the traditional and romantic Country Place Era style and the modern garden movement.

Since gardens are ephemeral by nature, photographs are often the only surviving visual records. These hand-painted lantern slides, commissioned by the Garden Club of America in the 1920s to record members' gardens, were donated to the Smithsonian's Archives of American Gardens in 1992.

Flanders continued her successful practice in the 1930s and 1940s by adapting designs to meet the needs of the owners of smaller urban and suburban gardens. Her former student, the landscape architect Alice Upham Smith, recalled one of Flanders's lectures in which she outlined her views: "To build a parapet on a country estate, to supervise construction of a bridge or turn a barren tract into a land of haunting loveliness demands a knowledge of architecture and engineering as well as botany. It is folly to take it up as a part-time interest for it demands so much energy and time. . . . Few people would try to paint without study, yet many plant gardens because they like flowers."

Flanders was named a fellow of the American Society of Landscape Architects in 1942, in recognition of her extensive work and her dedication to the advancement of the profession. She designed both public and private landscapes, lectured, and published extensively until her death at the age of fifty-eight. ■ —*KAC*

Opposite: Entrance into the "French Gardens" on the McCann estate in Oyster Bay, New York

This garden, located at the
Lowthorpe School of Landscape
Architecture for Women, was
designed by students. The school
opened its doors in 1901 and its
campus served as a living laboratory
for garden design and horticulture.

A Passion for Strings

❖ EDITH MABIE'S LOVE OF GUITARS
TURNED INTO A BUSINESS

By 1918, when sixteen-year-old Edith Mabie (1902–89) of Bluefield, West Virginia, was running her own music shop and winning mandolins in sales contests, a love for stringed instruments was already deeply embedded in her maternal line.

Her grandmother, Helen Garver, had studied guitar in the early 1850s at the Oxford Female Institute in Ohio. Garver had been homesick until she discovered the camaraderie that guitar playing could forge. Occasionally it landed her in trouble: one evening, while singing rambunctiously with her friends, the school dean banged on the door, suspecting that gentlemen had surreptitiously joined the party. Years later, Edith's mother played that same 1850 William Hall & Son guitar to provide accompaniment during church services, and also strummed "with gusto," as Edith recalled, "Polly Wolly Doodle" and other popular songs of the day.

Edith took her passion for guitars further. At a time when female entrepreneurship was restricted largely to domestic wares and services, she sought entry into the rapidly professionalizing music industry. After her return from an intensive 1918 summer music study in Cincinnati, she petitioned Kalamazoo, Michigan's Gibson Mandolin-Guitar Mfg. Co., Ltd. to become a sales representative. Upon her parents agreeing to cosign her contract, the Gibson company brought fifteen-year-old Mabie on board to develop the West Virginia market. She soon opened a Bluefield storefront to sell Gibson instruments and teach lessons on the guitar, steel guitar, and mandolin. Her success was immediate; in her first year, she outperformed all other Gibson representatives in her sales district. Nearly sixty years later, Edith Mabie donated four instruments to the National Museum of American History, including her grandmother's 1850 William Hall & Son guitar and the spoils from her victory in a Gibson sales contest: this exquisite top-of-the-line 1920 Gibson F4 Artist model mandolin. ∎ —JT

Twenty-year-old Edith Mabie won this 1920 Gibson F4 Artist model mandolin in a Gibson sales contest within a few years of opening her guitar store in Bluefield, West Virginia.

Madame Evanti's custom-made Fisher piano incorporates carvings of a lyre, a motif also found on her personal stationery. Her portrait (left) is the work of the Maurice Seymour Studios of Chicago.

Abroad to Succeed

MADAME EVANTI MAKING HER MARK IN EUROPE, THEN AT HOME

BORN IN WASHINGTON, DC, to a prominent family of black educators, Annie Lillian Evans (1890–1967) began singing in her early teens, honing her talent at community events with the goal of performing classical grand opera. Becasue of racial barriers, she decided that Europe offered more opportunities: "I'm going to learn to sing professionally under the best vocal teacher in Paris, then come back here and show what I can do." Known as Madame Evanti, in 1925 she became the first African American to sing with a European opera company.

Of her 1932 "home-coming concert" at the Belasco Theater in Washington, DC, one critic wrote, "She has a strikingly colorful voice—vibrant, dynamic, and compelling." She sang at the White House by invitation of First Lady Eleanor Roosevelt and performed with the National Negro Opera Company. Evanti was also an accomplished composer who published with W. C. Handy. "All of this has taken hard work," she told an interviewer. "But if you have some place to go, there is no other alternative." ■ —JM

Louise Bourgeois, *The Blind Leading the Blind*, ca. 1947–49

Before Her Time

❖ **LOUISE BOURGEOIS'S UNUSUAL CREATIONS HAD POLITICAL BITE**

LOUISE BOURGEOIS CREATED a vast, haunting, and much-admired body of work. The seminal *The Blind Leading the Blind* (ca. 1947–49), a precarious-seeming progression of paired vertical "legs" tapered at the bottom and anchored from above by a horizontal beam, is perhaps her best-known sculpture of the 1940s. Standing nearly six feet tall, the legs march in step without clear direction, unified yet idiosyncratic and offbeat.

Several versions of the work exist. The first was originally titled *The Blind Vigils*. Bourgeois (1911–2010) changed the title following her appearance before the House Un-American Activities Committee that same year, in reference to the oft-quoted biblical parable from Matthew 15:14, where Jesus describes the folly of the Pharisees and scribes: "Let them alone, they are blind guides. And if a blind man leads a blind man, both will fall into a pit."

The artist wielded the title both in contempt for the committee's actions and in reference to the egoism of certain artistic predecessors. In her words, "[André] Breton and [Marcel] Duchamp made me violent. . . . *The Blind Leading the Blind* refers to the old men who drive you over the precipice." Like much of Bourgeois's work, *The Blind Leading the Blind* assumes a sinister cast, its physicality perilous, charismatic, and ominous. ■ —AR

For the design of this cup and saucer in 1935, Kogan drew upon the influences of European avant-garde artistic movements and adapted them for a modern American audience.

The Spirit of the New

❖ INDUSTRIAL DESIGNER BELLE KOGAN MARRIED SOPHISTICATION WITH AFFORDABILITY

"NO WOMAN KNOWS machinery" was the narrow-minded view of manufacturers when Belle Kogan (1902–2000) started designing objects for mass production. Prevailing against this attitude, she distinguished herself as one of the few American women industrial designers active during the founding years of the profession in the late 1920s. She was the first woman to establish her own independent consulting firm, building a staff of three female designers by 1939. Reflecting on her career path, Kogan mused, "You sort of grow into a job like this. I started out as an art student, a portrait painter, then I got into the jewelry business, designed silver, then picked up the rest." She achieved financial success with an astute understanding of manufacturing and the marketplace, producing designs that married sophistication, affordability, and practicality. Working seamlessly across media, she earned praise for her work in silverware, electrical appliances, jewelry, clocks, ceramics, plastics, and more. She was an outspoken leader in her field, frequently lecturing on how to produce good, salable design.

Kogan noticed a taste for modern design in pottery, and sensing a more progressive consumer market for tableware, she produced this Metropolis-pattern cup and saucer and its accompanying dinner service in 1935. Described as embodying "the spirit of today," its motif of a stylized cityscape and rigid C-shaped handle marked it as modern. With a keen sense of color and form, gained by her training and experience in various artistic sectors, Kogan used concentric circles and painterly decoration in bold accent colors to offset the cup and saucer's dominant ivory—a color she often relied on as "the jack of all trades." She shrewdly patented the distinctive teacup form with its geometric handle.

Beginning in 1959, Kogan bequeathed a number of examples of her stylistic output, including molded melamine dishware and accompanying process drawings, to Cooper Hewitt, Smithsonian Design Museum. A later gift to the collection, this cup and saucer were presented to the museum by the designer in 1994. ■ —EMO

A Deep Devotion to Science and Politics

❖ **ON MOUNTAINS AND PICKET LINES, AGNES CHASE CHANGED VIEWS OF WOMEN**

AGNES CHASE (1869–1963), a diminutive but determined botanist, was among the radical suffrage demonstrators arrested for picketing the Wilson White House in 1918–19, and she participated in the jailed suffragists' hunger strike. Chase worked for the United States Department of Agriculture (USDA) as a grass specialist, stationed at the Smithsonian US National Herbarium. The USDA threatened to fire her for "conduct unbecoming a government employee," but her supervisor, A. S. Hitchcock, declared her too valuable to dismiss.

Born Mary Agnes Meara in rural Illinois, Chase had endured a traumatic childhood; both her alcoholic, abusive father and her brother were murdered in 1871. Forced to leave school for work at a young age, she learned botany on her own and was fascinated by grasses, which she described as "what hold the earth together." She was widowed after just a year of marriage to William Chase in 1888. Determined to ensure that others lived better lives than she had, and a strong advocate for equal rights, she joined the Woman's Christian Temperance Union and the NAACP.

Her childhood love of the natural world led to a career as a scientific illustrator and then as a renowned curator of grasses at the United States National Museum. She and Hitchcock published the definitive works on the grasses of the Americas. In 1922 she published *The First Book of Grasses: The Structure of Grasses Explained for Beginners*, so amateurs could learn about these important plants.

This popular volume with Chase's illustrations remains in print today. Denied access to funded expeditions because she was a woman, Chase fearlessly set off on self-financed solo field trips across South America in the early twentieth century. She also mentored young Latin American scholars, especially women, who affectionately called her "Grandma." She took them to her beloved operas, and they often stayed in her home, nicknamed Casa Contenta, where she cooked gourmet meals.

Scientific illustration was a way for nineteenth-century women to enter science, and botany was more receptive to women than other fields. Hitchcock was a supportive mentor who opened doors for her, and Chase in turn opened doors for women on the picket line, in the field, and in the museum. ■ —*PMH*

Specimen of *Arthrostylidium sarmentosum*, a bamboo, collected by Chase in 1913, with her scientific illustration of it

Left: In 1924, botanist Chase (far left) and her student Maria Bandeira (1902–92) climbed the second-highest peak in Brazil, collecting plants for Brazilian and US museums. Chase was a pioneer in conducting independent fieldwork across the Americas and mentored generations of women scientists. In this photograph from 1925, the botanists take a break from collecting to sit atop Mount Itatiaia.

A Latina Star and Hollywood Success

❖ MEXICAN ACTOR DOLORES DEL RÍO'S RAPID RISE IN AMERICAN FILM

"IF I EVER SEE MY NAME in incandescent lights, I know I will walk around the block five times to look at it, I will be so thrilled." So declared twenty-two-year-old Mexican actress Dolores del Río (1904–83) to the *Los Angeles Times* in a 1926 article. As she said those words, they were becoming reality. That year she was selected by Fox Film Corporation to play her first leading role, the French barmaid Charmaine in the World War I silent comedy drama *What Price Glory*. From then on, she was a major box-office draw.

Only six months earlier, she had arrived in Hollywood at the invitation of film director Edwin Carewe, who had "discovered" her at a soirée while vacationing in Mexico. Struck by her beauty, Carewe asked del Río if she would like to make a movie, to which she replied "Yes," uttering the only word she knew in English.

Del Río's debut turned her into the first internationally revered Mexican movie star and one of the very few Latinas in Hollywood at the time. Her extraordinary beauty and expressive face earned her principal roles in *The Trail of '98* (1928) and *Ramona* (1928), among other films. As the silent era ended and talkies were introduced, del Río was among the few actors who survived the transition. Owing to her accent, however, she was often typecast as ethnic and exotic characters, among them a Polynesian princess in *Bird of Paradise* (1932) and a Brazilian belle in *Flying Down to Rio* (1933). At the same time, her fair skin and aristocratic bearing made her ideal for such European characters as the mistress of Louis XV in *Madame Du Barry* (1934). All the while, she fought to be recognized as a Mexican actress in Hollywood, particularly when the media repeatedly referred to her as Spanish.

By the early 1940s, del Río's career in the United States was starting to decline, and she went back to her home country, where she became one of the divas of Mexican cinema's Golden Age. ■ —*TC*

This gelatin silver print portrait (1927) by celebrity photographers Benjamin Strauss and Homer Peyton captures Dolores del Río during her rise to become one of Hollywood's divas.

Opposite: Amalia Mesa-Bains (1943–), *An Ofrenda for Dolores del Rio*, 1984, revised 1991, mixed media installation including found objects, dried flowers, and glitter. The sumptuous *ofrenda*, or offering to the deceased, transforms domestic altar-making practices to commemorate Dolores del Río, a role model for many Chicanas in the United States.

A Trailblazing Life in Aviation

P LAGUED BY electrical storms and icy conditions, Amelia Earhart (1897–1937) crossed the Atlantic alone in this vibrant red Lockheed Vega 5B in 1932. She landed in an Irish pasture, becoming the first woman to make the solo trip. Later, Earhart wrote about her motivations for the flight, saying in part, "It was, in a measure, a self-justification—proving to me, and to anyone else interested, that a woman with adequate experience could do it."

Adventurous from an early age, Earhart constructed a wooden rollercoaster as a child in Atchison, Kansas, fearlessly testing and improving it. In 1918, while working as a nurse's aide in Toronto and tending to World War I soldiers, a visit to a local flying field ignited a spark in her. Drifting from college and uninterested in marriage and motherhood, Earhart learned to fly in 1921, bought a Kinner Airster biplane, and promptly set a women's altitude record in 1922. Six years later, she joined aviators Wilmer Stultz and Louis Gordon in a transatlantic flight, becoming the first woman to fly as a passenger across the Atlantic Ocean.

In 1930, Earhart bought this trusty Vega 5B. Despite an issue with fuel leakage, the aircraft carried her safely during her famed fifteen-hour transatlantic solo flight in 1932. Later that year, she flew the Vega 5B nonstop across the United States—another first for a woman.

Although flying undoubtedly carried risk, Earhart cherished her independence and felt far more daunted when her public relations manager, George Putnam, proposed marriage. Dismissing the "medieval code of faithfulness," she married him on her own terms in an open and equal partnership, which included an escape clause to part in a year if they did not find happiness. They remained married. In 1935, Putnam commissioned celebrated cabinetmaker Albert Wood and Five Sons to build a chest for her growing collection of aviation trophies, plaques, and memorabilia.

Two years later, Earhart set out to fly around the world with navigator Fred Noonan—fatefully, with a flawed communications plan. Quietly starting her world flight from Oakland, California, in late May, Earhart and Noonan left Miami on June 1 and flew twenty-two thousand miles over the next twenty-eight days. On July 2,

Piloting this Lockheed Vega 5B, Amelia Earhart became the first woman to cross the Atlantic Ocean alone in 1932. She loved the speedy, streamlined Vega and flew several from 1929 to 1935.

Below: Earhart challenged female stereotypes and encouraged society, policymakers, and other women to do the same. This mid-1930s portrait highlights her standard flight clothing and her elegant hands.

over the vast Pacific Ocean, the pair came tantalizingly close to tiny Howland Island but couldn't locate land. The US Coast Guard cutter *Itasca* heard Earhart's sporadic but strong radio calls—"I must be on you but cannot see you"—until there was radio silence. Search parties failed to find them.

Although a lifelong adventurer herself, Earhart empathized with conventional women, encouraging them to seek independence, education, equality, and opportunity. Her commitment to women's rights, the National Woman's Party, and the Women's International League for Peace and Freedom earned her widespread respect—famously from First Lady Eleanor Roosevelt, possibly the only woman more popular in the 1930s.

In the male-dominated world of early aviation, Earhart defied gender roles by building a legendary flight career, earning the Distinguished Flying Cross and other honors, and consistently landing on the women's lists of most admired and best dressed. In this mid-1930s portrait, the pioneering pilot appears confidently poised for the next adventure. ■ —DSC

Above: Despite misplacing these goggles (ca. 1920s) at her first stop in the 1929 Women's Air Derby competition, Earhart flew on, placing third.

Right: Early airplanes offered scant weather protection, so Earhart wore this wool-lined leather flight suit on long-distance flights (ca. 1928–35).

Below: Earhart kept trophies and plaques in this teakwood chest (1935), which highlights her three milestone solo flights: transatlantic, Honolulu–Oakland, and Mexico City–Newark.

Opposite: To support her endeavors, Earhart sold travel memorabilia like this signed, stamped envelope (1935) from her solo flight from Los Angeles to Mexico City and Newark.

AMELIA EARHART

May 8-9, 1935

One of 35 covers franked with the "Earhart" stamp issued by the Mexican Government for her non-stop, record breaking flight from Mexico to United States,
May 8-9th 1935.

O'Keeffe's Manhattan Abstractions

❖ **SUBVERTING THE MASCULINE SKYSCRAPER, FORESHADOWING FEMINIST ART**

THE DIZZYING HEIGHTS and soaring vertical faces of New York's skyscrapers command the eye in *Manhattan*—at approximately seven feet tall and four feet wide, the largest canvas ever painted by Georgia O'Keeffe (1887–1986). One of the most celebrated artists of the twentieth century, O'Keeffe is best known for her bold paintings of bones, flowers, and the New Mexico desert, but she created this legendary piece for a storied exhibition.

It was 1932, and the country was mired in the Great Depression. New York's Museum of Modern Art arranged a large exhibition of sixty-odd American artists, hoping the show would encourage architects to offer the painters mural commissions. O'Keeffe was thrilled upon being invited to exhibit. She had been thinking about painting the city but had been told it was impossible, and that "even the men hadn't done too well with it."

O'Keeffe painted this piece while living in an apartment in the Shelton Towers Hotel, which, at thirty-one stories, was considered the tallest hotel in the world when it was built in 1924. By the end of the Roaring Twenties, skyscrapers in steel, stone, and glass had sprung up across the city, becoming quintessential symbols of masculine striving. O'Keeffe adorned hers with falling roses in pink, coral, and sky blue.

On the day of the exhibition, O'Keeffe's clean, modernist vision of New York stood out among the many industrial and agricultural scenes that harkened to more prosperous times. To her delight, the Rockefeller family offered her a mural commission for the women's powder room in Radio City Music Hall. However, Alfred Stieglitz, O'Keeffe's husband and dealer, was convinced that a mural project might jeopardize her career. Reluctantly, she declined the proposal. In an ironic twist, *Manhattan* is now considered one of O'Keeffe's crowning achievements as the foremother of feminist art. ■ —*VMM*

New York City's spectacular views inspired some of Georgia O'Keeffe's most memorable paintings, among them *Manhattan* (1932). O'Keeffe was one of the first American artists to live in a skyscraper.

Anni Albers's *Ancient Writing*, made with cotton and rayon, is one of two highly innovative, influential weavings made by the artist in 1936.

Transforming Textile Art

WEAVING ABSTRACT ELEMENTS INTO AN ANCIENT ART FORM

GERMAN AMERICAN TEXTILE ARTIST Anni Albers (1899–1994) made this monumental handloomed weaving in 1936, after traveling to Mexico and visiting ancient sites, such as Monte Albán and Teotihuacán. The title of the work, *Ancient Writing*, references both her studies of Andean art and the abstract shapes she arranges here to resemble blocks of text, hieroglyphs, or pictograms, as though intending them to be "read."

Following studies at the Bauhaus in Weimar and then in Dessau, Germany, Albers became one of the first teachers at North Carolina's Black Mountain College, a pivotal school that later nurtured such luminaries as Ruth Asawa and Robert Rauschenberg. She established the school's weaving workshop in 1933, inspiring future generations of fiber artists and textile designers with her radical approach to materials and techniques. She also innovated a dialogue between fiber art and abstract painting, leaving an indelible mark on contemporary art.

Experimenting with synthetic materials, such as cellophane and rayon—both of which were rarely used in textiles at the time—Albers explored depth and density. Her prolific output included curtain fabrics, furniture upholstery, rugs, and architectural screens, and her bold, integrated visions greatly influenced the evolution of the modern interior. ■ —AT

Aerobatic Wonder

❖ **BETTY SKELTON AND "LITTLE STINKER" WERE A PERFECT PAIR**

Betty Skelton's success also spelled success for the petite and agile Pitts biplane, designed by Curtis Pitts in 1946. It remains a popular aerobatic plane to this day.

Model airplanes, not dolls, were Betty Skelton's favorite childhood toys. Precocious and spunky, Skelton (1926–2011) illegally flew solo at twelve years old in 1938, earned her pilot license at sixteen, and worked as a clerk and flight instructor to earn pilot ratings. Frustrated by the prohibition of women pilots in the military and airlines, she learned aerobatics and built her career at air shows and competitions. While setting seventeen aviation and auto-racing records, she paved the way for women in aviation, sports, and business.

Skelton and "Little Stinker" (above) were a perfect pair. Light, small, with a short wingspan and high agility, the Pitts Special S-1C was ideal for aerobatics. (Skelton named it after exclaiming "Little Stinker!" following a complicated landing.) She became the first woman to perform an inverted ribbon cut (slicing a ribbon held aloft by two poles while upside down), succeeding on her second attempt after the engine quit on her first approach.

Admired for her charm and depth of personality, Skelton wrote for aviation magazines and hosted a radio show. Although she reached the pinnacle of aerobatics, gender barriers, combined with the loss of friends and lovers through aviation accidents, left her with little motivation to continue. She sold "Little Stinker" in 1951.

After meeting Bill France of NASCAR, Skelton began driving Daytona pace cars, becoming the auto industry's first female test driver. In 1962, she passed the same fitness tests as the NASA's Mercury astronauts but never had any illusions NASA would select a woman for the program. When asked about competing in male-dominated fields, Skelton stated simply, "Competing? No, I didn't really do that. I found that once I demonstrated I was capable, had the ability, I was accepted." ∎ —DSC

In this ca. 1920–25 photo (above) taken at Hano, Arizona, Nampeyo paints designs on a clay pot. Her daughter, Fannie, likely assisted her with this ca. 1930–40 polychrome pot (right).

Heritage Reclaimed

❖ **NAMPEYO REVIVED AN ANCESTRAL POTTERY**

HOPI-TEWA POTTER Nampeyo (1859–1942) was the first Pueblo potter to gain acclaim outside of the American Southwest. She is credited with reviving Sikyatki pottery, a style that previously flourished from the fourteenth to seventeenth centuries at Hopi Pueblo's First Mesa.

Nampeyo and her husband, Lesou, drew inspiration from the unusual designs they saw on shards of broken pottery found near an abandoned ancestral village in northeastern Arizona. In the 1890s, a Smithsonian excavation led by Jesse Walter Fewkes unearthed well-preserved examples of the ceramics.

Nampeyo rediscovered and began using the fine Sikyatki clay to produce pots ranging from cream or golden yellow to orange. Bird features—curving beaks, wings, and feathers—figure prominently in her painted designs. The shapes of the pots are also distinctive, including low, wide jars and bowls, sometimes with flattened shoulders or outward flaring lips.

The matriarch of an extended family of potters, Nampeyo kept this artisanal tradition alive, working with her daughters and grandchildren as her husband's role lessened. Other women of First Mesa followed her lead in resurrecting the style, and new generations have maintained and updated the form by innovating on Nampeyo's painted designs. ■ —*RHT*

Thousands of women operated telephone switchboards like this one, which dates from around 1910. Telephone switchboard operators still exist, though many work private systems.

"Hello, Operator?"

❖ **MAKING NATIONWIDE COMMUNICATION POSSIBLE**

Elizabeth Willauer (1901–93) operated this telephone switchboard for nearly forty-three years, plugging the cords in by hand to connect calls. Installed in Mount Victory, Ohio, in 1910, the oak Kellogg Switchboard & Supply Company unit served one hundred subscribers until an automatic dial system replaced it in 1962. When a subscriber lifted the phone's receiver, a light on the board illuminated, notifying Willauer to make the connection.

Early on, young men who had previously worked in the telegraph industry typically served as switchboard operators. But telephone managers quickly deemed them unprofessional and unruly, replacing them with young women who proved adept at multitasking and calm customer relations. They could also pay the women less than half of what men were paid. Even so, operators earned good wages and could be financially self-sufficient in one of the few professional occupations then acceptable for women. Both civilian and military organizations employed women operators, and they appeared regularly in this role in popular culture. Lily Tomlin's Ernestine from *Laugh-In* may be the best-known characterization of this occupation. ■ —CH

This electric corn grinder was used by Concha Sánchez in Fillmore, California, to make tortillas that she would sell to support her family.

Concha's American Journey

❖ AN IMMIGRANT MOTHER SUPPLEMENTS HER FAMILY INCOME WITH COOKING

THIS ELECTRIC *MOLINO* (corn mill) is rustic by modern standards, but it was a time-saving alternative to making tortillas by hand when it was manufactured in the 1920s. Concepción (Concha) Nieves Sánchez (1874–1962), a Mexican immigrant, used it to make the thin, flat pancakes of cornmeal that have been a mainstay of the Mesoamerican diet since ancient times.

Concha's son Arnulfo bought the mill for his mother, along with a *comal*, a griddle to cook the tortillas, and a hand-cranked *tortilladora*, a machine to shape the dough. With these tools, Concha could produce quantities large enough to sell on weekends directly from home and from Arnulfo's food store. For entrepreneurial migrant women, participating in an informal economy of weekend street vending offered flexibility and freedom as an alternative to low-wage labor or factory work.

Born in Guanajuato, Mexico, Concha immigrated to the United States with her husband and small children in 1906. The family's American journey took them through El Paso, Texas, to work on a cattle ranch, followed by employment on the Kansas railroads. Eventually they moved to Riverside, California, in 1912. Ever resourceful, Concha began selling tortillas after her husband, Abundio, was injured in an accident. Later the family relocated to Fillmore, California, where they opened Sánchez Brothers Mexican Mercantile.

The tortilla making was led by women. Concha produced *nixtamal* (softened corn), masa (corn dough), and tortillas with her daughters María, Irene, and Guadalupe, and later with her grandchildren. The family softened the corn on Friday nights and on Saturday mornings they rinsed and ground it. The children added water to make the masa, which was first dropped onto the press and then onto a conveyor belt and finally cooked on the griddle. The warm tortillas were counted, wrapped, and sold by the dozen. Concha's grandson told Smithsonian curators in a 2006 interview that his grandmother continued making her signature tortillas until she was eighty years old. ■ —*LSV*

Eleanor Roosevelt

I am told that the stars are millions and millions of miles away, though sometimes they look so near, but it seems to me, at times, to be almost as hard for people who have no curiosity to bridge the gap from one human being to another. Perhaps the day will come when our curiosity will not only carry us out of our homes and out of ourselves to a better understanding of material things, but will make us able to understand one another and to know what the Lord meant when He said, "He that hath ears to hear, let him hear." And we might well add: "He that hath eyes to see, let him see."

—Eleanor Roosevelt, *The Saturday Evening Post*, August 24, 1935

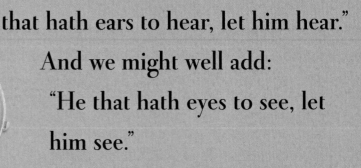

E LEANOR ROOSEVELT (1884–1962) spent her life looking beyond the class and culture into which she was born. As a young woman, she worked in city settlement houses. Once married to Franklin Delano Roosevelt, she advanced his aims when he became governor of New York and later president. But she also pursued her own goals while traveling the state, the country, and eventually the world, advocating for social, racial, and economic justice and for changes in government policies that would value the dignity of the individual. Her work culminated at the United Nations, where she guided the drafting and passage of the Universal Declaration of Human Rights. She called herself Franklin Roosevelt's eyes to minimize her power, but it was her own unique vision that made her one of the most influential women in the twentieth century. ■ —LKG

Wrapped tightly in a black fur coat, her famous face all but hidden, Eleanor Roosevelt nearly disappears from view in this ca. 1940 portrait by Charles Johnson Post. It underscores the intensely private woman behind the public persona.

Eleanor Roosevelt wore these white-gold reading glasses on a necklace chain. This pince-nez style of glasses was popular in the nineteenth century; they use a spring clip to cling to the bridge of the nose without support from temple

Della Hayden Raney worked as head of the nursing staff at the station hospital at Camp Beale, California, shortly after being promoted to captain in early 1945.

Left: Captain Hayden's scrapbook, assembled while stationed at home and abroad with the US Army Nurse Corps.

A Lifetime of Military Service

❖ **PERSISTING IN THE FACE OF RACIAL AND GENDER BIAS**

CAPTAIN DELLA HAYDEN RANEY's determined gaze in the photograph above, taken near the end of World War II, reflects her perseverance against gender and racial prejudice in the US military. She kept the image above in this scrapbook, assembled while stationed in military hospitals at home and abroad with the US Army Nurse Corps.

In 1940, a recent graduate of nursing school, the twenty-eight-year-old Raney (1912–87) applied to the Army Nurse Corps (ANC), which flatly rejected her because of her race. She persisted, eventually appealing to the head of the Red Cross. In 1941, in response to the need for a larger wartime workforce and to pressure from African American leaders and organizations, the ANC accepted fifty-six black women, limited to segregated wards. Raney thus became the first African American woman commissioned into the ANC since World War I. She remained in the corps, retiring as a major in 1978. This scrapbook provides a poignant reminder of her dedication to her country and her race. ■ —LEM AND KAS

In a League of Their Own

❖ DURING WORLD WAR II, WOMEN PILOTS PROVED THEY COULD FLY MILITARY AIRCRAFT

WHILE GIVING A FLYING lesson in her Piper Cub at Pearl Harbor on December 7, 1941, Cornelia Fort (1919–43) witnessed the attack of the Japanese air fleet. She was the first American pilot to do so, and she decided right then that she wanted to help her country. And she was not alone. When some enlightened military leaders agreed and approved the creation of the Women Airforce Service Pilots (WASP), about twenty-five thousand American women applied to be an auxiliary part of the home-front army. (A fraction of the applicants—1,820 in all—were accepted into the program; only 1,074 graduated.) Fort, an experienced pilot, joined the Women's Auxiliary Ferrying Squadron (WAFS), which later became part of the WASP.

The WASP flew sixty million miles of flight in all types of military aircraft, including fighters and B-17 and B-29 bombers, and paved the way for today's fully vested female military pilots. These women ferried aircraft, cargo, and personnel; tested repaired aircraft; and towed targets throughout the forty-eight states, filling gaps left by male pilots who had been sent to war. "We had to deliver the goods," Fort said, "or else there wouldn't ever be another chance for women pilots in any part of the service."

Although originally told they would become part of the military, the WASP instead were disbanded in December 1944, a casualty of rancor over unit independence, jobs, and gender roles toward the end of the war. Still, General Hap Arnold stated, "If ever there were a doubt in anyone's mind that women can become skillful pilots, the WASPs have dispelled that doubt." Never given any military benefits during the war, these women rallied to acquire veteran status in 1977. ■ —DSC

The civilian Women Airforce Service Pilots (WASP) adopted military-style dress, including this short field jacket. The group had its own insignia, the sprite-like Fifinella, designed by Walt Disney. In 2010, the WASP were awarded a Congressional Gold Medal in recognition of their service in World War II.

This lithograph, after artwork created by J. Howard Miller for Westinghouse factories during World War II, was purchased from the artist in 1985.

Flexing a Bicep for Uncle Sam

❖ AN EFFORT TO PLACE MORE WOMEN IN THE WARTIME WORKFORCE

Few graphics from the World War II era are as recognizable and enduring as J. Howard Miller's poster created for the War Production Co-Ordinating Committee at Westinghouse Electric and Manufacturing Company. It was displayed on the factory's bulletin boards for thirteen days in February 1943 as part of a series of posters designed by Miller (1915–90), a freelance Pittsburgh artist. Although a minor part of the war era's visual landscape, the poster was rediscovered and elevated to become an iconic feminist touchstone in later years.

The rapid military mobilization following the US entrance into World War II resulted in severe shortages of industrial workers for wartime production. To address this crisis, the War Manpower Commission orchestrated a campaign to fill these vacancies by drawing millions of women into industrial jobs they had previously been barred from taking. On assembly lines, in shipyards and munition factories, and throughout the economy, they replaced the women and men who entered military service. The appeal of these jobs was not simply a chance to support the war effort. Most of the women were already in the workforce, and although most companies paid them less than their male counterparts, they left lower-paying jobs for the higher wages of industrial work.

To help integrate so many new workers, the War Production Board urged companies to establish joint labor-management committees, which were intended to boost workplace morale and maintain shop discipline. One of their principal functions was arranging for a steady display of work-incentive posters throughout the plants. Although the posters carried direct messages to work harder, keep quiet, and conserve, the underlying and more important theme was to stress that workers were no longer just employees of the corporation, but rather Uncle Sam's soldiers on the industrial front line of the war.

The images were consciously created. Artists often chose to personify male American workers as "average Joes" to gain the common man's allegiance to production goals. The working woman, on the other hand, was idealized as a fashion model in denim. Carefully glamorized images were intended to convince women they would not have to sacrifice their femininity for war work. The symbolic image also reinforced the temporary role that government and business planners expected these women to play: fill the vacancies when needed and then leave once the veterans returned.

The posters Miller created for Westinghouse offer good examples on how companies blended traditional themes of workplace discipline and patriotism. With her strong gaze, rolled-up sleeves, and raised arm, the image emanates self-assurance and competence. But if there was any doubt about how far to take this new role, another poster

---

Few realize that this iconic poster was displayed for only thirteen days in 1943.

---

with an affable male manager counseled, "Any Questions about your work . . . Ask Your Supervisor." The transition for these women out of the factories would also be played out in Miller's posters, including one encouraging workers to "Do what you can to help returning veterans."

Although seen by only a few workers at the time, the *We Can Do It!* poster was introduced to the public in the 1980s and 1990s after it appeared in several publications and exhibitions commemorating the war. It was quickly reproduced, repackaged, personalized, and manipulated for new audiences, to be consumed as reproductions, pot holders, coffee mugs, lunch pails—and even as an action figure. Once freed from its historical context of wartime production and patriotism, the image became a powerful statement of feminist empowerment. ■ —*HRR*

"Farmerettes" Feed a Nation

❖ SERVING THE HOME FRONT IN
THE WOMEN'S LAND ARMY

W HILE MOST PEOPLE recognize World War II's
iconic Rosie the Riveter, her lesser-known com-
patriots in the Woman's Land Army of America (WLAA)
provided just as critical a service during the two world
wars. Women and schoolgirls like seventeen-year-old
Shirley Armstrong (shown here on the cover of *Life*)
worked on farms and in canneries to feed the nation
and ensure that crops did not spoil while millions of
farm laborers served in other wartime capacities.

The WLAA was initially established during World
War I by an array of civic clubs and organizations,
with women banding together to do the work of farm-
hands called to military service or factory jobs. Called
"farmerettes," the women were trained to cultivate
and harvest crops used to feed those on the home
front and abroad.

This invaluable civil organization was resur-
rected during World War II, this time under the US
Department of Agriculture's United States Crop
Corps, a federal agency tasked with overseeing
civilian agricultural efforts. With an estimated 1.5
million at work between 1943 and 1945 performing
duties as varied as driving tractors, picking fruit,
milking cows, and trucking produce, the WLAA helped
fuel the massive war effort. The organization also opened
opportunities for many women to work outside the home
for the first time and earn a wage.

Just like the millions of Americans who grew their
own victory gardens, land army enlistees came from
every walk of life, from wives and sisters of servicemen
to rural school teachers and urban office workers. Some
toiled full-time, while others lent support after work,
on weekends, or during summer vacations. Bolstered by
First Lady Eleanor Roosevelt and besting skeptics ranging from farmers to Secretary of Agriculture Claude R.
Wickard, the WLAA played an essential role in sustaining
America during World War II. Little wonder, then, that
Life chose to honor their contributions with this victori-
ous cover. ■ —*JMC*

During World War II, the Woman's Land Army of America
kept farms alive while soldiers fought overseas. This
September 27, 1943, cover of *Life* magazine shows land army
worker Shirley Armstrong (1926–2010) harvesting corn.

Wartime's Female Ideal

❖ **STOCKINGS GREW SCARCE DURING WORLD WAR II; THE REMEDY: LEG MAKEUP**

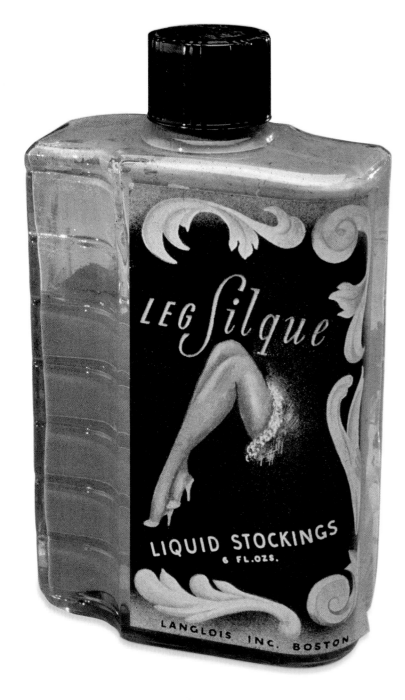

Rexall drugstores advised women to save their fabric hosiery for winter, since one bottle of Leg Silque provided "30 pairs" of snag-free liquid stockings.

WOMEN HAVE USED leg makeup since the late 1920s, when beauty editors raved that this revolutionary product would enable them to go without stockings during the hot summer months, feeling cooler, freer, and younger while still looking meticulously groomed. However, when World War II necessitated that nylon and silk be earmarked for parachutes and ropes, women's stockings suddenly became scarce. Just as suddenly, the popularity of leg makeup—or "liquid stockings"—surged.

Leg Silque's label conveys the glamorous, overtly flirtatious style that many women of the period embraced. "Cosmetic stockings" joined bright red lipstick and dark mascara as part of the wartime feminine ideal. Women painted on the hosiery-colored makeup. To heighten the illusion, some used eyebrow pencils to draw a seam running up the back of the leg.

Marketing for leg makeup reflected 1940s societal expectations about female bodies. The smooth, monotone look of stockings had become the norm, and bare legs were perceived as embarrassingly unfinished. Advertisements for leg makeup promised to make ankles appear smaller and legs look slimmer, and to conceal every blemish, freckle, and vein. Waterproof formulas claimed that women could swim without losing their perfected, velvety finish.

Leg Silque's Suntan shade reveals changing notions about ideal skin color. Since the 1930s, tanned skin on white women had evolved into a sign of healthy beauty—suggesting a lively, modern woman engaged in outdoor activities. Leg makeup advertisements vowed that legs would look sun-kissed or even deeply tanned, and brands offered shades with names such as Palm Beach Tan and Sun Copper. Other shades, such as Gypsy Tan and Mexitan, suggested an "exotic" ethnicity. Despite this emphasis on bronzed skin, Leg Silque, like most cosmetics from mainstream manufacturers of the time, was not offered in shades intended to look natural on darker skin tones—a reflection of the racial bias inherent in the period's beauty ideals. ■ —*RLA*

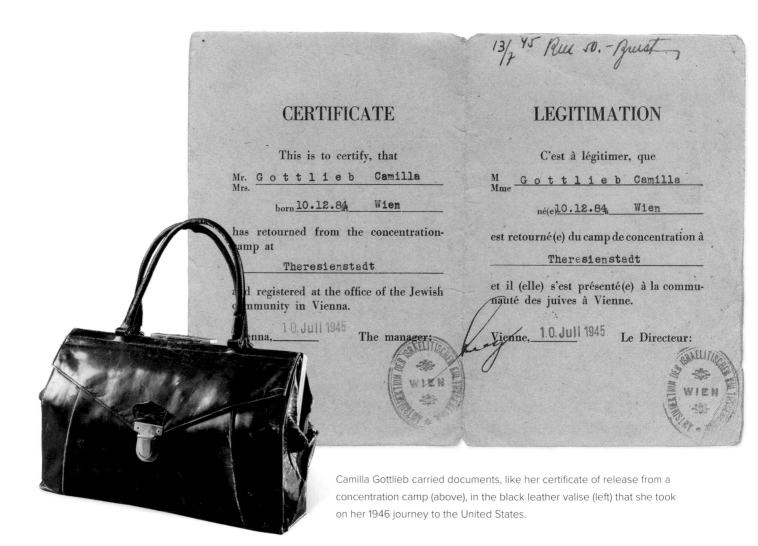

This is to certify, that

Mr. **G o t t l i e b Camilla**
Mrs.

born 10.12.84 Wien

has retourned from the concentration-camp at

Theresienstadt

and registered at the office of the Jewish community in Vienna.

Vienna, 10. Juli 1945

The manager:

LEGITIMATION

C'est à légitimer, que

M **G o t t l i e b Camilla**
Mme

né(e) 10.12.84 Wien

est retourné(e) du camp de concentration à

Theresienstadt

et il (elle) s'est présenté(e) à la communauté des juives à Vienne.

Vienne, 10. Juli 1945 Le Directeur:

Camilla Gottlieb carried documents, like her certificate of release from a concentration camp (above), in the black leather valise (left) that she took on her 1946 journey to the United States.

Unpacking History

❖ THE HOLOCAUST TOLD POIGNANTLY THROUGH ONE WOMAN'S POSSESSIONS

WHEN CAMILLA GOTTLIEB (1884–1964) arrived in America in 1946, her concentration camp memories were fresh. Like many Holocaust survivors, she spoke rarely of those nightmare years. Her testimony came after her death, in a leather valise tucked away in the back of a closet, where her grandson Robert Bodansky found it. It contained more than 250 letters and papers that trace her trials, triumphs, and journey. These documents reveal a compelling story of her Jewish heritage, imprisonment in Theresienstadt concentration camp, the death of loved ones, liberation, and her longing to reach her family in the United States.

"My pen cannot describe what I have endured," Camilla wrote to her daughter, Lony, in October 1945 while waiting to emigrate. "I might be able to tell you about it some other time. It was a God-given miracle that I lived to return here."

Fearing the growing Nazi anti-Semitism, Lony had fled their home in Vienna in 1938 and settled in Brooklyn. Following liberation, Camilla and Lony assaulted the bureaucratic wall of United States immigration policy. Finally successful, Camilla, carrying her valise, sailed to New York and resumed work as a seamstress and embroiderer, skills that may have improved her chances of survival in Theresienstadt. Her family only fully learned of her Holocaust experience when they poured over the contents of the valise. Now in the Smithsonian collection, Camilla's possessions tell a story of resilience in the face of horror. ■ —WHY

Above: A watercolor titled *Tanforan*, ca. 1942–44, depicts part of the incarceration campgrounds. Right: Citizen's Indefinite Leave card, 1944, issued to Sekimachi when she was finally permitted to leave Topaz, Utah.

Art in Isolation

❖ KAY SEKIMACHI FOUND SOLACE IN DRAWING AND PAINTING WHILE INTERNED

KAY SEKIMACHI WAS fifteen years old when she and her family arrived at the Japanese American camp known as Tanforan Assembly Center. She was one of the roughly 120,000 Japanese Americans living on the West Coast who were forcibly moved to incarceration camps during World War II. Like the Sekimachi family, many were US citizens.

Amid the crushing confinement of the camps, Sekimachi found solace in drawing and painting. She attended the Tanforan Art School founded by artist Chiura Obata (1885–1975), a fellow Japanese American prisoner who recognized the children's need for continuity and normalcy inside the camps and believed in the healing power of art. She learned from Miné Okubo (1912–2001), a Japanese American woman who became famous for her book *Citizen 13660*, which documented life inside the camps. Everyone at Tanforan was moved to another incarceration camp, the Topaz War Relocation Center in Utah, where Sekimachi attended high school and continued to take art classes. Sekimachi and her family left Topaz in 1944, settling in Cincinnati for a year before returning to Berkeley, California.

Sekimachi and Okubo became lifelong friends, supporting each other and their respective careers. Sekimachi went on to become a fiber artist of international renown. She leveraged the medium of fiber, especially weaving, to create sculptural pieces inspired by her Japanese heritage, an innovative approach that secured her reputation as a master weaver. ■ —*RU*

Hedy Lamarr's alluring beauty is the star attraction of this poster advertising the Italian release of her World War II propaganda film *The Conspirators* (1944).

Brain Power

❖ **HOLLYWOOD BEAUTY HEDY LAMARR DEVISED MILITARY TECHNOLOGY**

Celebrated as "the most beautiful woman in the world" during her Hollywood heyday in the 1940s, film star Hedy Lamarr (1913/14–2000) ultimately proved that her brain was even more extraordinary than her beauty. Without any formal training, she pursued childhood experiments in dismantling and rebuilding mechanical devices to see how they worked. Years later, when not in front of the cameras, she worked with scientific equipment in her home laboratory or on-set trailer.

Eager to aid Allied forces during World War II, she explored potential military applications for radio technology. She theorized that varying radio frequencies at irregular intervals would prevent interception or jamming of transmissions, thereby creating an innovative communication system. Lamarr shared her concept for utilizing "frequency hopping" with the US Navy and codeveloped a patent in 1941. But it was not until the Cuban missile crisis of 1962 that naval ships implemented her revolutionary idea for ensuring secure communications. Today, Lamarr's innovation makes possible a wide range of wireless communications technology, including Wi-Fi, GPS, and Bluetooth. ■ —RA

This portrait was taken by Nickolas Muray in 1937, the year in which Wong starred in the Hollywood film *Daughter of Shanghai.*

Not Just Exotic

❖ **ANNA MAY WONG FOUGHT TO BE VIEWED BEYOND STEREOTYPES IN HOLLYWOOD**

Anna May Wong (1905–61) was the first Chinese American actress to become a major box-office attraction. Initially finding success as the exotic Mongol slave in *The Thief of Bagdad* (1924), she went on to deliver commanding performances on Broadway and in several classic films.

At a time when women were typically relegated to romantic roles, Hollywood refused to cast Wong as the dame who got the guy—in large part because of strict miscegenation laws that existed in many states. Nevertheless, she achieved some starring roles, including acting shoulder to shoulder with Marlene Dietrich in the artistically pioneering *Shanghai Express* (1932). Wong also sought work in Europe. A quick study of languages, Wong recorded the dialogue for her films in English, French, and German.

When World War II broke out, she put her film career on hold and worked from the United States on Chinese war relief. While some Chinese Americans of the time reprimanded her for playing to stereotypes, many people today see her as a pioneer who succeeded in a hostile industry. ■ —*KCL*

Political Women: A Seat at the Table

When the Nineteenth Amendment was ratified in 1920, men ran the country. There were no women serving in the United States Congress or the president's cabinet. Jeannette Rankin, the first woman elected to the House of Representatives in 1916 (from Montana, where women had been voting since 1914), had lost her 1918 campaign for the Senate, and Oklahoma's Alice Robertson would not be sworn in until 1921.

Before World War II, most women representatives and senators gained their seats as widows appointed to complete their husbands' terms. Some declined to leave when their "placeholder" term expired and then went on to win elections in their own right and continue their careers as legislators. In the cabinet, whose members are nominated by the president, things moved more slowly. But in 1933, Frances Perkins (1882–1965) became the first woman in a presidential cabinet when Franklin D. Roosevelt named her secretary of labor.

A graduate of Mount Holyoke College, Perkins lived in settlement houses, trained as a social worker, and worked as a consumer lobbyist. After witnessing New York's Triangle Shirtwaist Factory fire in 1911, in which 146 workers—largely immigrant women and girls—died, she became a suffrage advocate and tackled issues surrounding labor, women, and children. In 1929, then-Governor Roosevelt named Perkins head of New York State's Department of Labor; four years later, she would begin a stint as the longest-serving secretary of labor in history. Twenty years passed before a second woman was named a cabinet secretary, with Oveta Culp Hobby appointed by President Dwight D. Eisenhower to head the newly formed Department of Health, Education, and Welfare. It took more than two decades longer for two or more women to serve in a cabinet at the same time. To date, three departments have still not been led by a woman: defense, treasury, and veterans affairs.

In the postwar years, women increasingly ran for office rather than inheriting it, and the women of the Capitol grew in legislative experience and seniority. In the 1960s and 1970s, this core of women was joined by activists and politicians from the women's and civil rights movements. Representative Patsy Mink of Hawai'i, the first woman of color elected to the House of Representatives, was the primary author of Title IX, which in 1972 amended the 1964 Civil Rights Act to include women. Following the example of the Congressional Black Caucus formed in 1971, women members of Congress elected from different parties and representing different constituencies and governing philosophies united in 1977 to form the Congressional Caucus for Women's Issues to discuss topics of mutual interest.

In 2019, nearly one hundred years after the ratification of the Nineteenth Amendment, there are more than one hundred women in Congress. Thirty-one women have served as cabinet secretaries, three have been secretary of state, and Nancy Pelosi is the Speaker of the House of Representatives. Although more women are at the table, their numbers are still not equal to men's. Doubtless, more women will follow the advice of Representative Shirley Chisholm: "If you wait for a man to give you a seat, you'll never have one! If they don't give you a seat at the table, bring in a folding chair." ■ —ECJ AND LKG

FRANCES PERKINS, IMMORTALIZED

Labor Secretary Frances Perkins was one of more than fifty notable Americans captured in bronze for the sculpture series *The Living Hall of Washington, 1944*. Commissioned by Washington, DC, publisher W. M. Kiplinger (1891–1967) and created by Max Kalish (1891–1945), the series was meant to be "an everlasting record of the men who held the reins of American life." Perkins was the only woman selected, as Eleanor Roosevelt had declined, saying she was not worthy of the collection.

Depicting Perkins at work, Kalish described her as "Not a typical business woman. Motherly type." Having pledged that the figures he was creating in one-third life-size scale would portray the subjects as they were, he offered to "take off some weight" from Secretary Perkins's statuette. While "it did not glamorize her," he said, it "did make improvement."

Recognized as the driving force behind the Social Security Act, Perkins also championed unemployment insurance, a federal minimum wage, the National Labor Relations Board, and the Bureau of Labor Standards. —ECJ

CHALLENGING FOR THE PRESIDENTIAL NOMINATION

Margaret Chase Smith (1897–1995) became the first woman to have her name placed in consideration for nomination at a major political party's national convention when she challenged Barry Goldwater to become the Republican presidential candidate in 1964. The senator from Maine is also remembered as the first member of Congress to speak out against the tactics of McCarthyism in 1950.

THE HAT MAKES THE WOMAN

Hats were Bella Abzug's trademark style. The New York congresswoman wore this brown felt hat while presiding over the National Women's Conference in Houston, Texas, in 1977. Known as "Battling Bella," Abzug (1920–98) took strong, sometimes controversial stands on women's equality, gay rights, the Vietnam War, government transparency, and child welfare. She served three terms in Congress and remained a powerful figure in the women's movement and an inspiration to aspiring female politicians at the end of her tenure.

PALIN FOR VICE PRESIDENT

As John McCain's 2008 running mate, Alaskan governor Sarah Palin was the first woman on a Republican presidential ticket. After the election, she continued to be a popular figure in conservative politics.

BRING U.S. TOGETHER

VOTE CHISHOLM 1972
UNBOUGHT AND UNBOSSED

A CATALYST FOR CHANGE

This daughter of working-class immigrant parents—a mother from Barbados and a father from Guyana—Shirley Chisholm (1924–2005) was the first black woman elected to Congress (1968) and the first to make a serious bid for the US presidency, represented by this 1972 campaign poster. Her career in education in Brooklyn led her to champion educational reforms and antipoverty programs during her years in Congress (1969–83). Assessing her life in public, she noted, "Of my two handicaps, being female put many more obstacles in my path than being black." —WSP

After serving as first lady, senator from New York, and secretary of state, Hillary Rodham Clinton came one step closer to breaking what she had once called "the highest and hardest glass ceiling" when she ran for president on the Democratic ticket in 2016. Clinton was the first woman to receive the presidential nomination from one of the country's two major political parties.

TAKING THE GAVEL

Nancy Pelosi received this gavel in 2007 when she became the first woman elected Speaker of the United States House of Representatives. One of the most influential figures in Democratic politics, Pelosi rose through the ranks as the first woman to serve as her party's whip and leader. She was elected speaker again in 2019.

DRESSED FOR POLITICAL SUCCESS

Geraldine Ferraro (1935–2011) wore this white dress in 1984 when she accepted the Democratic Party's nomination for vice president of the United States. As running mate to Walter Mondale, she was the first woman selected by a major political party for the presidential ticket. The three-term congresswoman's reputation for successfully meshing her own liberal and feminist views with the more conservative views of her Queens, New York, constituents helped secure her nomination.

Grandma Moses, American Icon

❖ **MOSES PAINTED A BUCOLIC VIEW OF AGARIAN LIFE**

IN THE MIDDLE of the twentieth century, an elderly woman from upstate New York turned the art world on its ear. Anna Mary (Robertson) Moses (1860–1961) became better known by the moniker "Grandma" when her paintings depicting rural traditions and family recollections made her the most famous female American artist of the day.

Moses was always artistically inclined, but she increasingly took to painting once her labor-intensive days as a farm wife were behind her. In 1938, after displaying her paintings at a country fair and a local drugstore, the seventy-eight-year-old self-taught artist caught the attention of New York City art collector Louis Caldor, who introduced her to the gallery owner Otto Kallir. Kallir's astute representation and the artist's quaint, grandmotherly persona propelled the amateur into international stardom. Moses provided a down-to-earth counterpoint to the rarified world of big-city art galleries. To her many admirers, she embodied the very essence of the American heartland.

In *Grandma Moses Goes to the Big City*, she reflects on a 1940 trip to New York City—her first, at age eighty. She was headed to see her own paintings on display at Gimbels department store. At the center, Moses (in black) prepares to depart her Eagle Bridge farm in the awaiting car while farm life bustles on. She poses herself at the crossroads of farm and fame—the moment when her horizons expanded both literally and figuratively. ■ —*LU*

Grandma Moses Goes to the Big City, oil on canvas, 1946

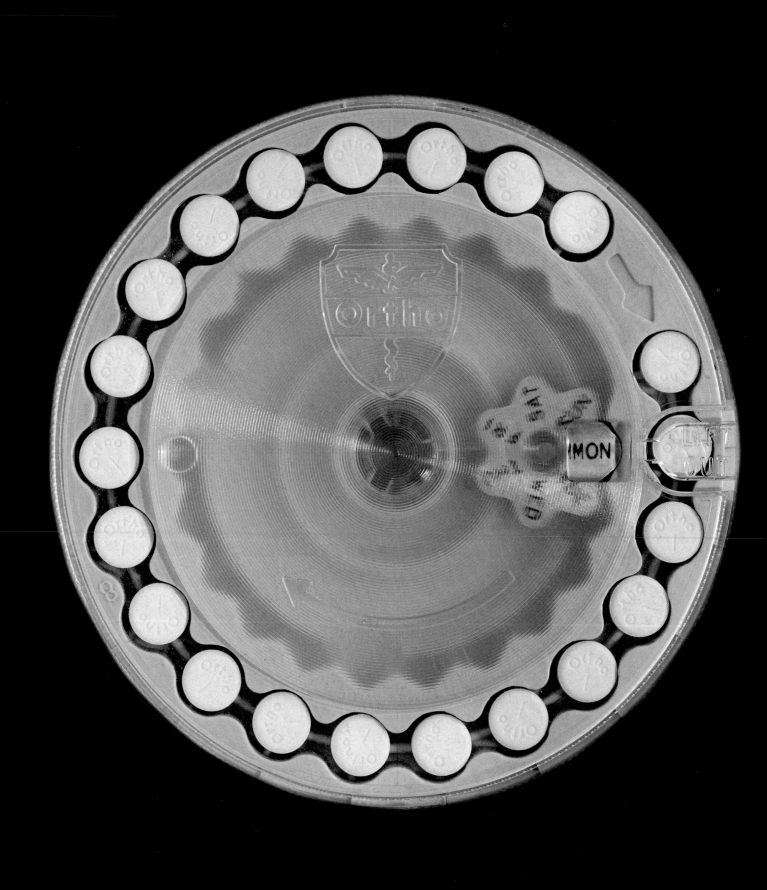

CHAPTER FOUR

1949-1967

Boycotts, Sit-Ins, and Civil Unrest

COMMUNISM AND THE COLD WAR held up a mirror to America as the world questioned whether the United States lived up to the promise of democracy. Popular culture papered over this anxiety with images of a return to a simpler America that had actually never existed. Images of the happy housewife and episodes of *Leave It to Beaver* competed with national events such as labor strikes, the McCarthy anticommunist hearings, and the 1963 publication of Betty Friedan's *The Feminine Mystique,* encouraging women to awaken to patriarchy.

Racial segregation, however, was perhaps the most public face of inequality. African American women employed the media to call attention to this injustice. In 1955, Mamie Till-Mobley insisted on an open casket at her son's funeral, showing the world Emmett Till's mutilated body following his lynching in Mississippi. That same year, activist Rosa Parks refused to give her bus seat to a white passenger, triggering the Montgomery bus boycott.

The question of civil rights extended beyond the boundaries of race, however. The year 1955 also marked the founding of the Daughters of Bilitis, the nation's first lesbian civil rights organization. And in 1962, Dolores Huerta cofounded the United Farm Workers with Cesar Chavez. By 1964, Congress passed the Civil Rights Act, addressing some issues of discrimination but leaving many more unresolved. ■

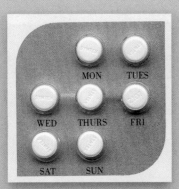

The first birth control pill container was a medicine bottle with loose tablets. Later designs helped women remember to take a pill each day.

PREVIOUS SPREAD

Game Changer

Approved for use in 1960 (but prescribed for married women only until 1962), the Pill quickly became the preferred method for delaying or preventing pregnancy. Existing methods of control, such as condoms, spermicides, diaphragms, and the rhythm method, were unreliable, and some held the risk of infection, migration of the device, or allergic reaction. The Pill, in contrast, was highly effective, with few side effects.

With the introduction of the round, efficient-to-use DialPak tablet dispenser in 1963, taking a pill seemed closer to medicine than immorality. That feeling was formalized with the disappearance in 1965 and 1972 of the last Comstock "vice" laws, legislation that had restricted the sale and advertisement of means of contraception. This wider access to the Pill meant that pregnancy now had to jockey with other aspirations—work life and education—in what it meant to be a fulfilled woman. —*KO*

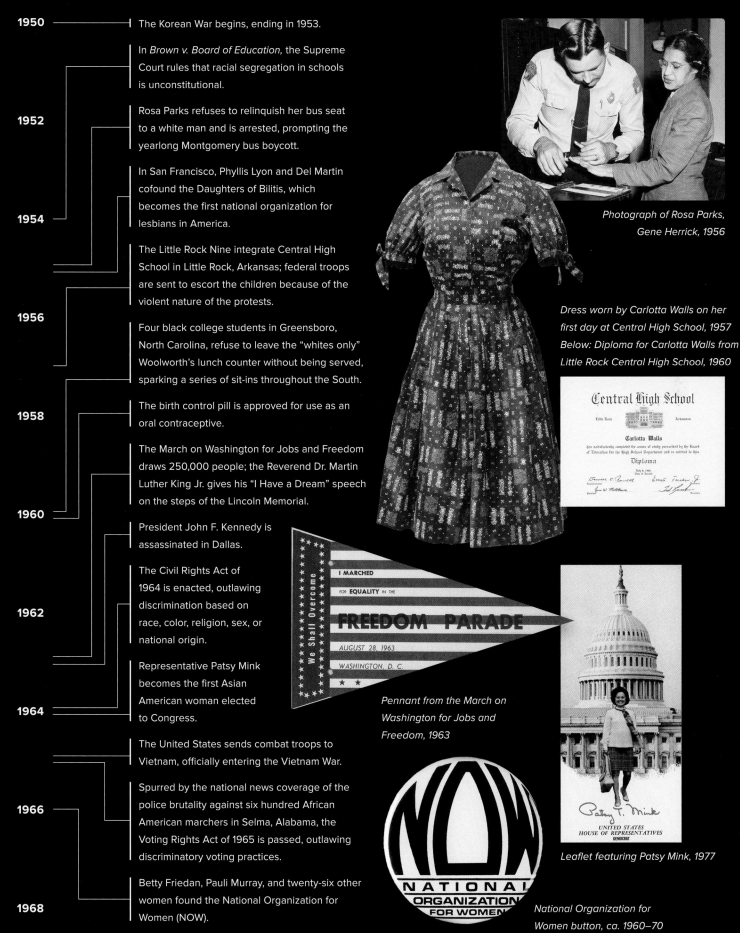

1950 — The Korean War begins, ending in 1953.	
1952 In *Brown v. Board of Education,* the Supreme Court rules that racial segregation in schools is unconstitutional.	
Rosa Parks refuses to relinquish her bus seat to a white man and is arrested, prompting the yearlong Montgomery bus boycott.	
1954 In San Francisco, Phyllis Lyon and Del Martin cofound the Daughters of Bilitis, which becomes the first national organization for lesbians in America.	

Photograph of Rosa Parks, Gene Herrick, 1956

The Little Rock Nine integrate Central High School in Little Rock, Arkansas; federal troops are sent to escort the children because of the violent nature of the protests.

1956

Four black college students in Greensboro, North Carolina, refuse to leave the "whites only" Woolworth's lunch counter without being served, sparking a series of sit-ins throughout the South.

1958 The birth control pill is approved for use as an oral contraceptive.

The March on Washington for Jobs and Freedom draws 250,000 people; the Reverend Dr. Martin Luther King Jr. gives his "I Have a Dream" speech on the steps of the Lincoln Memorial.

1960

President John F. Kennedy is assassinated in Dallas.

Dress worn by Carlotta Walls on her first day at Central High School, 1957 Below: Diploma for Carlotta Walls from Little Rock Central High School, 1960

The Civil Rights Act of 1964 is enacted, outlawing discrimination based on race, color, religion, sex, or national origin.

1962

Representative Patsy Mink becomes the first Asian American woman elected to Congress.

1964

The United States sends combat troops to Vietnam, officially entering the Vietnam War.

Spurred by the national news coverage of the police brutality against six hundred African American marchers in Selma, Alabama, the Voting Rights Act of 1965 is passed, outlawing discriminatory voting practices.

1966

Betty Friedan, Pauli Murray, and twenty-six other women found the National Organization for Women (NOW).

1968

Pennant from the March on Washington for Jobs and Freedom, 1963

Leaflet featuring Patsy Mink, 1977

National Organization for Women button, ca. 1960–70

A Mother's Grief Mobilizes the Nation

❖ REIGNITING PUBLIC AWARENESS OF THE CIVIL RIGHTS MOVEMENT

IN EARLY SEPTEMBER 1955, Mamie Till-Mobley (1921–2003) held an open-casket funeral for her brutally murdered son, Emmett Till (1941–55), shocking the nation into outrage. Weeks earlier, fourteen-year-old Emmett left his hometown of Chicago to visit with family in Money, Mississippi. He would not see his home or his mother again.

In late August, Carolyn Bryant, a young, white woman who owned a store in Money with her husband, Roy Bryant, accused Emmett Till of making unwanted advances. Three days later, authorities found the young boy's mutilated body in Mississippi's Tallahatchie River. Roy and his half brother, John Milam, were charged with the crime. An all-white, male jury acquitted both men.

Mamie Till-Mobley turned her grief into a national call to action. Refusing to let Emmett's murder be ignored, she demanded an open-casket funeral so the world could witness the inhumanity of racism and its violent consequences. This photograph (right) captures her wrenching grief as she buries her son. More than 100,000 people attended the funeral at Chicago's Roberts Temple Church of God, and hundreds of thousands more shook with disbelief when they saw photos of the boy's disfigured body in *Jet* magazine. As evidence of racism's toll, which included the lives of children, these images fueled a modern movement that transformed America.

Mamie Till-Mobley mobilized communities across the country. She spoke to large crowds at justice rallies, as shown in this New York City photograph by Grey Villet (left). She also helped increase membership for organizations like the National Association for the Advancement of Colored People.

In 2004, the US Justice Department reopened the Emmett Till case, as new evidence emerged suggesting that Roy Bryant and John Milam were not the only people involved in the murder. Although Bryant and Milam confessed to killing the teenager in *Look* magazine in January 1956, they were protected by the Fifth Amendment's double jeopardy clause and could not be tried again for the same crime. Decades later, Carolyn Bryant confessed to lying about what had happened in her grocery store that fateful day.

From the time of her son's murder until her death in 2003, Mamie Till-Mobley committed her life to social justice. Today, she stands as a courageous example of women who have led justice movements, demanded social change, and inspired communities to fight for equality. ■ —*AEB*

Till-Mobley addresses a crowd at an antilynching rally in New York following the September 1955 acquittal of Roy Bryant and John Milam for the murder of her son.

Right: This photograph by Dave Mann captures Mamie Till-Mobley (center) grieving as she buries her son, Emmett, in Chicago's Burr Oaks Cemetery, September 1955.

Mohegan Medicine Woman

❖ **PRESERVING NATIVE AMERICAN TRADITIONS AND BELIEFS**

Gladys Tantaquidgeon (1899–2005) brought an Indigenous worldview to her ethnobotanical research among the Delaware, Nanticoke, Cayuga, and Wampanoag tribes of the East Coast. She published significant works on tribal knowledge and on the use of local natural resources to create traditional herbal medicines, collecting samples like this medicinal snapwood plant, harvested in Massachusetts during fieldwork in 1929.

Born to Mohegan parents, Tantaquidgeon trained in Indigenous practices with Mohegan knowledge keepers Emma Baker, Mercy Mathews, and Fidelia Fielding. At age twenty, she was invited by respected anthropologist Frank Speck to deepen her studies at the University of Pennsylvania in a traditionally male-dominated discipline. She served as Speck's field assistant from 1919 to 1933.

Wanting to preserve her tribe's threatened culture for future generations, in 1931, Tantaquidgeon cofounded the Tantaquidgeon Indian Museum in Uncasville, Connecticut—the oldest museum in the United States owned and operated by Native Americans—with her brother and father. When the museum first opened its doors, she famously stated, "You can't hate someone [who] you know a lot about."

Committed to bettering the lives of Native peoples, Tantaquidgeon was a community worker on the Yankton Sioux Reservation in South Dakota in 1934. From 1938 to 1974, she promoted Indian art in the Dakotas, Montana, and Wyoming for the federal Indian Arts and Crafts Board. She also advocated for tribal religious freedom and helped revoke colonial prohibitions surrounding such traditional beliefs and practices as the sun dance and the rain dance.

During the 1970s, Tantaquidgeon returned home to serve as a member of the Mohegan Tribal Council. She was named Tribal Medicine Woman in 1992 and provided critical research in the landmark Mohegan case for federal recognition in 1994. On hearing the Mohegans had been granted tribal sovereignty, Tantaquidgeon replied, "That's wonderful. Now what do we do next?" ■ —*RM*

This snapwood specimen was one of the medicinal plants collected by pioneering anthropologist Gladys Tantaquidgeon among the Gay Head Wampanoag.

Below: In 1922, Tantaquidgeon and Nanticoke leaders successfully lobbied at the Delaware State Capitol for a school where Native American children could receive a modern education and learn traditional values.

Plath was at a turning point when this portrait was taken in 1959; she would soon become a mother. She strived to carefully balance motherhood and professional identity—a challenge for women of her era.

Poetic Portraiture

➤ THE ENIGMATIC POET SYLVIA PLATH, AS PHOTOGRAPHED BY ROLLIE MCKENNA

I N THIS PORTRAIT, Sylvia Plath (1932–63) appears deep in thought, clearly possessing a rich inner life. Photographer Rollie McKenna (1918–2003) took the photo in 1959 at the poet's 9 Willow Street apartment in Boston. At the time, Plath was emerging as a professional writer, cultivating her craft by auditing Robert Lowell's Boston University poetry seminar.

One of the most iconic American writers of the twentieth century, Plath used self-portraiture and carefully posed photographic portraits to cultivate her shifting persona, revealing a keen understanding of visual arts. In her writing, the groundbreaking poet imbued even the most mundane daily activities with the sublime. Plath was the first poet to win a Pulitzer Prize posthumously (for *The Collected Poems*) and wrote *The Colossus, Ariel,* and the best-selling novel *The Bell Jar*. Her work and life have captivated readers for generations.

McKenna captured many famous British and American poets, including Dylan Thomas, T. S. Eliot, Ted Hughes, Robert Lowell, and Anne Sexton. A number of her portraits have become defining images of her subjects, particularly in the case of Thomas and Plath. ■ —DM

Voice of Appalachia

❖ SINGER-SONGWRITER JEAN RITCHIE
REVIVED AN APPRECIATION OF FOLK MUSIC

JEAN RITCHIE (1922–2015) was one of America's finest and most beloved traditional singers, considered a national treasure for her work in preserving folkways. Born in Viper, Kentucky, she was the youngest of fourteen siblings. Her family was known for their rich repertoire of ballads and songs, many of which had originated in Britain and Ireland. Their singing—usually performed without accompaniment—was both a form of entertainment and part of church worship.

In 1946, Ritchie graduated with a degree in social work from the University of Kentucky and headed to New York City to work at the Henry Street Settlement. Even while working as a social worker, she became known as a singer and musician, giving her first formal concert in 1948. Her reputation grew steadily, and she became a performer and songwriter of international stature. In performance, Ritchie accompanied her songs on dulcimer, autoharp, and guitar, as well as singing unaccompanied. The eastern Kentucky coal country where she was raised proved creative fodder for the composing of such songs as "Blue Diamond Mines," "Black Waters," and "The L&N Don't Stop Here Anymore."

Ritchie met photographer and filmmaker George Pickow at a square dance in 1948. They married in 1950, and their life together was deeply collaborative. They mounted a song-collecting trip to England, Scotland, and Ireland, funded by a Fulbright scholarship that allowed Ritchie to explore the links between her family songs and those of her European forebears.

Ritchie is in large part responsible for the revival and popularization of the Appalachian dulcimer, which she often used to accompany her songs. Her father played the dulcimer and taught her to play when she was five or six years old. She made numerous recordings, many of which were issued on Folkways Records and on her family label, Greenhays Recordings. In 2002, the National Endowment for the Arts awarded Ritchie a National Heritage Fellowship. ■ —ss

Smithsonian Folkways Recordings

jean ritchie **ballads**
from her appalachian family tradition

The ballads on this recording, originally made in 1961, are outstanding Appalachian versions of the "Child ballads," English and Scottish narrative songs collected and published by scholar Francis James Child in the late nineteenth century.

Left: This teardrop-shaped plucked dulcimer was made by Ritchie's husband, George Pickow, in Viper, Kentucky, in 1951. Ritchie played this instrument, which she helped popularize, throughout her career. —SK

Betbeze's rounded tiara, with one central point, is far different from the iconic, four pointed tiara we know today, which first made its appearance in 1955.

Crown of Controversy

❖ YOLANDE BETBEZE CHALLENGED THE STEREOTYPES OF THE BEAUTY QUEEN

IN 1951, YOLANDE BETBEZE (1928–2016), a dark-haired beauty of French Basque descent, was crowned Miss America with this rhinestone tiara. The twenty-three-year-old won the pageant by unanimous vote, but if the judges thought they had chosen just a pretty face, they were quickly proved wrong. Betbeze broke from tradition, refusing to be photographed in Catalina swimwear advertisements: "I don't appear publicly in a bathing suit for anyone unless, of course, I'm going swimming."

A decidedly modern example of Miss America, Betbeze supported equal rights for women and minorities, joining NAACP protestors during civil rights demonstrations and criticizing the Miss America pageant for its lack of diversity. "'How could we say it's Miss America,' I asked, 'if it's not open to all Americans?'" she recalled in a 2011 book by Roy Hoffman. (The pageant's first African American contestant was Miss Iowa 1970.) Educated and well read, Betbeze often found herself refuting the stereotype of the less-than-intelligent beauty queen. The Miss America pageant has struggled with this image from the start, continually reinventing itself to keep up with changing mores.

Beginning in 1921 as a "photographic personality contest," Miss America was introduced through newsreels and newspapers. By the start of World War II, she was transformed into a symbol of patriotism. Educational scholarships for the winners attempted to modify the pageant's focus, but television continued to emphasize the glitzy, highly calculated image of the event.

Over time, the pageant shifted its focus to educational and professional goals, requiring contestants to address relevant social issues while educating the public—a change Betbeze welcomed. "I spoke out against the pageant when it was needed," she told *People* magazine in 2000. "The pageant has changed, thanks to me." ■ —*JR*

Mae Reeves (far right) and her millinery models presented fashion shows at local churches, restaurants, and hotels in Pennsylvania, Delaware, and New Jersey (photo ca. 1950). The events employed young women and raised money for business associations, community organizations, and charities.

Opposite: Reeves designed and created this signature turban. "When a woman gets a pretty hat it makes her pretty," she said at age 101. "You're not fully dressed unless you wear a hat."

Building Community through Fashion

❖ MAE'S MILLINERY SHOP, A BEACON OF BLACK STYLE AND CULTURE

A MID A NATIONWIDE depression and the Jim Crow era, a young black widow from the South did booming business as one of Philadelphia's premier hat makers. For more than fifty years, Mae Reeves's millinery operated in the bustling retail neighborhoods of Philadelphia. With creativity and business acumen, Reeves established herself as a one-of-a-kind ladies' hat maker who attracted customers from all walks of life. Mae of Philadelphia, as she became known, was also a community builder who epitomized the best qualities of her adopted home, the City of Brotherly Love.

Born in Vidalia, Georgia, Mae Reeves (1912–2016) created hats for her dolls as a child. As a young woman, she went to teachers college and taught in Lyons, Georgia. Following the death of her first husband, Reeves migrated north to Philadelphia during the Great Migration, when millions of African Americans left the rural South in search of freedom from racism. She worked in sales but found her calling during summers at millinery school in Chicago in the mid-1930s. There, she learned how to shape hats with special molds, using steam and wires to hold her designs in place. But her signature was the creation of "showstoppers"—elaborate creations adorned with feathers, flowers, bows, and other ornaments.

In 1940, Reeves secured a $500 loan from the Philadelphia-based Citizens and Southern Bank, an African American–owned institution that provided financial support to many migrants. The following year, she opened Mae's Millinery Shop on South Street, the center of black Philadelphia: a busy corridor lined with stores, nightclubs, and restaurants. Living in an apartment in

back with her eight-year-old son, Reeves quickly earned a reputation for the stylish hats she made for local women and entertainers.

Women soon came from as far north as Boston and as far south as Virginia to order Reeves's turbans, cocktail hats, and cloches. Equal parts artist and businesswoman, Reeves attracted black and white customers alike, including celebrities such as Ella Fitzgerald and Lena Horne and wealthy, white society women from such prominent families as the Annenbergs and the du Ponts. Most of her customers, however, came from local neighborhoods and churches. For African American women, Reeves's hats provided a source of pride and symbolic armor in the face of degrading stereotypes that demeaned black beauty. The black-and-white photograph pictured here shows Reeves and friends proudly donning her creations.

In 1953, Reeves and her second husband, Joel, purchased and renovated a building in West Philadelphia near the El train, and Mae Reeves became the first African American woman to own a business in the Sixtieth Street shopping area. The shop was downstairs and the Reeveses lived on the second floor with their children, Sonny, Donna, and Reginald. Across the decades, the family participated actively in neighborhood organizations, politics, and the NAACP. On election days, Mae's Millinery Shop served as a polling station.

Even after the decline of women's hat fashion, Reeves continued to inspire black women with her kindness, creativity, and entrepreneurial success. She kept the shop running by taking orders from special clients until 1997, when she was eighty-five years old. ■ —PG

Spanning a half century of women's fashion, Mae Reeves's elegant hats range from a simple cloche to her most complex showstoppers, adorned with feathers, flowers, and bows. Visible in all is the spirit of creativity, skill, and love that Reeves brought to her craft. Her creations helped black women reclaim their style and self-worth amid racial intolerance. In the welcoming atmosphere of Mae's Millinery Shop, they found a refuge of beauty, community, and empowerment.

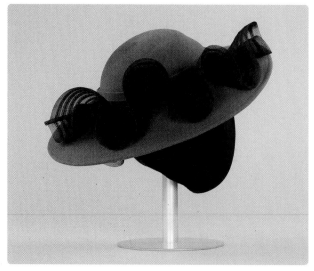

Through home sales parties featuring products like this Tupperware Wonderlier bowl (ca. 1954), women in the 1950s transformed business culture from the socially acceptable arena of their homes.

Wonder Bowl Women

❖ FINDING ENTREPRENEURIAL EMPOWERMENT IN AN ERA OF LIMITED OPPORTUNITY

A PROLIFIC INVENTOR, Earl Tupper (1907–83) designed and manufactured the hardy plastic Wonder Bowl, but women turned it into an empire.

During World War II, Tupper began experimenting with plastic goods for new suburban lifestyles and kitchens. He transformed polyethylene waste into a flexible, durable material and molded it into containers in translucent colors. After adding an innovative airtight seal in 1947, Tupper began marketing his Wonder Bowls through department stores, positioning them as food storage and entertaining solutions. Sales were slow.

In 1951, Tupper enlisted Brownie Wise (1913–92), a charismatic, divorced single mother, to lead a new Tupperware Home Parties sales organization. Wise had a knack for selling to women through home demonstrations; she demystified the bowl's patented two-step seal, showing how to expel the air like a "burp." The home demonstration model wasn't new, but Wise took it to the next level,

introducing fun games, hostess gifts, and extravagant dealer prizes. Sales skyrocketed as Wonder Bowls filled cupboards across the United States.

In an era that discouraged women's work outside the home, Tupperware parties offered women in new suburban communities, immigrant city neighborhoods, and rural regions unique opportunities to host neighbors, make friends, and earn money without upsetting the status quo. For women who had not graduated high school or college, Tupperware "jubilee" graduations offered both a diploma and public recognition.

As the first female corporate executive to grace the cover of *Business Week*, Brownie Wise left a legacy. Her pioneering approach set a standard for home-party selling through women's social networks that lives on in the twenty-first century. Today, as Tupperware parties and Wonder Bowls span the globe, they continue providing a means for women to seek opportunity amid marginalization. ■ —SKN

Empowering Embroidery

❖ **USING NEEDLEWORK TO CELEBRATE SELFHOOD AND SERVICE**

These kitchen towels were embroidered by women in the Ford family of Jersey City, New Jersey. The designs were among the most popular for kitchen towels and handkerchiefs in 1943.

I N AN ERA OF rigidly defined gender roles, many educated middle-class women gave up their professions after marriage and became homemakers. A well-kept home was considered a reflection of the taste and character of the lady of the house. Mass-produced do-it-yourself embroidery kits like the one for this set of kitchen towels made it possible for middle-class women to create personalized home decor. In the absence of multigenerational homes, many learned this traditional skill from kits, not elders. A 1948 advertisement for Paragon Needlecraft touted "easy-to-follow instruction sheets," and included photographs of a smiling, impeccably dressed woman displaying beautiful linens throughout her home and the slogan: "EVERYTHING for EVERY room in your own 'dream house.'"

For many women, these embroidered linens weren't just home decor; they were emblems of respectability and upstanding citizenship. Mary Thompson Ford (1861–1960) and her adult daughters Blanche (1897–1992) and Ethel (1899–) spent time and effort adorning the kitchen of their family home in Jersey City, New Jersey. The days-of-the-week motif they selected depicts a housewife's weekly tasks. On each kitchen towel, a young woman performs a daily domestic activity: washing on Monday, ironing on Tuesday, grocery shopping on Wednesday, sewing on Thursday, cleaning on Friday, baking on Saturday, and resting or attending church on Sunday. The structured weekly schedule paralleled office or factory work, suggesting that the modern homemaker's labor was equally necessary and worthy of admiration.

Middle-class women of all races took great pride in decorating their homes with their own handiwork. Because the patterns were so affordable, homemakers were able to stretch their household budgets, making room for things otherwise out of reach. Given the skill, creativity, and resourcefulness these women used to run their homes successfully, it's unsurprising that many, like the Fords, chose to commemorate their important role through needlework. ■ —*MD*

Abstract Expressionism's Unsung Heroes

❖ PIONEERING FEMALE PAINTERS
IN A MALE-DOMINATED WORLD

AT A TIME WHEN societal roles for women were severely constrained, some committed their lives to art, defying social and aesthetic conventions within an overtly sexist art world that celebrated audacity, individuality, and heroic spirit as intrinsically "male" qualities.

Since its emergence in the 1940s, the epoch-defining art movement of abstract expressionism has largely been associated with men. But pioneering women helped forge this important chapter of American modernism.

Among the few to garner recognition early in their careers were Helen Frankenthaler (1928–2011) and Joan Mitchell (1925–92). Frankenthaler's innovation of pouring diluted paint directly onto raw canvas to create luminous veils of color was highly influential. In this 1961 photo, she considers a work in progress in her New York studio. Mitchell was renowned for her bold compositional rhythm and explosive yet lyrical brushwork.

Critical attention came much later for others. A veteran of the Federal Art Project of the Works Progress Administration, Lee Krasner (1908–84) nourished the career of her husband, Jackson Pollock, for years to the detriment of her own. Her full artistic flourishing came only after his death.

Other female artists faced double marginalization by the art establishment, as women and as people of color. The first student to earn a fine arts degree from Howard University, African American artist Alma Thomas (1891–1978) spent years as a teacher, dedicating herself completely to painting only after she retired. Exhibiting at New York's Whitney Museum of American Art in 1972, Thomas remarked, "When I was a little girl . . . there were things we could do and things we couldn't. One of the things we couldn't do was go into museums, let alone think of hanging our work there. My, times have changed." ∎ —MH

Joan Mitchell's bold, gestural style of abstraction registers the artist's physical actions while conveying emotional and psychological states. Both *Marlin* (1960), at top, and *Cercando un Ago* (1959), at bottom, feature dense networks of turbulent brushstrokes in dark hues and brighter highlights. While decidedly abstract, the paintings' complex spatial structures also call to mind the more traditional genre of landscape. —EH

Opposite: Helen Frankenthaler in her studio on East Eighty-Third Street and Third Avenue, New York City, 1961

Above, left: The rich color and unexpected forms in Helen Frankenthaler's *Small's Paradise* (1964) were achieved by staining raw canvas with thinned paint, a method that inspired a generation of color field painters.

Above, right: A transplant to New York from Puerto Rico, Olga Albizu (1924–2005) created rhythmic compositions that vibrate with blocks of pigment, as in *Radiante* (1967). Like other abstract expressionists, she harnessed the emotive power of color.

Right: An early painting by Lee Krasner, *Composition* (1940) demonstrates a geometric style informed by European modernism. She would go on to experiment with new painterly approaches and techniques throughout her long career.

Far right: In this photograph, Lee Krasner works on a painting (since lost) at the school run by Hans Hofmann, the influential German émigré artist with whom Krasner studied intermittently between 1937 and 1940.

Opposite: Alma Thomas is best known for abstract compositions, such as her *Earth Sermon—Beauty, Love and Peace* (1971), in which a vibrant palette and daub-like forms commingle to conjure fleeting elements of the landscape. —*EH*

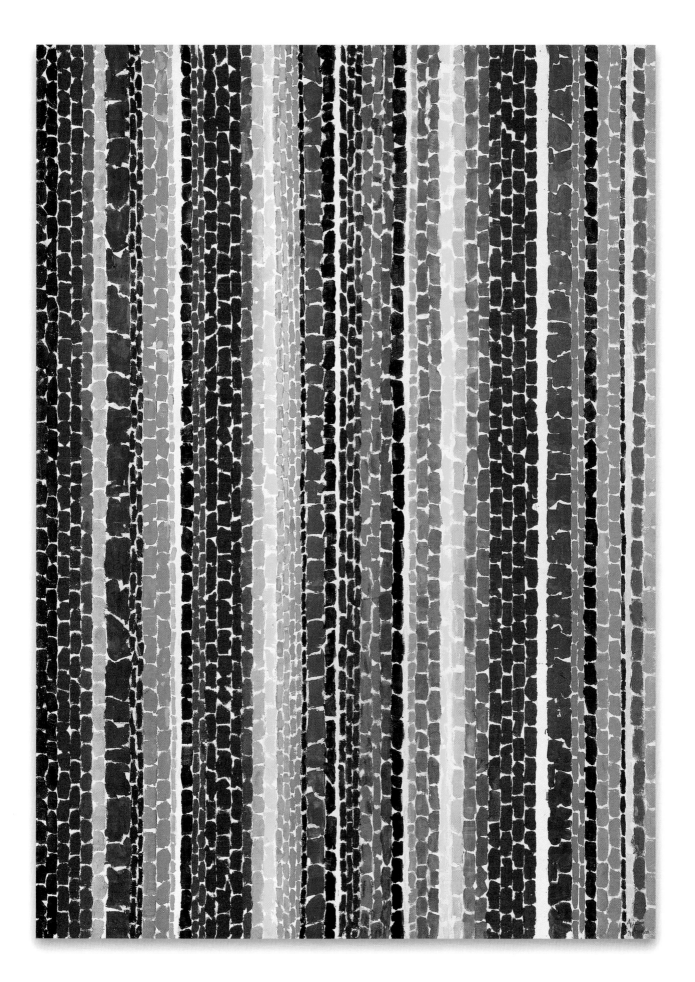

Smiling with confidence, Minnijean Brown wore this 1959 tea-length dress as she accepted her high school diploma. The teenager designed the gown, and her benefactors had it made as a graduation gift.

Opposite: Brown's 1958 school suspension notice signaled the end of her time in the Little Rock school system and was clearly the result of racial discrimination.

Resilience against Racism

❖ A FIFTEEN-YEAR-OLD GIRL'S BRAVE STAND AGAINST SEGREGATED EDUCATION

I N 1959, MINNIJEAN BROWN wore this elegant, white commencement dress as she, like many other teenage girls across the United States, celebrated graduation day. With its sheer overlay and delicate floral pattern, the dress belies the difficult—and at times ugly—journey of attending and graduating from an integrating high school in the 1950s.

In the battle for civil rights, fifteen-year-old Minnijean Brown made history as one of nine African American students who sought to attend all-white Little Rock Central High School in the fall of 1957. Three years earlier, the Supreme Court ruled that segregated schools were unconstitutional in the landmark case *Brown v. Board of Education of Topeka*, but federally mandated integration was slow to become reality. When the Little Rock Nine first attempted to enter Central High School, they were greeted by a mob screaming obscenities and by the Arkansas National Guard, who, under the governor's orders, blocked their entrance to school. President Dwight D. Eisenhower was called on to intervene, and the students entered school on September 25, three weeks after the academic year started.

Throughout the 1957–58 school year, the Little Rock Nine were frequently harassed at school, both verbally and physically. But it was Minnijean Brown who received a suspension notice from the Little Rock public school administration on February 6, 1958, for attempting to resist the daily torment. During an argument with a fellow classmate, Brown had called the girl "white trash," after which the student threw her large purse at Brown. School administrators expelled Brown; the white student went unpunished.

The school system claimed the expulsion was warranted, as Brown had been given a warning to resist retaliation for any bullying after receiving a six-day suspension for dumping a bowl of chili on an abusive white male student. Brown's parents appealed the suspension with a letter to the school board, stating that the repeated attacks against their daughter represented a concentrated effort to have her expelled, and that she had to defend herself because school officials had not intervened. The appeal was unsuccessful.

Fortunately, noted African American psychologists and researchers Drs. Kenneth B. and Mamie Clark invited Brown to live with them in New York City and attend New Lincoln High School. For Minnijean, it meant living away from family and friends for the remainder of high school, but she gained a better education from the private school's progressive curriculum. Her 1959 graduation from high school and subsequent degrees from Canada's Laurentian University and Carleton University represent a triumph over the adversity she faced within the Little Rock public school system. ∎ —DSJ

Suspension Notice
LITTLE ROCK PUBLIC SCHOOLS
Date February 6, 1958

Name of Pupil Brown, Minniejean Birthdate Sept. 11, 1941 Grade 11th
(Last) (First) (Middle)

Name of Parent Mr. &Mrs. W.B. Brown Address 117 Ringo Phone (unlisted)
or Guardian

DEAR PATRON:
It becomes my duty to inform you that Minniejean Brown has been suspended
from Central High School, for the following reasons:

REASONS:
Reinstated on probation January 13, 1958, with the agreement that she would not retaliate verbally or physically, to any harassment but would leave the matter to school authorities to handle.
After provocation of girl student, she called the girl "white trash", after which the girl threw her purse at Minniejean.

Pupils in the Little Rock Public Schools who fail to adjust to their school program may be suspended from school for an indefinite period by the school principal. This pupil cannot again enter Little Rock Public Schools except by written permission from the Superintendent.
In order that this pupil may be reinstated in school, the parent or guardian must accompany her to the office of the Superintendent of Schools, Department of Pupil Personnel and Attendance, 800 Louisiana Street, Little Rock, Arkansas, for the purpose of discussing the problems relative to this suspension.

Very truly yours,

Jess W. Matthews

Principal

With authoritative science and poetic prose, Rachel Carson's *Silent Spring* (1962) stirred citizens and scientists to action. Investigations ordered by President John Kennedy confirmed Carson's findings, leading to stronger pesticide regulation.

Left: This gelatin silver print by Alfred Eisenstaedt shows Carson at work at her microscope in her home in Silver Spring, Maryland, in 1962.

Scientist, Author, and Activist

❖ **RACHEL CARSON'S RESEARCH AND WRITINGS RALLIED THE NATION AROUND ENVIRONMENTALISM**

IN 1962, RACHEL CARSON's revolutionary volume *Silent Spring* sounded an alarm. The shells of birds' eggs were being perilously weakened by exposure to dichlorodiphenyltrichloroethane (DDT), Carson warned; if environmental protections weren't enacted around synthetic pesticides, nature's delicate balance would be disrupted and humans would awaken to a silent spring. The book has sold millions of copies since publication, galvanizing environmental movements in the United States and beyond.

Rachel Louise Carson (1907–64) was a scientist and nature writer. She trained as a marine biologist and embarked on a career in government research in 1936. By the 1950s, she was also publishing award-winning books about the natural world, such as *The Sea Around Us,* and began science writing full-time. In *Silent Spring,* she turned her attention to the impact of synthetic pesticides, consulting scientists who found troubling side effects in some of the "miracle" pesticides developed during World War II.

The book met with fierce industry opposition, but Carson's research was irrefutable. Scientists and citizens mobilized, and six years after Carson's untimely death in 1964, the Environmental Protection Agency (EPA) was established. *Silent Spring* remains in print today. ∎ —*PMH*

Detecting Dark Matter

In the 1960s, using this image tube spectrograph built by W. Kent Ford Jr., Vera Rubin and Ford found evidence of dark matter.

Top: Rubin prepares for an evening of observing through the image tube spectrograph at the Lowell Observatory in 1965.

AT AGE TWELVE, Vera Rubin (1928–2016) preferred watching the stars to sleeping. Her childhood curiosity about astronomy would ultimately lead to a dramatic change in our understanding of the universe.

After earning a PhD in astronomy at Georgetown University in 1954, Rubin was hired as an astronomer by the Carnegie Institution's Department of Terrestrial Magnetism (DTM) in Washington, DC, at a time when few women worked in the field. The Carnegie was then pioneering a new magnetically focused electronic image tube that promised to amplify the sensitivity of telescopes of all kinds, allowing astronomers to record fainter objects faster. Collaborating with gifted instrument designer W. Kent Ford Jr., Rubin used Ford's DTM image tube spectrograph on various telescopes, starting with a large reflector at the Lowell Observatory in Flagstaff, Arizona, pictured here.

Scrutinizing our nearest galaxy, Rubin made a surprising discovery: the gas spinning around its edges orbited almost as quickly as the gas in the center. It didn't go more slowly, as one might expect. The galaxy contained an enormous amount of invisible mass, she surmised. But what was it exactly? Astronomers and physicists are still trying to find an answer for what continues to be called dark matter. For her groundbreaking work, Rubin received the 1993 National Medal of Science, among other honors. ■ —DHD

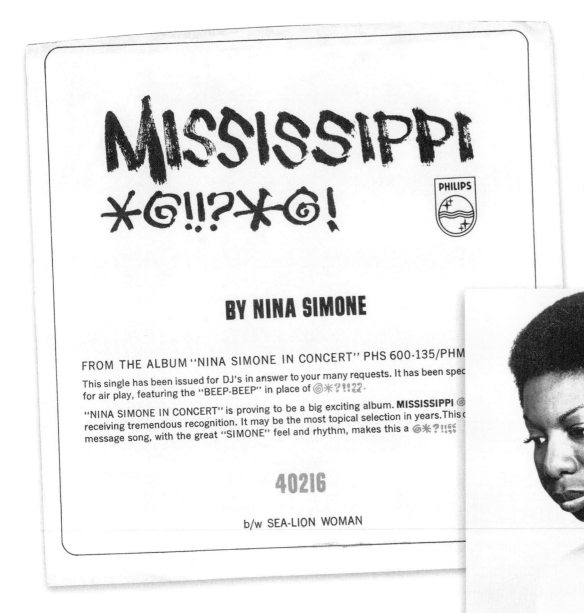

Left: Nina Simone described "Mississippi Goddam" as her "first civil rights song." The record sold well—except in the South, where racism blocked its distribution. "Mississippi Goddam" promotional record, 1964.

Below: This photograph was taken to promote Simone's 1970 *Black Gold* album. It featured her song, "To Be Young, Gifted and Black," written for the late playwright and activist Lorraine Hansberry, a friend.

Civil Rights Artist and Activist

❖ SINGER-SONGWRITER
NINA SIMONE DEMANDED
RACIAL JUSTICE

"MISSISSIPPI GODDAM" MARKED a turning point in Nina Simone's career. The young singer, pianist, and songwriter wrote the song in 1964 in response to the assassination of Mississippi civil rights activist Medgar Evers and the bombing of the Sixteenth Street Baptist Church in Birmingham, Alabama, in which four young girls were killed. Using lyrics to channel her outrage over the injustices of racism and segregation, Simone demanded a call for action. She debuted the anthem at a Carnegie Hall performance, shocking audiences who'd known her for her interpretation of popular standards.

Born Eunice Waymon in Tryon, North Carolina, Simone (1933–2003) had dreams of becoming a classical pianist. Despite having studied at Julliard, she was denied admission to Philadelphia's Curtis Institute of Music. Undeterred, she changed her name and started singing professionally.

Politically awakened by the Evers and Birmingham church incidents, Simone harnessed the power of music to address racism, sexism, and other injustices, often meeting controversy. She commanded a space for black women in the narratives of cultural nationalism and black liberation, paving the way for the black power and feminist movements of the late 1960s and early 1970s. ■ —DRR

Champion of Gay Rights

❖ BARABARA GITTINGS CHANGED TWENTIETH-CENTURY VIEWS ABOUT GAY LIFE

SEXUAL PREFERENCE
IS
IRRELEVANT
TO
FEDERAL EMPLOYMENT

Barbara Gittings (1932–2007), arguably the most public lesbian of the twentieth century, wore this dress on many gay-rights picket lines. She relentlessly pushed American society to understand and accept gay people back when being gay was often dangerous and even criminal. In the 1960s, nearly every state had laws on the books that forbade same-sex relations and cross-dressing.

Gittings wore this dress at Philadelphia's Independence Hall on July 4, 1965, at the Reminder Day demonstration, an event designed to remind the public that gay Americans did not have basic civil rights. To emphasize the injustice, the protestors wore respectable suits and ties, and Gittings wore the Marimekko striped dress that she and her partner had purchased in Harvard Square.

The year 1965 was a landmark for gay protests, with activists picketing the White House, the United Nations, the Civil Service Commission, the State Department, and elsewhere. Gittings, who had deep and lifelong movement roots, participated in most of these protests and was also at the first gay pride march, the 1970 Christopher Street Liberation Day March. She edited *The Ladder* (the lesbian-focused journal of the Daughters of Bilitis) and, with fellow activist Frank Kameny, advised numerous people who sued over employment rights or revoked security clearances.

With other activists, Gittings worked to remove homosexuality as an alleged illness from the American Psychiatric Association's list of mental disorders, and organized the landmark 1972 panel at the association that asserted "Gay, Proud, and Healthy." The following year, the association removed homosexuality from its list. Barbara Gittings rightfully is considered the mother of the modern gay rights movement. ■ —KO

Gittings came of age at a time when LGBTQ+ people believed that fitting in and appearing responsible were of great importance, reflected in this dress.

Above, right: Gittings carried this poster at actions in the 1960s.

Dolores Huerta

"I never felt overlooked because I didn't expect any kind of recognition. I think that's very typical of women. I had been acculturated to be supportive, to be accommodating, to support men in the work they do. We never think of getting credit or recognition or even taking the power. We didn't think in those terms. Of course I think that's changing now and there's a surge of women who are not only running for office, but getting elected. That could make an incredible amount of difference in our world. We will never have peace in the world until feminists take power."

— Dolores Huerta, *Time* magazine, March 27, 2018

In the early 1960s, California's migrant farmworkers toiled in deplorable conditions, laboring ten to fourteen hours a day for less than minimum wage. By 1965, they'd had enough; fifteen hundred Filipino grape pickers, members of the Agricultural Workers Organizing Committee, walked out of the fields. The strikers asked the National Farm Workers Association—a largely Mexican American union formed in 1962 by American labor leaders Dolores Huerta and Cesar Chavez—to join the struggle. Out of the grape strike, the United Farm Workers (UFW) was born.

As vice president of the UFW, Huerta's unparalleled diplomacy skills, tactical expertise, and uncompromising character propelled the movement forward. In 1970, the union signed contracts with twenty-six grape growers, establishing the UFW as the nation's first successful agricultural workers union and a new voice in the struggle for social justice.

At age eighty-nine, Huerta continues to make public appearances and to train young organizers in building a more robust democracy. ■ —*TC*

DOLORES

To My Dear Beloved Barbara with respect, Dolores Huerta

Chicana artist Barbara Carrasco created this portrait in 1999 honoring Dolores Huerta as an "equal of Cesar Chavez and, historically, the most important UFW contract negotiator."

Opposite: To support the 1965 strike, the UFW, guided in part by Huerta, organized a successful national grape boycott, making the plight of farm laborers a national cause

Lieutenant Uhura's Legacy

❖ **BECOMING A ROLE MODEL FOR WOMEN AND PEOPLE OF COLOR**

O F ALL THE UNUSUAL and otherworldly imagery that captivated *Star Trek* fans from the start of its 1966 prime-time debut, few things made as big an impression as Nichelle Nichols: a black woman portraying a commanding officer on national television. Wearing this sleek red uniform, Nichols starred as Lieutenant Uhura, chief communications officer of the USS *Enterprise*. Nichols made history with the role, breaking significant ground for black women in television, film, and beyond.

During the mid-1960s, black actors were still largely relegated to secondary roles, playing domestic servants and comedic pawns who reinforced racial stereotypes and revealed the lasting, harmful legacy of early-nineteenth-century minstrel-show caricatures. By contrast, Nichols portrayed Uhura as an assured, capable, and complex individual, emerging as one of the first black women to star in a non-menial television role. In 1968, she famously shared one of the first interracial kisses in television history with costar William Shatner.

A versatile performer and accomplished singer and dancer, Nichols considered leaving the series after one season to pursue Broadway aspirations. She continued on, however, after a chance conversation with the Reverend Dr. Martin Luther King Jr. at a NAACP fundraiser. A fan of the show's multicultural vision of the future, King persuaded Nichols of Lieutenant Uhura's positive impact and her importance as a role model for black children and young women. Nichols went on to break more barriers as the first black woman to have an ongoing costarring role in a televised series.

Nichols leveraged her influence for various causes, including volunteering her time as a recruiter of women and minorities for NASA. She inspired a generation of women and people of color to enter the fields of aeronautical and aerospace engineering, among them famed astronauts Dr. Mae Jemison and Guion Bluford. ■ —*KMS*

Actress Nichelle Nichols wore this iconic red Starfleet uniform—a 1960s minidress—while handling communications for the USS *Enterprise* on *Star Trek*. Designed by William Ware Theiss, 1966–67.

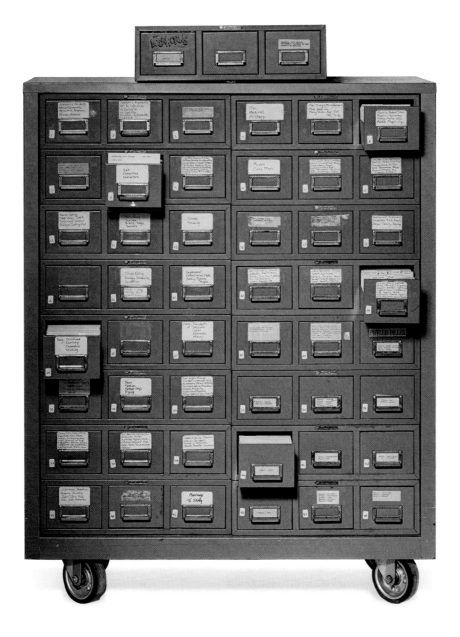

Phyllis Diller used this steel cabinet to organize her material during the peak of her career, from 1962 to 1994. Some jokes are short one-liners, while others span several index cards.

Phyllis Diller's Gag File

FROM THE 1960S TO THE 1990S, Phyllis Diller (1917–2012) organized her jokes in this fifty-one-drawer cabinet containing 52,569 three-by-five index cards, each holding a typewritten joke or gag. She arranged her material alphabetically, poking fun at everything from divorce and dogs to doctors and dislikes (and that's just drawer number 14). Among the colorful costumes, comedy albums, and awards she donated to the museum in 2003, the file is the pièce de résistance.

Diller became the nation's first female stand-up comedy star by being a horrible housewife—at least that's what the thirty-seven-year-old married mother of five told audiences when she first took the stage in 1955. Mocking the myth of the idealized American wife and mother, Diller upended gender stereotypes with jokes about how she couldn't cook, clean, or get along with her fictionalized husband, Fang. She was famous for her self-deprecating style and outlandish outfits, including a signature fright wig and cigarette holder.

A seasoned performer on stage, television, and film, Diller also traveled with comedian Bob Hope and the USO to entertain troops around the world. Throughout the latter half of the twentieth century, Diller's humor cut straight to the heart of what Americans were talking, joking, and worrying about. ■ —HB

Suiting Up for the Sky

❖ **BANNED FROM THE COCKPIT, WOMEN NONETHELESS FOUND CAREERS IN FLIGHT**

I OWA NATIVE ELLEN CHURCH (1904–65) was a nurse and a licensed pilot, but in the male-dominated world of early aviation, no commercial airline would hire her to fly. So in 1930, she approached Boeing Air Transport with an idea: placing nurses aboard airliners to assist travelers and pour drinks. Boeing accepted her pitch. On May 15, Church and seven other nurses donned crisp, professional green wool uniforms and took to the skies as the country's first flight attendants.

Soon, other airlines were hiring stewardesses. "There is still a newness about air travel," reads an excerpt from a 1935 airline magazine, "and, though statistics demonstrate its safety, the psychological effect of having a girl on board is enormous."

Pan American hired its first stewardesses after World War II. The airline emulated luxurious ocean liner service, calling their pilots "captains" and dressing crews in naval-style uniforms that included double-breasted blue jackets with rank insignia. Other airlines followed suit.

Air travel's newfound popularity provoked fierce competition. Because airfares were government regulated, airlines began attracting passengers—especially business-men—with such amenities as better food, drinks, movies, and fashionable staff uniforms. In the 1960s, uniforms evolved from conservative and military to colorful and stylish, reflecting changing social attitudes. Appealing to their mostly male travelers, airlines introduced miniskirts and hot pants to the dismay of many flight attendants.

"When a tired businessman gets on an airplane, we think he ought to be allowed to look at a pretty girl," a Braniff advertising executive said in *Business Week* in 1967. Airline deregulation in 1978 meant that cabin crews could return to more conservative, practical military-style uniforms. ■ —*FRV*

Left: In 1935, Thelma Jean Harman (ca. 1914–2001) became the first TWA stewardess. She wore this jaunty summer uniform while flying aboard Ford Tri-Motor aircrafts from New York to Los Angeles on the "Lindbergh Line," as TWA was then known.

Opposite: In 1930, Ellen Church (1904–65)—the first American stewardess and one of United Airlines' "Original Eight"—wore a dark green wool uniform much like this 1956 replica, made in her honor.

Above: As the nation changed, so did flight fashions. Stewardess Macivor Celeste (1930–2004) wore this green uniform aboard Colonial Airlines in the 1950s; by the 1960s, Air California stewardesses were donning festive ponchos and hats.

Breaking into Elite Sports

❖ **RISING ABOVE BIAS TO BECOME THE FIRST AFRICAN AMERICAN GRAND SLAM CHAMPION**

Born into a sharecropping family in South Carolina, Althea Gibson (1927–2003) spent most of her formative years in Harlem, where she was first introduced to the game of tennis as a teenager. A "country club" sport, amateur tennis was expensive and required strict adherence to the dictates of its elite, genteel culture. Gibson had to learn the strokes of the game as well as how to fit into the exclusive environment. Defying racist stereotypes, she proved that African Americans could comport themselves—and excel—in the most exclusive, elite spaces in society.

At age twenty, Gibson won the first of ten straight titles at the national tournament of the American Tennis Association, the first African American sports association founded under segregation. At the time, major tennis tournaments were held in whites-only private clubs. Tennis was not among the most popular sports in black America, but Gibson received tremendous support from African Americans as they rallied round her ascent in tennis. Supporters lobbied on Gibson's behalf, and in 1950, she broke the race barrier in the US National Championships.

Despite her success in the early 1950s, Gibson wasn't selected to represent the United States in the Wightman Cup tournament until 1957, by which time she had already won two of her five grand slam titles: the 1956 French Nationals championship and the 1957 Wimbledon title. Founded in 1923, the Wightman, an annual women's team tennis competition between the United States and Great Britain, was the most prestigious women's team tennis event in the world. Gibson's race and class background made her a groundbreaking choice for the team.

After her tremendous run of accomplishment in amateur tennis, Gibson, who earned a bachelor's degree from Florida A&M University in 1953, continued breaking barriers. In 1963, she became the first African American woman to compete in the Ladies Professional Golf Association tour. More than a decade later, she was named New Jersey's commissioner of athletics, becoming the first woman to head a state's athletic commission. ■ —*DLT*

This high-quality Apollo tennis racket made by the Wilson brand was from Gibson's personal collection.

Top: This elegant glamour shot was taken in 1959 by Wallace Seawell, a photographer most known for photographing Hollywood stars.

Civil Rights Frontrunner

❖ **BRINGING RACIAL INTEGRATION TO CLARKSVILLE, TENNESSEE**

Wilma Rudolph overcame major obstacles to become an Olympic champion. "I love what the Olympics stand for," she said in her memoir, *Wilma*. "They'll always be a part of me."

Right: Rudolph insisted African Americans be treated as equals during the citywide "Wilma Randolph Day" festivities in Clarksville. This pamphlet celebrates her 1960 Olympic wins.

ELEVEN SECONDS FLAT—that's how long it took for Wilma Rudolph (1940–94) to streak to victory in the 100-meter sprint and claim Olympic gold at the 1960 Summer Games in Rome, a moment captured here by *Life* magazine photographer George Silk. Nicknamed "Skeeter," the twenty-year-old sprinter triumphed in the 200-meter sprint and the 4 x 100-meter relay as well, becoming the first American woman to win three gold medals in track and field at a single Olympics.

Rudolph had overcome tremendous odds to reach the pinnacle in her sport. Growing up in poverty in the racially segregated city of Clarksville, Tennessee, in the 1940s, she endured a series of devastating illnesses that left her with a partially paralyzed leg. Rudolph's family spent their meager resources traveling ninety miles round trip several times weekly to seek treatment, as the segregated medical facilities closer to home wouldn't treat her. Following years of physical therapy, Rudolph not only regained full use of her leg but also became a lightning-fast runner.

After Rudolph's historic performance in Rome, her hometown planned a "Welcome Wilma" parade and banquet to honor her as "Clarksville's gift to the Olympics." Even as officials celebrated the city's newfound fame as home of "the fastest woman in the world," their decision to enforce segregation at the homecoming festivities was a stark reminder of how unwelcoming Clarksville and the South were to African Americans. Rudolph took a bold stand and refused to attend.

Because of her unwillingness to participate, city officials relented. On October 4, 1960, Clarksville honored Rudolph's victories in the city's first-ever integrated event. For the African American community—including Rudolph's family—both the athlete's Olympic wins and stand against segregation were reasons to celebrate.

Wilma Rudolph is acknowledged as an all-time great track and field athlete, but her actions as an activist athlete are often overlooked. As someone who used her fame to fight for equality and opportunity for African Americans, her contributions off the field are equally important. ■ —*AMS AND DLT*

Coding the First Lunar Landing

❖ HOW MARGARET HAMILTON'S COMPLEX CODE HELPED GUIDE APOLLO 11 ASTRONAUTS TO THE MOON

O N JULY 20, 1969, millions of people worldwide watched via television as Neil Armstrong and Buzz Aldrin took their first steps on the Moon. The safe and successful landing of Apollo 11 on that day would never have been possible without a hardworking crew in the NASA centers—and a complex navigation code, created by a team led by a young woman.

A few years after graduating from Earlham College in 1958 with a BA in mathematics, Margaret Hamilton took charge of software development—then an emerging field—for the Apollo program in the Charles Stark Draper Laboratory at the Massachusetts Institute of Technology. Like all digital computers, the Apollo guidance computer stored its information as sequences of ones and zeros. This logic was mirrored in the machine's hardware, which featured doughnut-shaped pieces of magnetic material, called "cores," threaded with wires. If a wire passed through the core, it sensed a one, and if the wire bypassed the core, a zero. The computer memory was called a "core rope." While overseeing the rope's production, Hamilton earned the name "Rope Mother."

Hamilton and her coders developed the navigation code itself on a large mainframe computer, which printed the results on great reams of paper, a sample of which is shown here. For the next step, they rigorously checked the listings, after which the computer directed a machine to position the cores for proper threading. Programmers didn't weave the ropes directly; they enlisted women from nearby factories, choosing them for their dexterity. Getting the programs correct was crucial, as once woven, it was very difficult to fix an error.

To ensure accuracy, Hamilton pored over her data, verifying every decision and line of code in great detail. "There was no second chance," she later said. "We all knew that."

The software was seamless. No "bugs" appeared in any of the six missions that took human beings to the Moon and back. Today, Hamilton's work stands among the great legacies of the Apollo program and the field of software engineering. She received the Medal of Freedom from President Barack Obama in 2016. ■ —PEC

S TIME   1640 AGC TIME   1639•56 ID 777   PAGE 1

25   FLASH O   DSPTAB +11 00000
25   FLASH O   DSPTAB +11 00000

                S/C ATTITUDE MATRIX
13   -•41226554   •79156518   -•45106578
23   •00031686   -•49497294   •20380950
91   -•91106343   -•35836411   •20380950

          LOS DR   LOS ALT   LOS CR
                           •00   -•00
R ERROR   •00   -•00   •00
V ERROR   •00

      VY   VZ   RSS   TIME
5821•87   -3317•27   7758•94   1640•42
5821•87   -3317•27   7758•94
   •00   •00   -•00

5787•80   -3297•51   7740•17   1640•42
5787•80   -3297•51   7740•17
   •00   •00   -•00

   AZIMUTH   ELEVATION   RANGE   RANGE RATE
    -•37   32•24   40713•0   -40•35

FLAGWD 5 40200   FLAGWD 6 00000   FLAGWD 7 00100

CADR+1   73174   CADR+2   10132   FAILREG 00000
FLAG 10   00000   FLAG 11 00000   OPTMODES 00120
IMODE 33 26000   CHAN 11 01000   CHAN 12 00000
CHAN 33 67767

    -19•76440   ADOT/   -•3012188
    -57•75513   AK2   2•186279
    2372•820   BEST I   •0000000
R Y1 -•2367206E-01 STAR Z1 •5000000
R Y2 1•219482   STAR Z2   •0000000
-RREC 575738•0   VGTIG X   -85•17761
T/OBP -1•256434 ADOT/OBY   •3407679
TAD X -•5163574 THETAD Y -64•36890
    •1301066   TEVENT   2372•820
    -•1428223   ERRORY   58•55713
ORX -•   THETAD X   5•778809
O/OCY •5621408E-01 Y CG   •3071489
G   8•466005   IYY   79900•74
     31119•44   WX DEG/S -•3497057E-02
     1424•454   AYSCM/S2 -•1329155E-02
CM/S2 -•9327403E-03
RI

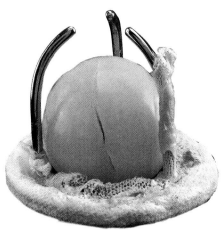

Margaret Hamilton's work was critical to the success of the six Moon landings between 1969 and 1972. Here, she is shown at work in MIT's Draper Laboratory, ca. 1970.

Top: The onboard flight software for the Apollo Program's LM (lunar module) and CM (command module) filled thousands of pages, all of which were carefully checked by Hamilton.

An Early Heart Valve

❖ **A PIONEERING INVENTION FROM THE FIRST FEMALE OPEN-HEART SURGEON**

IN THE MID-1960S, when male physicians dominated hospitals and operating rooms across the United States, Nina Starr Braunwald (1928–92) was performing open-heart surgery. She was also developing artificial heart valves like this one, the Braunwald-Cutter valve, created in conjunction with Cutter Laboratories.

The objective was to design a cloth-covered caged ball valve that could replace malfunctioning human heart valves. Although dozens of similar models were developed between the 1950s and 1980s, Dr. Braunwald was the first to suggest covering the titanium frame with Dacron

In 1960, Dr. Nina Starr Braunwald led a team that implanted the first mitral artificial heart valve. A decade later, she developed this Braunwald-Cutter valve.

tubing to reduce clotting. Initial tests were encouraging, and clinical use of the valve began in 1972.

Unfortunately, the device was taken off the market in 1979 when a significant number of the devices showed fabric wear and abrasions that caused the silicone ball to escape its cage. The valve you see here was surgically implanted and then removed. There is, however, a documented case of a patient living with a Braunwald-Cutter valve for forty-three years.

A pioneer in the discipline of cardiac surgery, Dr. Braunwald was the first woman elected to the American Association for Thoracic Surgery. She was also the first woman to perform open-heart surgery—then an emerging field. ■ —JMC

The Self as Subject

What is a self-portrait? Countless artists—women and men alike—have claimed to make them because their own mirror image is the cheapest model available. But the genre is rarely a simple exercise in self-depiction, as you can see in this commanding self-portrait painted by artist Romaine Brooks (1874–1970) in 1923. Living in Paris, the lesbian artist challenged gender norms with her androgynous appearance and tailored suits. Here, she portrays herself gazing confidently at the viewer, yet her face is partly shaded, suggesting a true self that remains private.

The traversal between the public and private self is part of what makes self-portraits so compelling. The artist's gaze offers up a likeness while raising questions about identity and intent. We feel a strong sense of intimacy, immediacy, and presence as we are offered a private glimpse into the artist's inner world through her expression, pose, and the objects included in the portrait.

Women have long employed the genre to raise questions about shifting conventions of beauty and gender. In Alice Neel's provocative *Self-Portrait* (see page 184), created in 1980, the artist demands that we notice her naked, aging body and situate her portrait within the long history of more traditional female nudes. A pioneer among women artists, Neel painted with a style and approach uniquely her own.

In Janine Antoni's *Lick and Lather* series (1993–94), Antoni subverts ideas about classical sculpture and likeness by using quotidian materials: chocolate and soap (see page 184). Licking and washing the sculptures, she reshapes her image to question assumptions of classical aesthetics.

As technology advanced in the twentieth century, some artists began shifting their gaze away from the mirror. Abandoning painterly, sculpted, and drawn surfaces, they opted instead to look through the camera, documenting their existence through photographs and video. While an artist's depicted self may or may not reveal her true character, we can often discern something of her activism, self-perception, and engagement with the tradition of art and self-portraiture.

Since the 1960s, conceptual artist Adrian Piper has used drawings, paintings, photographs, multimedia installations, videos, and performances to challenge viewers' notions about the "other." For her provocative *The Mythic Being* project (1972–81), Piper adopted the invented persona of a young African American male doing everyday activities in urban environments. The two photos on page 185, *The Mythic Being: Loitering*, invite audiences to challenge their own assumptions about race, gender, class, and identity.

The self-portraits shown here represent just a few of the myriad ways in which women have explored their identities through self-portraiture over the years, with deeply affecting results.

These days, countless women post "selfies" on social media sites across the Internet, offering viewers clues to their social status, connections, and hopes. While most of these images are far less involved than more carefully crafted works, might some of them be considered works of art in their own right?

Within the contemporary culture of the quick smartphone self-portrait and fast-paced social media, it's perhaps more important than ever to take the time to examine thoughtfully created self-portraits made by women from all walks of life, racial backgrounds, and gender expressions. ■ —*BBF*

SELF-PORTRAIT, ROMAINE BROOKS, 1923

Although born into a wealthy Rhode Island family, Beatrice Romaine Goddard had a childhood filled with abuse and neglect. She studied art in France and Italy in the 1890s, married briefly, and then settled among the intellectual elites of Paris. Within those circles, she received high praise for her portraits of friends and lovers, including writers Jean Cocteau and Gabriele D'Annunzio, and her partner and fellow American heiress, Natalie Clifford Barney. But the artist never sought, nor attained, widespread public acclaim. Today, Brooks's works call attention to the obstacles she faced pursuing professional and sexual freedom as an open lesbian. —*CAM*

Since the mid-1990s, New York–based artist Janine Antoni has employed her body as a tool, in her words, to create art. Process is as important as the end result for Antoni, who uses intimate activities—eating, washing, nursing, sleeping—to shape her works and explore gender stereotypes. In her *Lick and Lather* series, shown here, Antoni molded her own likeness in soap and chocolate, before bathing with the former and licking the latter until the surfaces were abraded and her features obscured.

Neel (1900–84) that
it the mark but do not
artist's penetrating yet
n her celebrated figure
e postwar abstract
nt, Neel adhered to
nsequently ignored by
, her career was reignited
ospective exhibitions held
"Life begins at seventy!"
nd revival.

s shocking and utterly
trait, one of just two she
e years to complete the
calling the process, she
neeks got so pink was that
paint that I almost killed
lenging centuries-old
d femininity and female
artists, this striking work
ceptance of her aging

Challenging conventional notions of beauty, these sculptures are the end result of a performance centered on the body of the artist. While evocative of classical busts made with more traditional media, such as marble or bronze, Antoni's sculptures are fashioned from more prosaic materials and reshaped with unorthodox techniques. *Lick and Lather* thus upends portrait traditions premised on likeness by erasing the subject and posing questions about cultural definitions of feminine identity. —*EH*

THE MYTHIC BEING: LOITERING, ADRIAN PIPER, 1974

Conceptual artist and philosopher Adrian Piper works across disciplines to explore identity, race, gender, and class. In the 1970s, drawing on social and political upheavals like the Vietnam War, women's liberation, and the civil rights movement, Piper created performative and visual works to encourage—and occasionally jolt—viewers into experiencing the xenophobia and marginalization of "otherness." These two photographs (gelatin silver prints on paper) are part of *The Mythic Being*, a multiyear project involving photographs, drawings, performances, and advertisements. In these photos, Piper, a light-skinned black woman, dresses as a young, urban black male. Wearing an Afro, mustache, and reflective sunglasses and smoking a cigar, she circulated in the subway, art galleries, and museums. The invented "mythic being" persona offered Piper a framework to reconsider her own identity, while inviting people on streets and in galleries to question their assumptions about the "other." For a moment, viewers must acknowledge the structures that uphold racism and sexism—and, perhaps, find empathy. —*SAG*

CHAPTER FIVE

1968–2019

Breakthroughs and Backlash

I N THE WAKE OF 1960s civil rights legislation, American women pressed for a fuller expression of their rights. But what would those rights be? Women's abilities, women's bodies, and women's right to self-expression took center stage on the nightly news and popular television shows. The nation was divided on whether women could perform in the workplace, in government, in the arts, and on the playing field. Seen as a contest between men and women, millions tuned in on September 1973 as tennis champ Billie Jean King played Bobby Riggs and won. At the same time, many women worked for legislative victories and for the ratification of the Equal Rights Amendment (ERA) to abolish sex discrimination. Headed for ratification in the late 1970s, the ERA was stopped in its tracks by conservative activist Phyllis Schlafly.

Women's activism followed many paths. At times women converged on issues like equal pay and sexual harassment, but diverged on mainstream beauty standards and sex-positivity. These points of solidarity and difference made the women's movement stronger, as did the voicing of broader perspectives by trans women and women of color. In 2017, both the million-strong Women's March and the #MeToo campaign against sexual violence gave fresh momentum to diverse campaigns for women's rights. ∎

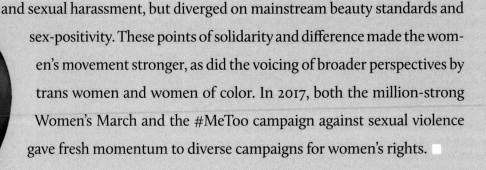

Above: Proceeds from GN4LW merchandise like this 2015 protective helmet support micro-grants and nonprofits that encourage girls in skateboarding.

Previous pages: With its pink wheels and gold-colored trucks, this 2013 GN4LW skateboard conveys a definite feminine vibe, but the skulls and Cindy Whitehead's distinctive logo bring that skater-girl edge.

PREVIOUS SPREAD

Skater Girl Gear

A skateboarding pioneer, Cindy Whitehead turned pro at seventeen, skating both pool and half-pipe and becoming one of the top-ranked vert skaters while competing against the boys. But Whitehead had no choice but to wear boys' shorts when competing; there were no skate products for girls in the 1970s. She changed that in 2013 with her girl-empowered brand Girl is NOT a 4 Letter Word (GN4LW). This skateboard, adorned with Whitehead's artwork, was the brand's first product; equipment and apparel came next. She designed this helmet for safety, comfort, and style and manufactured it through a female-owned company.

To afford women opportunities and recognition lacking in skateboarding, Whitehead fields an all-girl skate team through her GN4LW brand and is fiercely dedicated to supporting girls in action sports. Her personal motto reflects her powerful commitment: "Live life balls to the wall. Do epic shit. Take every dare that comes your way. You can sleep when you're dead." —*JR*

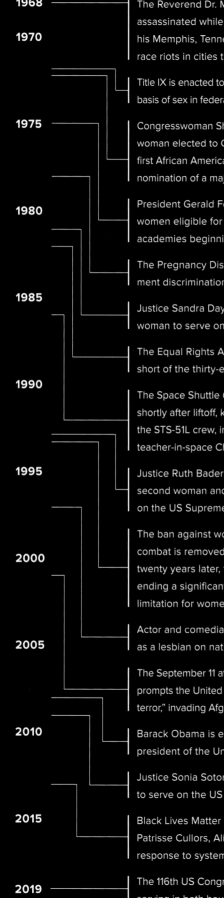

1968	The Reverend Dr. Martin Luther King Jr. is assassinated while standing on the balcony of his Memphis, Tennessee, motel room, igniting race riots in cities throughout America.
1970	
	Title IX is enacted to prohibit discrimination on the basis of sex in federally funded education programs.
1975	Congresswoman Shirley Chisholm, the first black woman elected to Congress in 1968, becomes the first African American to run for the presidential nomination of a major political party.
1980	President Gerald Ford signs law making women eligible for admission to the US military academies beginning in 1976.
	The Pregnancy Discrimination Act bans employment discrimination against pregnant women.
1985	Justice Sandra Day O'Connor becomes the first woman to serve on the US Supreme Court.
	The Equal Rights Amendment falls three states short of the thirty-eight required to ratify.
1990	The Space Shuttle Challenger breaks apart shortly after liftoff, killing all seven members of the STS-51L crew, including Judith Resnik and teacher-in-space Christa McAuliffe.
1995	Justice Ruth Bader Ginsburg becomes the second woman and first Jewish woman to serve on the US Supreme Court.
2000	The ban against women serving in military combat is removed, first in aviation and then, twenty years later, throughout the US services, ending a significant command and promotion limitation for women in military service.
2005	Actor and comedian Ellen DeGeneres comes out as a lesbian on national television.
	The September 11 attacks coordinated by al-Qaeda prompts the United States to begin the "war on terror," invading Afghanistan and later Iraq.
2010	Barack Obama is elected as the first black president of the United States.
	Justice Sonia Sotomayor becomes the first Latina to serve on the US Supreme Court.
2015	Black Lives Matter is founded by activists Patrisse Cullors, Alicia Garza, and Opal Tometi in response to systemic violence against blacks.
2019	The 116th US Congress has a record 131 women serving in both houses.

Pinback button for the Shirley Chisholm presidential campaign, 1972

Portrait of Ruth Bader Ginsburg, Everett Raymond Kinstler, 1996

Challenger Button, STS-51-L, ca. 1986

Ellen poster, Timothy White, ca. 1996

Untitled, Sheila Pree Bright, 2015

Early in her career, Celia Cruz performed in the traditional *bata cubana*, which includes Spanish, French, and African influences. Cuban-born designer José Arteaga made this orange *bata* for Cruz around 1992.

Opposite: Cuban-born photographer Alexis Rodríguez-Duarte, in collaboration with Tico Torres, took this 1994 photograph of Cruz as part of the *Cuba Out of Cuba* series. Cruz wanted people all over the world to see her brightly colored, elegant *batas* and know that Cubans produced beautiful things.

Celia Cruz: An Unapologetic Force

❖ ASSERTING LATINX PRESENCE AND IDENTITY THROUGH MUSIC AND STYLE

THIS DRESS BELONGED to the legendary Úrsula Hilaria Celia de la Caridad Cruz Alfonso (1925–2003), better known as Celia Cruz, the Queen of Salsa. Cruz's costume style, especially early in her career, was an adaptation of a Cuban rumba dress, or *bata cubana.* Its formfitting seams made it sculpturally elegant, while its ruffles moved dramatically on the sleeves and train during performances. In 1997, Cruz told Smithsonian curator Marvette Perez that she liked to wear *batas* in concert halls when "I know I'm going to sing some Afro-Cuban number slow, beautiful . . . . I can walk on the stage and flaunt the train."

Celia Cruz was a force. The only female member of the legendary Fania All-Stars, she was one of few women of her time to succeed in the male-dominated salsa world. With her impassioned songs and dazzling costumes, she harnessed the power of music to affirm Latinx identity and community.

As a teenager in 1940s Havana, Cruz rejected her father's outdated ideas about vocations for respectable women and pursued music. She gained fame by singing in radio contests and, in 1950, became the voice of Cuba's popular band, La Sonora Matancera. The band traveled to Mexico after the 1959 Cuban Revolution and never returned. In 1961, Cruz and her partner, Pedro Knight—former trumpeter for La Sonora Matancera—moved to the United States and settled in New Jersey to join New York's burgeoning Latin music scene. She performed with Tito Puente and the Fania All-Stars before embarking on a successful solo career.

Cruz's star rose in the United States during a period of demographic change, ethnic pride, and activism. From 1960 to 1980, the Latinx population in the New York City area doubled, as Puerto Ricans, Cubans, and Dominicans moved there. Cruz's Afro-Caribbean rhythms and Spanish language—she joked that her English was "not very good looking"—helped affirm the nation's growing Latinx population. Audiences cheered at her signature cry, *¡Azúcar!* (literally, "sugar"). For decades, Cruz was the sound of pan-Latinx identity across generations and genres, her music evolving to encompass rumba, salsa, hip-hop, and even reggaeton.

Cruz's global popularity had as much to do with the power of her alto voice as with her brightly sequined costumes, colorful wigs, and extremely high heels—an aesthetic she vowed to uphold even when she reached ninety years old. Unfortunately, she passed away at the age of seventy-eight. This iconic portrait, taken in 1994, shows the artist beaming in a yellow *bata.*

With a Grammy Lifetime Achievement Award and a host of other honors and awards to her name, Cruz was a trailblazing Afro-Cuban who carved success in male-dominated spaces. She was radiantly and unapologetically black, Cuban, Spanish speaking, Caribbean, Latina, and woman. ■ —*AAC*

ERA: Fast Track to Slow Defeat

❖ TWO WOMEN DRIVE THE HISTORY OF THE EQUAL RIGHTS AMENDMENT

IN 1920, THE Nineteenth Amendment removed sex as an obstacle to women voting, but women still lacked equality in other areas. Three years later, women's suffrage leader Alice Paul (1885–1977) and the National Woman's Party proposed the Equal Rights Amendment (ERA), seeking to complete the equalization of men and women in American law and life. Beginning in 1923, the ERA was introduced without success in every congressional session.

The amendment was controversial from the beginning, even among women, but by the 1940s, both Republicans and Democrats had added ratification of the ERA as a plank to their party platforms.

The 1960s and the growth of the women's movement brought increased agitation and public support for the ERA. Activists argued that existing laws protecting women

---

> "It's been a half a century since women began fighting for the amendment. It would make the Constitution apply fully to women for the first time."
>
> —GLORIA STEINEM

> ERA "will take away the right to be a woman."
>
> —PHYLLIS SCHLAFLY

---

from discrimination could be repealed or selectively enforced. Believing that a constitutional amendment was required to ensure equal treatment permanently, women's rights activists, including the newly formed National Organization for Women (NOW), began pressuring legislators to finally move on the amendment.

Success, it seemed, was in sight. In 1972, both the House and the Senate passed the ERA with large bipartisan majorities and, after forty-nine years, sent it to the states for ratification. On March 22, the same day the amendment passed Congress, Hawai'i voted for ratification.

Although thirty-three other states quickly followed Hawai'i's lead, support for the ERA was slowly diminishing, largely due to the efforts of Republican activist Phyllis Schlafly (1924–2016), who had lost her own races for the House of Representatives in 1952 and 1970. In her nationally circulated newsletter, Schlafly skillfully swayed politicians and the public with convincingly articulated arguments against the amendment. The equal protection clause of the Fourteenth Amendment rendered the ERA unnecessary, she insisted. She also warned that the ERA would condone federally funded abortions, gay marriage, unisex bathrooms, federally controlled child care, and the drafting of women into the military. She founded a grassroots organization called STOP ERA, garnered support from religious groups and the conservative wing of the Republican Party, and lobbied national and state legislators. In 1977, Schlafly staged what was called "a pro family rally" in Houston, about five miles away from the site of the National Women's Conference. The latter was being held to develop national plans for women's legislative action, with the ERA among its key proposals. The competing conferences painted very different visions of women in America.

Schlafly almost singlehandedly prevented the remaining states from ratifying, and many historians argue that her work was one of the contributing factors in the rise of the religious right, the culture wars, and the nation's current political divisiveness. The ERA became more than a constitutional amendment. It was a cultural flashpoint, a symbol of what was right or wrong—depending on one's perspective—with America in the last half of the twentieth century. ■ —ECJ AND LKG

Alice Paul created four bracelets of charms engraved with the dates each state ratified the ERA. The first bracelet begins with Hawai'i (3/22/1972) and ends with New Jersey (4/17/1972).

Left: The National Committee to Stop ERA drew support from political, cultural, and religious conservatives. STOP ERA (as shown on this 1978 button) was an acronym for Stop Taking Our Privileges.

Choreopoem for Colored Girls

❖ **BRINGING AFRICAN AMERICAN WOMEN'S VOICES TO MAINSTREAM THEATER**

Adorned in the colors of the rainbow, seven women electrified Broadway audiences in 1976 with an innovative blend of dance, music, poetry, and storytelling that placed African American women's lives and voices in mainstream theater. Ntozake Shange's spectacular first play, *for colored girls who have considered suicide / when the rainbow is enuf*, was the second show by an African American woman to open on Broadway. In Shange's powerful choreopoem, the seven female characters present poetic monologues conveying struggles with racism, sexism, and other forms of discrimination and violence, while the rainbow symbolizes the celebration of their survival and hope for a brighter future.

A leading poet, novelist, and playwright during the 1970s and 1980s, Ntozake Shange (1948–2018) developed and performed *for colored girls* with her own California theater company before moving to New York a year prior to the play's Broadway opening at the Booth Theatre.

The provocative *for colored girls* ran nearly two years on Broadway, where it earned both glowing and harsh reviews. Since then, the play has cleared a path for the Broadway success of other black playwrights; has launched the acting careers of countless men and women who have starred in the television and film adaptations; and has inspired and enriched the work of black theater groups, which continue to create stirring productions of *for colored girls*. This 1977 playbill represents Shange's innovative work and its iconic place in African American literature, in black feminist writings, and in American theater. ■ *—DTS*

With its rainbow-colored cover, this *for colored girls* playbill from 1977 boldly embodies Ntozake Shange's pioneering choreopoem mixing the vibrancy of dance, music, poetry, and storytelling.

Dressed for the Bench

❖ **THE UNIFORM WORN BY THE NATION'S FIRST WOMAN SUPREME COURT JUSTICE**

I T'S A PLAIN BLACK ROBE, the kind worn by judges across the United States. But the woman it belonged to, Sandra Day O'Connor, wore it on September 25, 1981, the day she was sworn in as an associate justice of the Supreme Court of the United States. O'Connor's robe is hemmed to fall to the length of a skirt. Like the gold stripes that William Rehnquist added to his robe to designate his role as chief justice, this detail illustrates O'Connor's unique position on the high court: the first woman after a succession of 101 men.

O'Connor first wore this robe in 1975, when she was elected to the bench in Arizona as a superior court judge, and took it with her to Washington. In 1985, she ordered a replacement and, at the request of the museum, quietly donated the robe that symbolized a milestone in her judicial career and in women's history to the national collections.

In her twenty-five years on the Supreme Court, she earned a reputation as a pragmatic centrist voice, judging each case on its individual merits and specializing in narrowly crafted opinions. She played a powerful role, often casting the pivotal vote in cases concerning reproductive rights, affirmative action, privacy rights, campaign finance, and the line between separation of church and state.

Of the judicial robes she wore while casting such key votes, O'Connor wrote in a 2013 *Smithsonian* magazine article, "I am fond of the symbolism of this tradition. It shows that all of us judges are engaged in upholding the Constitution and the rule of law. We have a common responsibility."

O'Connor's investiture marked the first time a woman served on the Supreme Court, and her skillful performance as a justice smoothed the way for the next woman to be appointed. In 1993, Justice Ruth Bader Ginsburg joined her on the bench. ■ —*LKG*

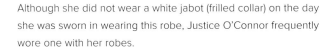

Although she did not wear a white jabot (frilled collar) on the day she was sworn in wearing this robe, Justice O'Connor frequently wore one with her robes.

Above right: Artist Jean Marcellino painted this portrait in October 2006. O'Connor sat for twenty-five artists, each of whom created a portrait of the retiring justice as part of a special exhibition.

A Room of One's Own, Reimagined

❖ FINDING FREEDOM OF EXPRESSION IN FEMINIST ART

WITH THE ARRIVAL of feminism in the 1960s and 1970s, the widely held assumption that women couldn't be professional artists changed radically, altering the world of contemporary art. Not only did more women dedicate themselves to professional art careers but they also insisted on their right to do so without conforming to artistic criteria and rules not of their making. They built new institutions to bypass existing gatekeepers and reach new audiences, while challenging ideologies that kept women and minorities from the art world's upper echelons.

In 1970, California artist Judy Chicago founded the first-ever Feminist Art Program (FAP) in the United States

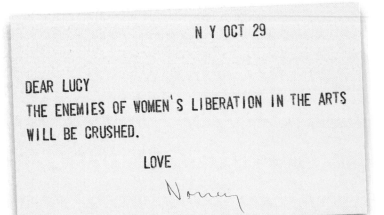

NY OCT 29

DEAR LUCY
THE ENEMIES OF WOMEN'S LIBERATION IN THE ARTS
WILL BE CRUSHED.

LOVE

Nancy

at Fresno State College (now California State University, Fresno), after realizing she and her students were poorly served by the patriarchal curriculum. The following year, Chicago introduced the program at the California Institute of the Arts (CalArts), where painter Miriam Schapiro (1923–2015) became codirector. Teachers and students explored innovative art making, from setting off vibrantly colored flares to "feminize" the desert to turning a condemned Hollywood mansion into *Womanhouse*, an immersive exhibition on enforced domesticity. *Dollhouse*

(1972), a collaborative work by Schapiro and artist Sherry Brody, was on display in that installation. Playing with the prim stylization of earlier versions, the sculpture contains handkerchiefs, miniature furniture, and curios collected from women across the United States to illustrate the conflicting demands of artist, wife, and mother. Contrasting abstract art trends of the previous period, the work is pointedly politically illustrative: its tiny rooms evoke both childhood flights of imagination and cells where those aspirations are constrained.

Artists Senga Nengudi and Judith Baca played animating roles in Los Angeles's burgeoning art scene as well, merging innovative individual practice and feminist concerns with efforts to build community among African American and Latinx artists and audiences. Nengudi's sculptures prompted collective performances under freeways and in galleries, while Baca's gallery-scaled installations and monumental community murals explored racial and gender stereotypes.

In 1970s New York, critic and curator Lucy Lippard joined Women Artists in Revolution and other activist groups in demanding equal representation for women and nonwhite artists in major museums. These organizations picketed, projected excluded artists onto museum facades, and strategically engaged the media to advance their case. Lippard also organized all-women artist exhibitions, started The Slide Registry of Women's Art so others could do the same, and, over decades, connected a national network of artists, activists, and academics.

In the mid-1980s, an anonymous collective called the Guerrilla Girls carried Lippard's creative activism forward, plastering the city with eye-catching posters attacking the persistent sexism and racism in the art world. Today, the Guerrilla Girls continues using humor, facts, and flamboyant visuals to expose gender and ethnic bias, while emphasizing feminism's necessity in twenty-first-century art and society. ■ —SG

In Miriam Shapiro and Sherry Brody's *Dollhouse* (1972), a kitchen, a Hollywood star's bedroom, a "harem" room, and a nursery illustrate the many roles women are taught to embrace and shuffle among from an early age.

Opposite: Artist and activist Nancy Spero made women the sole figural subjects of her artwork from 1976 onward. In this excerpt from a 1971 letter to fellow activist Lucy Lippard, she doesn't mince words.

Judy Chicago took her FAP students into the desert to perform rituals, release flares, and produce *Smoke Bodies* (1972), one of a series of photographs documenting these ephemeral land artworks.

Left, top (four details): Although best known for her performances, Carolee Schneemann (1939–2019) primarily considered herself a painter interested in liberating paint from the canvas. *Eye Body: 36 Transformative Actions* (1963–73) consists of thirty-six nude photographs of Schneemann immersed in her monumental painting installation, *Four Fur Cutting Boards* (1962–63). Denounced by critics who insisted that she had to keep her clothes on to be taken seriously, Schneemann nevertheless continued utilizing her body as a material in her artwork throughout her career, demonstrating that a woman can be both "image and image-maker." —BJ

Left, bottom: Appropriating an image from art history, this 1989 Guerrilla Girls poster, *Do women have to be naked to get into the MET museum? (from Portfolio Compleat: 1985-2012)*, combats gender inequities at the Metropolitan Museum of Art with facts gathered from a "weenie count" of the museum. —SAG

Opposite: Investigating learned and performed identities, Judith Baca's *Las Tres Marías* (1976) features two life-size drawings of the same Chicana woman flanking a mirror that reflects the viewer as a third possible María.

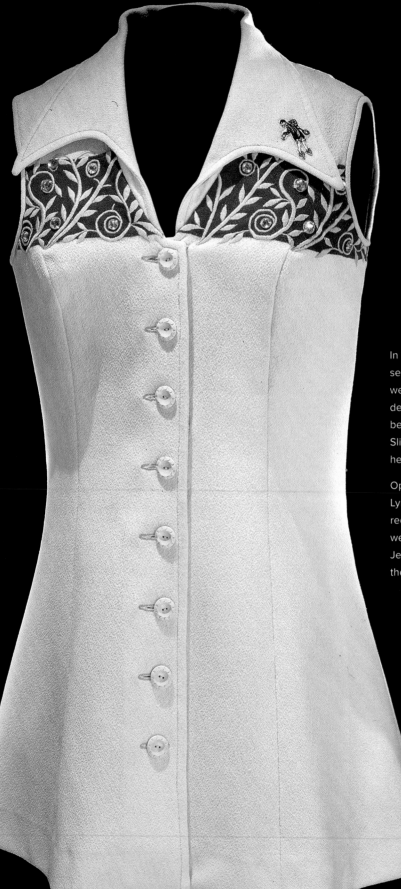

In 1973, Billie Jean King served sexism a crushing defeat while wearing this dress. Created by designer Ted Tinling, its collar bears the logo of the Virginia Slims women's tennis tour King helped found three years prior.

Opposite: In 1981, photographer Lynn Gilbert published a book recognizing forty-six women who were pioneers in their field. Billie Jean King is shown here, racket at the ready.

Winning the "Battle of the Sexes"

❖ BILLIE JEAN KING'S FIGHT AGAINST CHAUVINISM ON AND OFF THE COURT

GROUNDBREAKING TENNIS player Billie Jean King wore this custom blue-and-green dress while defeating self-proclaimed "male chauvinist" Robert "Bobby" Riggs (1918–95) in their legendary "Battle of the Sexes" exhibition tennis match in 1973. "I would never have worn pink," King later said of her outfit choice.

At the time of the match, King was one of the sport's most dominant players. The native Californian had recently become one of just a few athletes to win a singles title at each of the four Grand Slam events. King used her fame to become a vocal advocate for better recognition and equal pay for women in the sport. Tennis was more popular than ever, but a massive wage gap remained between male and female competitors. Three years earlier, she'd been instrumental in the founding of the Virginia Slims Circuit, a women's tour. The tour's success led to the founding of the Women's Tennis Association in 1973, the world's first professional organization for female tennis players.

King's fight was part of a larger wave of demands for increased respect and opportunities by America's growing female workforce. As women tried to expand the nature of the American labor force, some people resisted the change, digging in their heels and reinforcing stereotypes and rhetoric.

Wanting to cash in on the cultural debate, former tennis champion Bobby Riggs made outrageous claims about women's inferiority, insisting that he, even at the age of fifty-five, could defeat any professional woman player in a tennis match. Riggs made an open challenge to the female tennis community, daring them to face him in an exhibition match.

After tennis star Margaret Court lost to Riggs in such a match, King stepped up to the challenge to dispel any doubts about women's athletic abilities. On September 20, 1973, she faced off against Riggs in Houston's massive Astrodome as ninety million television viewers looked on worldwide. The $100,000 winner-take-all competition was the most-viewed tennis match in history.

King handily defeated her male opponent in three straight sets. Her victory, celebrated around the world, helped to destigmatize female participation in athletics and invigorated the women's liberation movement. "I thought it would set us back fifty years if I didn't win that match," King said.

In addition to being one of the most successful players of all time, including winning thirty-nine Grand Slam titles in her career, King has been an influential advocate for women's and LGBTQ+ rights off the court. When receiving the Presidential Medal of Freedom in 2009, she said, "Tennis is a platform, and I fight for everybody." ■ —*EWJ*

A Powerful Voice for Social Change

❖ "MY LIFE BELONGS TO THE STRUGGLE."—FREEDOM FIGHTER ANGELA DAVIS

I N THIS VIBRANT PORTRAIT, artist Wadsworth Jarrell captures the intensity and power of legendary black activist, writer, and scholar Angela Davis. *Revolutionary* (1972) evokes the social turmoil of a nation grappling with civil rights, the Vietnam War, the rising tide of feminism, authoritarian policing practices, and more.

Davis was born in Birmingham, Alabama, in 1944. Her parents, middle-class school teachers, were active in the civil rights movement. She studied with Marxist philosopher Herbert Marcuse at Brandeis University and became a professor of philosophy at UCLA, where she developed ties with the American Communist Party and the Black Panther Party for Self-Defense. In 1970, the University of California Board of Regents—pressured by Governor Ronald Reagan—fired Davis for her Communist connections, causing international outcry. A judge ruled that her freedom of speech had been violated and reinstated her, but she was fired a second time for "inflammatory language."

The next year, Davis was charged with kidnapping and murder; guns she had legally owned and registered had been used in an attempt to free three black inmates accused of killing a Soledad Prison guard in California. Davis eluded authorities for two months before the FBI captured her. Her sixteen-month imprisonment and trial became an international cause célèbre, inspiring a variety of "Free Angela" ephemera as nearly 300 defense committees formed worldwide. An all-white jury acquitted her in 1972, the same year she campaigned for Communist Party candidates.

Davis taught at the University of California, Santa Cruz, from 1991 to 2008. Since then, she has continued to be an internationally acclaimed activist on issues of race, class, feminism, mass incarceration, and social justice. ■ —*WSP*

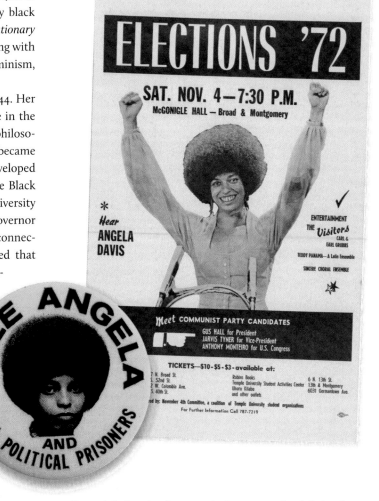

Above, left: People often wore buttons supporting jailed antiwar and civil rights activists like Angela Davis. Above, right: This 1972 poster drew crowd eager to hear Davis speak in support of Communist Party candidates.

Opposite: This 1972 portrait of Davis, *Revolutionary*, was painted by Wadsworth A. Jarrell Sr. He cofounded AfriCOBRA (African Commune of Bad Relevant Artists), an artists' collective internationally acclaimed for politically themed art.

Navigating Change

❖ **THE FIRST OFFICIAL MATERNITY UNIFORM FOR PREGNANT PILOTS**

I N THE EARLY 1990S, while cruising across the sky in a Boeing 737, a pregnant Captain Cynthia Berkeley wore this accommodating uniform bearing the United Airlines wings. It was the first company-issued pilot's maternity uniform; in the past, pregnant pilots had sewn their own.

Decades earlier, the dramatic social and cultural changes of the 1960s and 1970s profoundly affected commercial aviation. For years, female employees typically stepped away from their jobs when they married—sometimes voluntarily and sometimes not. When women married someone at their own institution, antinepotism laws were often used against them, whereas their husbands were able to keep their jobs. But as the nation wrestled with issues surrounding civil rights and discrimination, barriers against women and people of color began to fall. Airlines started to hire women and African Americans as pilots.

In January 1973, a Colorado-born pilot named Emily Howell landed a pilot job at Frontier Airlines, becoming the first American woman to fly for a scheduled US commercial airline. An experienced pilot when the regional carrier hired her as a second officer, Howell soon advanced to first officer (copilot) and then captain. Several months after Howell broke the gender barrier, Bonnie Tiburzi earned her American Airlines wings, becoming the first American woman to fly for a major airline.

Traditional attitudes about women working reflected class bias as well. Working-class women often continued to hold jobs after marriage and childbirth, while white-collar women were expected to stay at home and tend to the children. As these attitudes gradually changed, many businesses recognized the need to extend full rights to all employees, including expectant mothers.

By the early 1990s, both the aviation industry and the traveling public had accepted that all qualified people, regardless of race or gender, could pilot an airliner. At the time Captain Berkeley wore the maternity uniform shown here, she had been expertly navigating the skies for United Airlines since 1979. ■ —*FRV*

Wearing this dark blue wool maternity uniform with her rank insignia on both shoulders, Captain Cynthia Berkeley flew Boeing 737s for United Airlines during her pregnancy in the 1990s.

The Voyager Development Test Model was a structural prototype for *Voyager 1* and *2*, twin spacecrafts sent to investigate the solar system. The mission launched the careers of a generation of women in planetary science.

The Women of Voyager

❖ BREAKING INTO PLANETARY SCIENCE, EXPLORING THE OUTER SOLAR SYSTEM

IN THE SUMMER OF 1977, NASA sent two robotic probes on flyby missions to explore our outer solar system. By the end of their first twelve-year mission, *Voyager 1* and *2* (each identical to the engineering model pictured here) had flown by Jupiter, Saturn, Neptune, and Uranus. The spacecraft gathered imagery and data from the planets, their rings, and many of their moons—including close-up views of Saturn's largest moon, Titan. Although the two probes didn't visit Pluto, they effectively completed the first phase of human-robotic solar system exploration. In contrast with previous planetary missions, women played prominent, public roles in Voyager program explorations.

Planetary scientist and astrophysicist Fran Bagenal, co-investigator on the Voyager Plasma Science Experiment, studied the electrons and ions trapped by the outer planets' magnetic fields. Planetary astronomer Heidi Hammel, a brand-new PhD at the time of the 1989 Neptune flyby, was already the world's expert on Neptune's clouds. Candice Hansen was a member of the Voyager imaging team; during the initial mission, she went from holding a bachelor's degree in physics to being a PhD candidate in earth and space science. Carolyn Porco wrote her PhD dissertation on the rings of Saturn before joining the *Voyager 2* imaging team in 1983 to study the faint rings around Uranus and Neptune.

Before the Voyager program, planetary science was a male-dominated field. Breaking into these ranks was no small feat. Talking to the National Air and Space Museum in 2018, Hammel explained, "There was a cohort of young women in the late 1970s who were recipients of the feminist movement. We just plowed ahead and went into the fields we found most exciting. When people said 'You can't do that,' we just said, 'Yeah we can. And here we are, we're doing it.'"

All four women went on to become distinguished members of the planetary science community, holding leadership roles on new planetary missions and helping to grow the planetary science community. As for *Voyager 1* and *2*, they are still flying on an interstellar mission exploring the space between stars. ■ —*MBS*

A Woman's Place: In Outer Space

❖ PIONEERING NASA WOMEN AMONG THE FIRST TO SUIT UP FOR SPACEFLIGHT

AMERICA'S FIRST FEMALE astronaut was Miss Astronaut Barbie, introduced in 1965 during the Space Race era. At the time, American women didn't qualify to be astronauts simply because they weren't men. An all-male astronaut corps of fighter pilots and test pilots manned American spacecraft for almost twenty years, but in the 1970s, things began to change.

After the Moon landings in the late 1960s and early 1970s, NASA changed course with an orbital spaceplane—the Space Shuttle. The nation was changing course, too, moving toward equal opportunity and equal rights. In 1978, with the introduction of six women, three African American men, and an Asian American man, the astronaut corps began to look more like America. Subsequent recruitments yielded more racial and ethnic diversity. Democratizing spaceflight, NASA expanded its astronaut corps to include more scientists, engineers, physicians, and even veterinarians, who were all needed for research and technical work in orbit.

From 1978 through 2018, fifty-seven women were selected into the United States astronaut corps. Insisting they be referred to as astronauts, not "women astronauts," they neither sought nor accepted differences in training, treatment, or performance. Of these pioneers, three are among the most renowned.

Wearing this blue flight jacket, astrophysicist Sally Ride (1951–2012)—one of the most vocal about equality—flew aboard the Space Shuttle *Challenger* in 1983, becoming the first American woman in space. Ride flew again in 1984 on the first mission with two women.

Engineer and physician Mae Jemison earned her wings on a 1992 research mission as the first female African American astronaut. Five more African American women followed in her wake, as gender and race barriers to spaceflight had decisively fallen.

During the 1990s, Eileen Collins, US Air Force, became the first woman to occupy the pilot's seat, and then the commander's seat, in the course of her four Space Shuttle missions. She capably piloted two complex missions and commanded two others between 1995 and 2005.

No one needs an astronaut doll for inspiration now. Real women inspire that dream. ■ —VN

This 1999 portrait by Annie Leibovitz shows pilot-commander astronaut Eileen Collins in the shuttle Launch-Entry Suit, or "pumpkin suit," worn by astronauts after the 1986 *Challenger* tragedy.

Opposite, top: Mae Jemison, the first female African American astronaut, was issued this leather name tag embossed with NASA civilian wings (ca. 1992).

Opposite, bottom: Sally Ride wore this flight suit in 1983 on the seventh Space Shuttle mission (STS-7), making history as America's first woman in space.

Mapping the Universe

I N 1986, ASTRONOMER Margaret Geller and her colleagues at the Harvard-Smithsonian Center for Astrophysics mapped a sliver of the universe, offering revolutionary insights into the spatial distribution of nearby galaxies. Geller discovered that, contrary to what most people previously believed, the universe had a distinct structure of galaxy clusters and empty spaces; she likened their patterns to soap bubbles. The soap bubble walls of galaxies connected to create a stickman pattern, which you can see in the center of this map. It was the largest-known superstructure of galaxies in the universe at the time.

Growing up in the 1950s, Geller spent time in her physicist father's laboratory at Bell Labs, where he nurtured her investigative tendencies. She discovered the importance of creativity in science and found role models in his female colleagues. Despite battling gender discrimination during graduate school, she persisted, in 1974 becoming only the second woman to earn a PhD in physics at Princeton. Joining the Harvard-Smithsonian Center for Astrophysics, she went on to teach at Harvard during the 1980s, but she was not offered tenure—despite many awards and membership in the prestigious National Academy of Sciences. However, Geller found an intellectual home at the Smithsonian Astrophysical Observatory, working with long-time collaborator John Huchra, who gathered the data Geller used to create her maps.

In 1990, Geller won a MacArthur Fellowship "Genius Grant." She used it to produce the award-winning films *Where the Galaxies Are* and *So Many Galaxies . . . So Little Time,* employing brilliant visuals and accessible language to share her discoveries. Geller's films have since been viewed by millions of people in science museums across the world.

A senior scientist at Smithsonian since 1991, Geller fosters the collegiality that was missing in her own graduate experience; on joint publications, she insists the students she collaborates with are listed first. Today she continues charting our vast, mysterious universe, improving on her original maps, and sharing an infectious enthusiasm for exploring nature's unanswered questions. ■ —*LF*

In this 1990 photograph, astronomer Margaret Geller explains her revolutionary map of the universe, which led to the discovery of what was then the largest-known superstructure of galaxies.

Barbara McClintock

❖ A MICROSCOPE, A UNIQUE VISION, AND A NOBEL–PRIZE WINNING DISCOVERY

BARBARA MCCLINTOCK's experimental corn gardens yielded crucial clues about the plant's genetic material. While working at Cold Spring Harbor Laboratory in New York in the 1940s, she selectively bred maize in an abundant array of colors and patterns ranging from red and yellow to purple, white, spotted, and striped. Seeking patterns and anomalies within the complex variability of her plants, McClintock (1902–92) was hoping to answer questions about their genes: the basic units responsible for passing traits from one generation to the next.

McClintock looked past the corn's cell walls into the nucleus and at the chromosomes within. In 1929, she became the first person to identify all ten maize chromosomes. Although individual genes were beyond the reach of her microscope, she inferred their location on the corn chromosomes by analyzing the visible traits of offspring created through her crossbreeding.

In the late 1940s, while studying the tendency of a specific chromosome to break, she discovered that some genes can move to a new location on a chromosome; not all genes were fixed in place, as was generally believed. McClintock continued to research how these mobile genetic elements controlled the expression of other genes within the maize plants.

Although she was a well-respected geneticist, the wider scientific community didn't immediately celebrate her discovery, and many were puzzled by it. Regarding the lack of interest in her early 1950s publications, McClintock concluded "no amount of published evidence would be effective."

Perhaps it was too hard to follow. Or maybe it was because it straddled two different scientific communities concerned with genetics and development. Perhaps McClintock's treasured independence isolated her as well. The combination of all of these factors, and a myriad of others, meant that it took decades for her work to be widely recognized.

In 1983, more than thirty years later, McClintock received the Nobel Prize in Physiology or Medicine at the age of eighty-one. We keep returning to her published evidence after all, fascinated not just with what she saw when she looked through her microscope but with the uniqueness of her vision. ■ —KFF

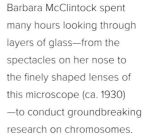

Barbara McClintock spent many hours looking through layers of glass—from the spectacles on her nose to the finely shaped lenses of this microscope (ca. 1930) —to conduct groundbreaking research on chromosomes.

Stitching Together a Nation's History

Today, the word *quilt* is defined as a bedcover or hanging made with a decorative top layer, a filling or interlining, and a backing fabric, all held together with lines of hand or machine stitching. But quilts are more than just bedcovers or wall art. The stories they embody can illuminate the lives, activities, artistic skills, and aspirations of American women and girls across our nation's history.

Quilting is both the process of making a quilt and the actual finishing stitching. Quilts can be made of a single fabric (whole cloth); they can be stitched together from cut-up cloth or clothing (pieced); they can be created by cutting out designs and applying them on a whole cloth surface (appliqué); or they can be some combination of these approaches. Within those limits, quilt makers have always had an extraordinary variety of options.

Most of the quilts in the Smithsonian collections were made by women, though men have been and continue to be quilt makers. Representing every level of income and social status, these objects range from utilitarian scrap quilts, such as the sock-top quilts of Ada Chitwood Jones (1903–1997), to those made as conscious self-expression, such as the 2008 *Tribute to the Mohawk Ironworkers* by Carla Hemlock (1961–). Some of the designs are unique, but others come from traditional patterns that were traded among friends and, beginning in the 1800s, from pictures in women's magazines and handicraft manuals. For quilt makers, creativity and aesthetics were—and are—as important as thrift. Political and religious beliefs, ties of family and friendship, engagement in community, and measuring their skills against other quilters at fairs and shows were also essential elements. By the 1960s, artists were appropriating traditional quilting techniques to make contemporary art for walls as well as beds.

Quilts are three-dimensional and tactile, making them an intimate art form. Each quilt maker infuses the work with her or his personality and style, even when using a popular pattern. The choices are many: materials, colors, scale, overall composition, and how to combine the imagery of the quilt top with the quilting stitchery. The only limits are the availability and/or affordability of materials. These details—of fabric, thread, stitching, filling, design—can help confirm, flesh out, or contradict the stories that accompany many quilts. Every quilt invites inquiry into the circumstances of its maker and making and its history of use.

Close examination encourages questions. Who made the quilt? Was it the work of one individual, or was it a group effort, like the "Seamstresses' Quilt"? What can fabric choice tell us about the maker's life and world? Why was she inspired to create this particular quilt, and why was it considered important enough to preserve? How does it now offer insight into the past? A legion of quilt scholars has contributed to our understanding of these objects through electronic and print publications and through state quilt-documentation projects and national, regional, and local quilt guilds, museums, and historical societies.

American quilts embody American history. The women who created the quilts in these pages may have led ordinary lives for their times, but they left us a legacy of extraordinary work for all time. ■ —*MCS*

SLOTHOWER FAMILY QUILT

Sometimes referred to as the "Seamstresses' Quilt," this striking appliquéd quilt came from the George Slothower (1802–77) family of Baltimore County, Maryland. From 1800 to 1850, Baltimore was second only to New York City in the number of immigrants entering through its port. Census records from 1840 to 1850 indicate the Slothowers had German-born servants and seamstresses; family history attributes this quilt to their work. George Slothower may have hired them either through the city's German Society or the Lutherville Female Seminary, in which he played active roles. The servants probably stayed with the family long enough to learn English and to make connections in the community, which could lead to marriage or a better job.

George Slothower was a wholesale dry goods merchant and, after 1852, owned a cotton mill that produced Osnaburg, a coarse cloth often sold for clothing for enslaved workers. The high-quality fabrics used in this quilt (ca. 1840–60), however, were probably produced by New England's cotton mills—and their largely female labor force. —*VE AND MCS*

FOLK QUILT, MODERN ART

Harriet Powers (1837–1910), an African American farm woman of Clarke County, Georgia, made this extraordinary quilt around 1886. Born enslaved in 1837 on a small plantation, Harriet married Armstead Powers in 1855, and the couple had at least nine children. In the 1880s, she began quilting as a creative expression; she had likely quilted of necessity while raising her family. Her remarkable pictorial design illustrates several stories from the Bible. Powers exhibited this quilt at the Athens Cotton Fair of 1886, where it captured the imagination of Jennie Smith, a young, internationally trained local artist. Initially, Powers did not want to sell the quilt, but later, during a period of hard times, she sold it to Smith for five dollars. Smith kept careful notes of Harriet's comments on the design. This quilt has been called a masterpiece of folk art. And yet, the imagery foreshadows modern art of the early twentieth century. Perhaps, then, Harriet Powers should be remembered not only as a former enslaved worker who created folk art quilts but also as one of the earliest modern artists. —VE AND MCS

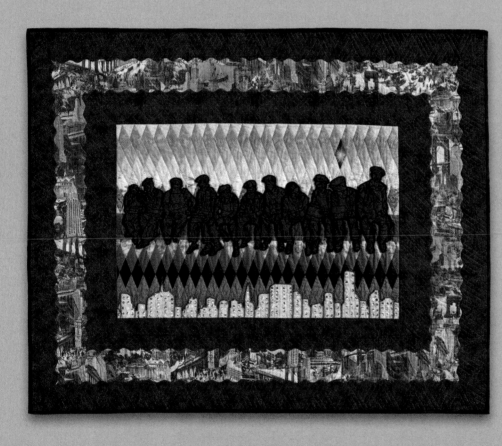

ART ROOTED IN MOHAWK HISTORY

A social commentary, Carla Hemlock's *Tribute to Mohawk Ironworkers* (2008) pays homage to generations of Mohawk construction workers who helped build New York City's bridges and high-rises, and lost their lives doing so. The quilt was inspired by an iconic 1932 photograph of ironworkers perched on a suspended I-beam—an image that hangs in countless Mohawk homes. The star on the quilt symbolizes those who have passed. After sixty-five Mohawk men died building the Quebec Bridge in 1907, Mohawk women told their skilled ironworker husbands, brothers, and sons to continue their profession—but never in large numbers on the same site. Throughout the twentieth century, Mohawk men heeded this counsel, as they helped build and, in the case of the World Trade Center, disassemble New York City's most famous high-rises. Hemlock's quilt is a tribute to this ongoing history, steeped in pride and pain. —CRG

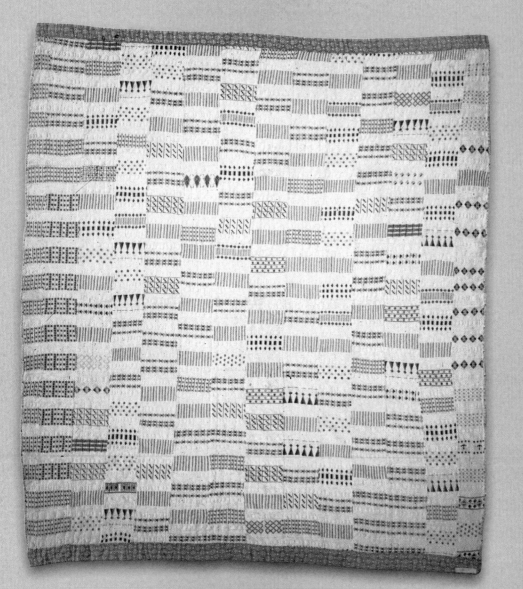

This quilt, made by South Carolina fabric chronicler, author, and musician Dorothy Montgomery, depicts a powerful reunion. In 1997, two women separated by many miles and very diverse life experiences mingled their tears and sang a song connecting them across time, the horrors of slavery, and the dramatic changes suffered by Africa in the nineteenth and twentieth centuries. Mary Moran of Harris Neck, Georgia, and Baindu Jabati of Senehun Ngola, Sierra Leone, stood side by side at a grave singing a funeral song that returned to Africa two hundred years after traveling to America with an enslaved Mende woman. Moran learned the "A Wa Ka" song from her mother, Amelia Dawley; in 1932, Lorenzo Dow Turner recorded Dawley singing it. In the 1990s, scholars Joseph Opala, Cynthia Schmidt, and Tazieff Koroma discovered the recording at the Archives of Traditional Music at Indiana University and brought the two women together. An elder at the African village summed up the momentous occasion by quoting an ancient proverb: "You can identify a person's tribe by the language they cry in." —AMA

ART OF NECESSITY

Art can flourish in spite of hard times and scant leisure. The 1940 US census describes Ada Chitwood Jones (1903–97) of Fyffe, Alabama, as a wife, farm laborer, and unpaid family worker. Her schooling did not go beyond the eighth grade. Married at sixteen, she and her husband, James, owned their farm and worked it themselves. She was also an accomplished quilt maker, and among her many original designs were quilts made from machine-knitted sock tops. The quilt shown here, made in 1934, is backed with a printed cotton fabric that the Agricultural Extension Office in Auburn, Alabama, distributed to farm women as part of a New Deal self-help program during the depths of the Depression. The filling is a batt of cotton fiber from the family farm. Ada's sister-in-law supplied Ada with hundreds of sock tops, discarded from the showroom of her employer in Fort Payne, Alabama, the "Sock Capital of the World." From these castoffs Ada fashioned bedcovers that were both utilitarian and creative. —VE AND MCS

Women Warriors Breaking Boundaries

❖ DISPLAYING VALOR AND LEADERSHIP IN THE MILITARY

WEARING THE UNIFORM below, Major Rhonda Cornum stepped off a plane on March 6, 1991, on being released from Iraqi captivity. A prisoner of war for a week during the Persian Gulf War, Major Cornum had broken both arms, smashed her knee, and taken a bullet when her helicopter was gunned down. She continued in service, retiring twenty-one years later as a brigadier general.

Indomitable women have long been vital in the United States military, though gender limited their contribution for years. During the Revolutionary War, women supported troops as nurses and cooks, but in World War I, they began serving in uniformed auxiliaries, as thirteen thousand women joined the navy and the Marine Corps. Female troops enlisted for different reasons: economic advantages, a path to higher education, a steady career, patriotism, and the opportunity to prove their strength.

During World War II, 350,000 women joined the military as full members, serving in each branch and showing their mettle. President Harry S. Truman signed the Women's Armed Services Integration Act into law in 1948, establishing women's permanent presence in the military. When the armed forces moved to an all-volunteer force after the Vietnam War and the end of the draft, even more women began to pursue not only military careers but also parity. In 1976, Congress ordered the integration of the female services into the armed forces. Prestigious military service academies started opening their doors to women such as Jane McKeon, who graduated in 1980 from the United States Military Academy at West Point in the first gender-integrated class.

Still, for decades, women were excluded from ground combat, combat ships, and air combat assignments. In 1993, Congress redefined the combat exclusion, making a quarter of a million jobs available to women, including fighter-pilot training in the United States Air Force. In 2006 and 2007, Major Nicole Malachowski—the first female pilot to fly with the Thunderbirds—wore this bright pink Gentex HGU-55/P protective helmet at more than 140 events.

Since the lifting of the ground combat exclusion in 2013, which opened all assignments and training opportunities to women, American women have become four-star generals and admirals, infantry officers, fighter pilots, carrier strike group commanders, and Army Rangers. Nearly forty thousand women mobilized for the Gulf War, over four times more than in Vietnam; many were wives and mothers, which sparked public debate. Women entered new combat roles during the Iraq and Afghanistan wars, earning valor awards for combat actions. Today, women continue breaking new barriers in the military, setting examples of what all women can do for their teammates, their country, and themselves. ■

—MSL AND KAG

Major Nicole "FiFi" Malachowski, the first female pilot selected to fly with the Thunderbirds, wore this helmet while performing during the 2006–2007 flying season. Thunderbirds demonstrations highlight the skills and training of the US Air Force. —AS

Opposite: Major Rhonda Cornum, a flight surgeon, was captured during the Gulf War while attempting to aid a downed fighter pilot. This is the POW uniform she wore upon her release, including the slings for her broken arms.

Opposite: In the 2013 presidential inaugural parade, Mitchelene BigMan (Crow/Hidatsa) wore this jingle dress (powwow dress) with military patches representing her status as a Native American woman, US Army veteran, and founding president of Native American Women Warriors. —*RHT*

Above: This graduation ring belonged to Second Lieutenant Emily Jazmin Tatum Perez, who has the heartbreaking distinction of being both the highest-ranking black female cadet in West Point history and the first black female officer in US history to die in combat.

Right: Jane (Perkins) McKeon wore this West Point cadet dress uniform coat in 1980, the year her class became the first class in the history of the United States Military Academy at West Point to graduate women.

Below: Admiral Michelle Howard proudly wore this naval dress cap when she became the first African American woman to command a US Navy ship, the USS *Rushmore*, in 1999. —*LEM*

Sylvia Rivera (center) sits with her partner, Julia Murray (right), and friend Christina Hayworth in New York City's Bryant Park in June 2000 at the Saturday rally before the next day's gay pride parade.

Tireless Transgender Advocate

❖ **A LIFELONG CRUSADER FOR TRANS RIGHTS**

A FORERUNNER IN THE FIGHT against gender identity discrimination, Sylvia Rivera (1951–2002) walked New York's Times Square district as a transgender sex worker after being cast out by her grandmother at just eleven years old. On the night of June 28, 1969, as riots broke out during a police raid at the Stonewall Inn, seventeen-year-old Rivera reportedly said to her lover, "I'm not missing a minute of this. It's the revolution!"

Politicized by this turning point in the modern LGBTQ+ struggle for equality, Rivera campaigned with the Gay Activist Alliance (GAA) in urging the city to enact a nondiscrimination ordinance in housing and employment. But as a trans Latina, Rivera was an outlier among white gay men and lesbian feminists. In 1970, she cofounded the militant group and youth shelter STAR (Street Transvestite Action Revolutionaries) with African American trans activist Marsha P. Johnson (1945–92), providing vulnerable and homeless trans teenagers with food and clothing.

Rejected for years by the LGBTQ+ movement, Rivera was finally embraced in the 1990s as one of its pivotal figures. She died in February 2002, and in January 2003, the New York City Sexual Orientation Non-Discrimination Act she had championed went into effect. ■ —TC

Left: This quilt, featuring the Delta Sigma Theta logo at its center, celebrates the eighty-year anniversary of the sorority's founding.

Bottom, right: These Sigma Ghamma Rho Converse sneakers were worn by member MC Lyte, a pioneering musical artist and the first female rapper to achieve a gold record.

Bottom, left: The pin for the diamond anniversary of the Alpha Kappa Alpha sorority includes ivy leaves, which symbolize strength, endurance, and lasting friendship.

Symbols of Sisterhood

▸ FINDING SOLIDARITY AND SELF-SUFFICIENCY THROUGH BLACK SORORITIES

In the jim crow era, Ethel Hedgeman (1887–1950), a young coed at Howard University in Washington, DC, helped form Alpha Kappa Alpha, the first sorority founded by and for African American women. The sorority celebrated its seventy-five-year diamond anniversary in 1983 with this commemorative gold pin.

Amid societal hostility, black Greek letter organizations fostered self-help, solidarity, and a sense of cultural pride and connectedness on college campuses, helping young women forge life-long bonds through rituals and shared experiences. From 2005 to 2010, Sigma Gamma Rho member and Butler University student MC Lyte wore these customized Converse sneakers, which proudly bear the sorority colors and founding date as if to declare, "We're still here!"

Not just social clubs, sororities have long been committed to community service and uplift through educational, economic, and political projects that reach far beyond campus. Among the symbols in this 2000 quilt from Delta Sigma Theta is the Habitat for Humanity logo, representing a partnership to build homes for those in need in the United States and abroad.

Black sororities continue to thrive today, helping women connect to their past, engage in the present, and look toward a better future. ■ —MGM

A Patriarchy-Smashing Publication

"I'm a woman. I'm a black woman. I'm a poor woman. I'm a fat woman. I'm a middle-aged woman. And I'm on welfare.

"In this country, if you're any one of those things you count less as a human being. If you're all those things, you don't count at all. Except as a statistic.

"I am 45 years old. I have raised six children. There are millions of statistics like me. Some on welfare. Some not. And some, really poor, who don't even know they're entitled to welfare. Not all of them are black. Not at all. In fact, the majority—about two-thirds—of all the poor families in the country are white.

"Welfare's like a traffic accident. It can happen to anybody, but especially it happens to women."

—Johnnie Tillmon, "Welfare Is a Women's Issue," *Ms.* magazine, 1972

When Gloria Steinem and Dorothy Pitman Hughes published *Ms.* magazine as a sample insert in the December 1971 issue of *New York* magazine, they invigorated the feminist movement. In eight days, all three hundred thousand copies were gone. Subscriptions soared and letters poured in from women around the nation. In July 1972, the inaugural issue of *Ms.*—with Wonder Woman on the cover—sold out within days.

With its unflinching editorials on issues such as reproductive health and domestic violence, *Ms.* brought thousands of new feminists into the fold of second-wave feminism. Women of color did not always feel included in the magazine's content, and some feminists felt it was not radical enough; even so, *Ms.* magazine's pioneering efforts paved the way for second- and third-wave feminist magazines, such as *Lilith, Bitch,* and *Bust.* In the Internet age, all four publications continue to encourage women of all ages to smash the patriarchy. ■ —*JAS*

On the July 1972 inaugural issue of *Ms.* magazine, a larger-than-life Wonder Woman towers over an American city, with war-torn Vietnam in the background. This cover made the superhero a women's liberation icon.

Opposite: In 1970, feminist Gloria Steinem and child welfare advocate Dorothy Pitman Hughes joined forces to galvanize grassroots support for women's issues. In this photograph, they signal their solidarity with a raised-fist salute.

1996 Olympics "Summer of the Women"

❖ **HOW TEAM USA'S FEMALE ATHLETES INSPIRED A GENERATION**

Aᴍᴇʀɪᴄᴀɴ ᴡᴏᴍᴇɴ have shared the Olympic spotlight with men since 1900, but in the 1996 Atlanta games, they dominated. That summer, a record-breaking 292 female athletes took the fields, courts, track, and pool by storm, outnumbering men on the 555-member US team and marking the largest number of women to represent a nation in the history of the games.

These female athletes were among the generation raised after Title IX, a law designed to eliminate gender inequality in college education and athletics. When Title IX passed in 1972, only 15 percent of college athletes were women; by 1996, that number had soared above 40 percent.

In 1996, women competed on the soccer field for the first time. Wearing this jersey, Mia Hamm led Team USA on an undefeated run to the gold. The win kicked off an era of triumph—including a celebrated 1999 World Cup victory—and generated an explosion of interest in soccer among girls.

The women's basketball team swept the Olympic tournament, claiming gold and serving as a springboard for a professional women's league. The following year, Rebecca Lobo—whose uniform you see here—helped found the new Women's National Basketball Association.

Before 1996, a number of US women won gold in gymnastics, but in Atlanta, the "Magnificent Seven" became the first US team to reach the championship podium, defeating perennial favorites Russia and Romania. Among the seven, Dominique Dawes became the first black athlete from any country to win gold in gymnastics. Her leotard is preserved in the national collections.

Inspiring generations, the 1996 women of Team USA sparked public conversation surrounding women's expanding role in sports, paving the way for future generations of female athletes and Olympians. ■ —*EWJ*

Stamping Out Breast Cancer

❖ **FUNDING THE FIGHT FOR A CURE**

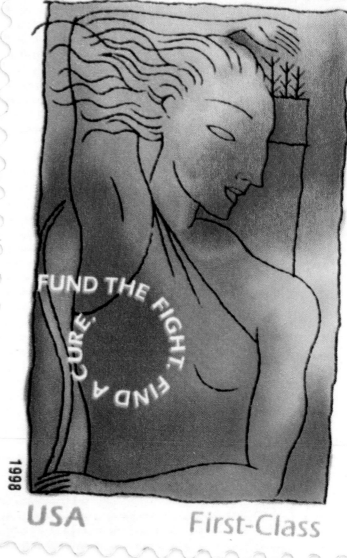

Although the USPS had previously issued stamps promoting breast cancer awareness and screenings, this 1998 stamp—designed by a survivor—was the first to raise funds.

THIS STAMP, designed by a breast cancer survivor, raised millions of dollars for breast cancer research. In the mid-1990s, as health professionals and patients alike began calling for more open, public dialogue on treatment options and long-term care, the *New York Times Magazine* proclaimed breast cancer a "hot charity." Women's health advocates began lobbying the United States Postal Service (USPS) to issue a postage stamp to fund research.

Other countries had been using semipostals (fund-raising stamps) for years, selling them for a few pennies above the regular price and donating the surplus to charity. But the USPS resisted, arguing that it was an inefficient fund-raising strategy that would lead to endless similar requests from worthy causes. Proponents shifted their strategy to Congress and won. In July 1997, the Stamp Out Breast Cancer Act mandated the USPS to issue a breast cancer research semipostal within one year. The charitable revenue was to be split between the National Cancer Institute of the National Institutes of Health and the Breast Cancer Research Program of the Department of Defense.

For the design, the USPS enlisted Ethel Kessler, one of its newest art directors and a breast cancer survivor. Kessler initially drafted designs bearing a pink ribbon—the symbol of breast cancer awareness popularized in the early 1990s. Changing course, she commissioned illustrator Whitney Sherman, who drew an image symbolizing patients' heroic fight. In the finished stamp, a stylized version of Diana, Roman goddess of the hunt, reaches behind her back for an arrow. Surrounding the right breast are the words "Fund the fight. Find a cure."

Issued on July 29, 1998, at a White House ceremony, the stamps sold for forty cents apiece, with eight cents going toward research. They have since been used for more than two decades, making the design the longest-running and best-selling commemorative stamp in US history. In December 2015, after the sale of the one-billionth stamp, the USPS announced that $81 million had been disbursed to NIH and DOD for peer-reviewed, competitively chosen breast cancer research projects. ■ —*DP*

Below: Oprah Winfrey encouraged guests to talk candidly about race, gender, sexuality, and more on this sofa from the Harpo Studios set of *The Oprah Winfrey Show*.

Bottom: This portrait of Oprah by Brigitte Lacombe was taken in 2009, the same year Winfrey announced the show would conclude in 2011, after twenty-five years on air.

In America's Living Room

❖ OPRAH WINFREY AND HER INVITING COUCH GOT PEOPLE TALKING

I N 2005, BARACK OBAMA made an appearance on this leather sectional—one among many iconic moments on *The Oprah Winfrey Show*.

The legendary program dominated daytime television and ran for twenty-five seasons—a total of 4,561 episodes—from September 8, 1986, to May 25, 2011. Millions of viewers from more than 150 countries tuned in weekdays to watch Winfrey dish with celebrities, quiz beauty experts, and console families touched by personal trauma and national tragedy. The highest-rated talk show in history, the program placed into public conversation issues surrounding race and racism, gender roles, and sexuality, while emphasizing women's experiences and perspectives. It provided a platform for people from all walks of life to share their stories.

But it was Winfrey—as host, executive producer, and eventually celebrity brand—who was the charismatic center and driving force of the show's phenomenal success. Winfrey and her production team carefully planned each episode to keep viewers tuning in at four o'clock weekday afternoons. The set of *The Oprah Winfrey Show*, with its tasteful decor and comfortable couch, provided a space for Winfrey to interact with her guests and studio audience. It also served as an idealized extension of television viewers' living rooms, encouraging them to feel as if they were at home with Winfrey.

Born in rural Mississippi, Winfrey knew from an early age she wanted to be a journalist. She started her career in radio during high school and landed a job as a reporter in college. But her love of interacting with people eventually led her away from the news desk and to hosting her own talk show. Today, Oprah Winfrey is—through her various business ventures, television network, and magazine—one of the most influential Americans in modern history. ■ *—RLC*

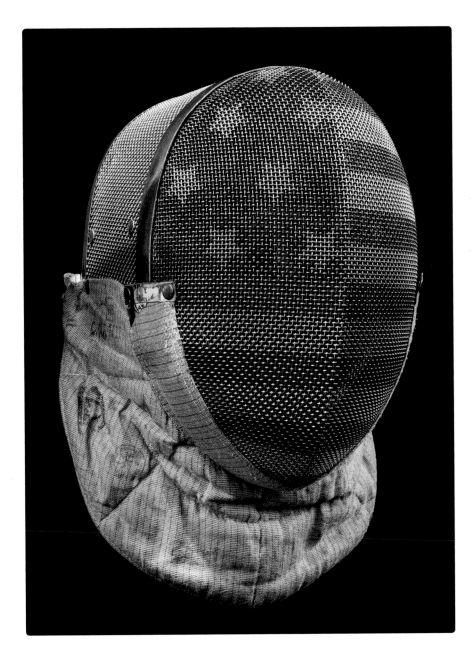

Saber fencer Ibtihaj Muhammad wore this mask adorned with the American flag, a strong patriotic symbol, while earning the bronze team medal at the 2016 Olympic Games.

Olympic Debut in a Hijab

❖ **ENCOURAGING ACCEPTANCE THROUGH SPORT**

For generations, US Olympic athletes have proudly worn the American flag—a symbol of independence, patriotism, and revolution. At the 2016 Rio de Janeiro Olympics, American saber fencer Ibtihaj Muhammad embodied all three qualities. Wearing this mask over her hijab, the traditional head covering of Muslim women, she became the first Muslim American athlete to compete in a headscarf *and* the first Muslim American woman to earn an Olympic medal. "America is all that I know," she later told reporters. "I feel American down to my bones."

Growing up in New Jersey, Muhammad played a variety of sports but ultimately chose fencing because its modest uniform and mask allowed her to honor her Islamic faith. Navigating the exclusive world of fencing proved challenging at times, but now Muhammad empowers others through sports, seeking an end to discrimination through inclusion.

Muhammad is not defined by her religion, but it shapes her narrative. "My skin color, wearing the hijab, being a Muslim and being a woman of color, these things have the power to shape how people treat me within the sport," she said. Her journey continues to inspire a new generation of Muslim women and aspiring athletes. ■ —JR

Science writer Maia Weinstock designed a Women of NASA LEGO® prototype in 2018 and pitched her proposal with the headline "Ladies rock outer space!" The inspiring kit was a hit. The women represented in the prototype are, from left to right, Margaret Hamilton, Katherine Johnson, Sally Ride, Nancy Grace Roman, and Mae Jemison.

Building Blocks That Inspire

❖ IMMORTALIZING NASA WOMEN IN LEGO® MINIFIGURE PROTOTYPES

Science writer and LEGO® enthusiast Maia Weinstock had an idea in 2016: create minifigures (called "minifigs" by fans) celebrating notable NASA women. "I didn't want this set to focus solely on space travelers," she later explained. "I designed it to . . . recognize some of the women who've been underappreciated for their critical work behind the scenes as computer scientists, as mathematicians, as engineers, and more."

Weinstock built her prototypes by "kit bashing," combining existing bricks with altered or custom-made ones. For a finishing touch, she posed her creations in LEGO® stages depicting historic moments based on well-known photographs. MIT's Margaret Hamilton, who developed the onboard flight software for Apollo lunar missions, stood beside tall stacks of code. Mathematician and NASA human computer Katherine Johnson, famously depicted in the 2016 movie *Hidden Figures*, worked at her desk. Trailblazing astronomer Nancy Grace Roman (1925–2018), considered the mother of the Hubble Space Telescope, was shown next to a miniature version of that astronomical instrument. A Space Shuttle orbiter accompanied two storied NASA astronauts: Sally K. Ride (1951–2012), the first American woman in space, and Mae Jemison, the first African American woman in space.

That summer, Weinstock posted images of her prototypes on the LEGO® Ideas website, where the company hosts a competition for possible new products. Propelled by social media and online articles, Weinstock's idea reached the required ten thousand votes in less than two weeks. LEGO® accepted her proposal, and she helped its designers create the 231-piece commercially available set (Johnson declined to participate in the final kit). Within its first twenty-four hours on Amazon.com in November 2017, the Women of NASA set became the site's best-selling toy. At the LEGO® store in Manhattan, customers lined up out the door for the kit's first day of sale.

"I certainly hope all kids can see from this set that women have been a part of the space program for a long time, and will continue to be," Weinstock told Space.com. She added that she hoped the toys would spark interest among girls in pursuing careers with NASA. ∎ —*MW*

Immortalized in Medicine and Canvas

❖ THE CONTROVERSIAL, LIFESAVING LEGACY OF HENRIETTA LACKS

THE RADIANT WOMAN in this portrait saved countless lives—without ever knowing it. Born into a family of impoverished tobacco farmers, Henrietta Lacks (1920–51) had an immense global impact on medicine, although her controversial story was ignored, hidden, falsified, and left untold for decades.

Raised in rural Virginia, Lacks was descended from enslaved individuals. After her mother died, Lacks's grandfather raised her on the family farm, where she worked in the tobacco fields with her cousins. She had her first child at fourteen, and a second before marrying their father, David "Day" Lacks, in 1940. During World War II, the family moved to Turner Station, Maryland, so Day could work at the United States Steel Sparrows Point mill.

In March 1951, after the birth of her fifth child, Lacks went to Johns Hopkins Hospital complaining of a "knot" on her womb. She was diagnosed with cervical cancer. Despite receiving standard radium treatments, she died at thirty-one.

While Lacks was alive, a surgeon removed a tissue sample from the tumor in her cervix without requesting permission or even informing Lacks—a common but not universal practice at the time—and delivered it to the laboratory of Dr. George Gey, a cancer researcher at Johns Hopkins. Gey was a leader in the decades-long effort to cultivate a line of living cells for experimental uses. Unexpectedly and for reasons scientists still don't fully understand, Lacks's cells survived and even thrived, duplicating themselves at an astonishing rate. Soon, samples were being distributed to laboratories around the world.

Named HeLa for the first two letters of Lacks's given name and surname, the cells were dubbed the first "immortal" cell line available for medical research. They've been used in research ever since, aiding more than seventeen thousand patents in treatments for conditions ranging from polio and Parkinson's disease to AIDS, hemophilia, and infertility.

Researchers were curious about the source of these immortal cells, but Gey's laboratory and its successors provided fictional names. Lacks's true identity remained unknown until her name appeared in a 1971 tribute to Gey in the journal *Obstetrics & Gynecology*.

Soon after, doctors at Johns Hopkins asked Lacks's children to participate in medical tests, though they were confused and angry about their mother's legacy. While others benefitted from HeLa cells, the Lackses—who lived in poverty—were unable to afford medical insurance and first-rate care. Meanwhile, Lacks's medical records and familial genetic information were made public without the family's permission. Although standards in biomedical ethics and privacy have since improved, the Lacks family was deeply shortchanged.

Lacks's story is part of a centuries-long history of medical experimentation on African Americans, enslaved and free, without their consent or knowledge. Only with the 2010 publication of Rebecca Skloot's revelatory book, *The Immortal Life of Henrietta Lacks*, did Lacks's story come to widespread public attention. In a conciliatory gesture, the university has included the Lacks family in a committee overseeing the uses of HeLa cells and has named in her honor two medical symposia, a scholarship, and a building.

Henrietta Lacks (HeLa): The Mother of Modern Medicine, this 2017 portrait by Kadir Nelson, commemorates Lacks's life and legacy. The gold-and-blue "flower of life" motif on the wallpaper represents immortality; the geometric figures on her dress echo the structure of cells; and the two missing buttons from her deep red dress symbolize the cells removed from her body without consent. ■ —*WSP AND DM*

Leading up to HBO's 2017 film about Lacks's "immortal cells," the network commissioned artist Kadir Nelson (1974–) to paint this portrait, *Henrietta Lacks (HeLa): The Mother of Modern Medicine.*

Coming of Age, Latina Style

❖ **A DRESS, A TRADITION, AND THE TRANSITION TO SEÑORITA**

I N THE EMBROIDERED stems and flowers on this resplendent dress, Chicagoan Natalia Flores saw a metaphor: a self reaching for the future while remaining firmly rooted in tradition. The gown seemed the perfect option for her quinceañera (or simply quince), a coming-of-age celebration held throughout Latin America and Latinx communities. Part birthday party and part religious rite of passage, the event marks the symbolic moment when a fifteen-year-old Latina becomes a young woman.

Quinceañera ceremonies typically begin at a Catholic church, with a blessing attended by close family and friends. Beforehand, girls take mandatory preparation classes on faith, church, and sacraments. After the ceremony, the elegant *niña* heads to a jubilant reception rich in symbolism. She is crowned with a tiara, receives the gift of her last doll, and dances with her father or father figure. After the formalities, the teens take over, dancing to Mexican and American music, sometimes performing choreographed dances. As the tradition evolves, new generations are shaping quinces on their own terms.

Quinceañera celebrations vary from the frugal to the extravagant. Flores's mother hails from Guanajuato, Mexico; as she never had a quince, her daughter's celebration was particularly monumental.

When asked if Natalia would hold a quince for her own future daughters, she said, "I want to apply what my parents have taught me and keep my quinceañera tradition with my family, regardless if my kids are mixed or full-blooded Latinos. I want this tradition to keep on going, and not just die off."

In a society where some Latinx people suffer from discrimination, the quince reinforces cultural traditions. It brings Latinx families and friends together to send girls confidently into womanhood with strong social and economic networks. The dress is a central element of the tradition. This one grounds Natalia in both her Mexican roots and her Latin American community, helping her carve out an identity uniquely her own. ■ —*LSV*

In 2006, Chicagoan Natalia Flores wore this gown for her quinceañera, a celebration of her fifteenth birthday. The dress is an important element of this Latina tradition, one that binds culture and generations.

Michelle LaVaughn Robinson Obama, 2018. Artist Amy Sherald and Michelle Obama are deeply committed to ensuring that girls of color see themselves on the walls of national museums.

The Power of a Portrait

PAINTING PROGRESS, EMPOWERMENT, AND STRONG FEMALE LEADERSHIP

THIS ICONIC 2018 portrait immortalizes both a woman and a watershed moment. Michelle Obama became the first African American first lady in 2009. When selecting an artist for her official portrait, she chose Amy Sherald, who, in 2016, became the first woman *and* the first African American artist to win the National Portrait Gallery's prestigious Outwin Boochever Portrait Competition. Painting this dress, Sherald referenced quilts sewn by the Gee's Bend quilt makers—generations of African American women who descended from enslaved people in Alabama.

Born in 1964, Michelle Robinson grew up on Chicago's South Side with parents who raised her to be outspoken and unafraid. After earning degrees from Princeton and Harvard Law School, she joined Sidley Austin LLP in Chicago, where she met the man who would become her husband—and the country's first African American president. Wanting to improve her community, she left the firm in the mid-1990s and began a career in public service. During Barack Obama's two presidential campaigns, she spoke passionately about her family's commitment to serve. As first lady, she fought for women's rights, LBGTQ+ rights, children's health, and military families.

In a *New York Times* interview, Sherald described Obama as someone "women can relate to—no matter what shape, size, race, or color. We see our best selves in her." ■ —DM

Antiracist Activism

❖ **ONE WOMAN'S SOCIAL MEDIA POST SPARKS A GLOBAL MOVEMENT**

IN FEBRUARY 2012, a seventeen-year-old African American child named Trayvon Martin (1995–2012) was shot and killed by a neighborhood watchman in Sanford, Florida. His shooter, George Zimmerman, was acquitted a year later. In response, Alicia Garza, a gender rights activist based in Oakland, California, shared her heartbreak and outrage through social media. She ended her post by saying, "Our lives matter." The post would plant the seeds for a contemporary social justice movement.

Patrice Cullors, another activist and colleague, shared Garza's post, adding the following hashtag: #BlackLivesMatter. Immigration-rights advocate Opal Tometi leveraged the power of social media to connect #BlackLivesMatter with other online communities. The hashtag went viral, and a movement was born.

Following the deaths of Michael Brown (1996–2014), Tamir Rice (2002–14), Eric Garner (1970–2014), Sandra Bland (1987–2015), and other African Americans in subsequent years, the Black Lives Matter (BLM) movement quickly expanded as activists organized around the organization. Known for driving conversations on discrimination and violence against marginalized people and communities, BLM now has more than forty chapters around the world.

In 2015, a demonstrator held this Black Lives Matter sign in Baltimore, Maryland, during a rally organized by the People's Power Assembly to protest the death of twenty-five-year-old Freddie Gray (1990–2015), who died in police custody. Writer and activist Rahiel Tesfamariam wore the muscle shirt in Saint Louis, Missouri, during a 2015 rally commemorating the one-year anniversary of Michael Brown's death in a shooting by a white police officer.

Throughout history, men have typically led large, highly visible social justice movements, whereas women's contributions have too often been overlooked and undervalued.

#BlackLivesMatter serves as a reminder that throughout US history—from abolition and antilynching movements to voting rights, civil rights, and present-day struggles against inequality—women have taken the lead in social progress and change. ■ —*AEB*

The back of this shirt (below) reads "Hands Up United," which is the name of the group that helped organize the 2015 rally commemorating the shooting of unarmed teenager Michael Brown, where this sign (above) was also used.

Drawing inspiration from the official pattern, the non-knitter who wore this peachy-pink crocheted pussyhat gave it more prominent ears and an opening in the top for her ponytail.

Pussy(hat) Power

❖ FROM SEXUAL SLANG TO SYMBOL OF FEMALE EMPOWERMENT

O N JANUARY 21, 2017, the National Mall in Washington, DC, was awash in pink. Protesters wearing handmade "pussyhats" in shades ranging from magenta to peach overflowed the space occupied the day before by revelers in red "Make America Great Again" caps. Held the day after the presidential inauguration, the Women's March on Washington was born of the anger and frustration felt by many women following the 2016 presidential campaign and election.

In the words of the Women's March website, women and their allies came together to "harness the political power of diverse women and their communities to create transformative social change." The pussyhat became the march's ubiquitous symbol.

The original concept was the brainchild of artists and feminists Jayna Zweiman and Krista Suh. They conceived of the hats in response to obscene comments made by Donald Trump about grabbing women, which had surfaced during his 2016 presidential campaign. The official pussyhat pattern was designed by Kat Coyle—Zweiman's and Suh's knitting teacher—and distributed by the Pussyhat Project. The hat's name, cat-eared design, and pink color were meant to reclaim the word *pussy*, transforming it from derogatory slang for female genitalia to a term of female empowerment.

Handmade by women across the country, the hats brought people together, harkening back to long traditions of female crafting and knitting circles. Some who could not attend a march contributed instead by crafting hats for those who lacked the time or skill. The hat pictured here was worn by an off-duty Smithsonian staffer attending the march.

As quickly as the pussyhat gained popularity as a unifying symbol, it became a source of tension. Some were concerned that the visual of the hat was not as inclusive as the movement itself. Did it privilege white, cisgender women and exclude women of color, transgender women, and nonbinary people? While planning anniversary marches for 2018, some organizers encouraged participants to find alternative headgear. As with all evocative symbols, the meaning of a pussyhat depends on who is wearing it, who is looking at it, and who is interpreting it. ■ —BB AND LKG

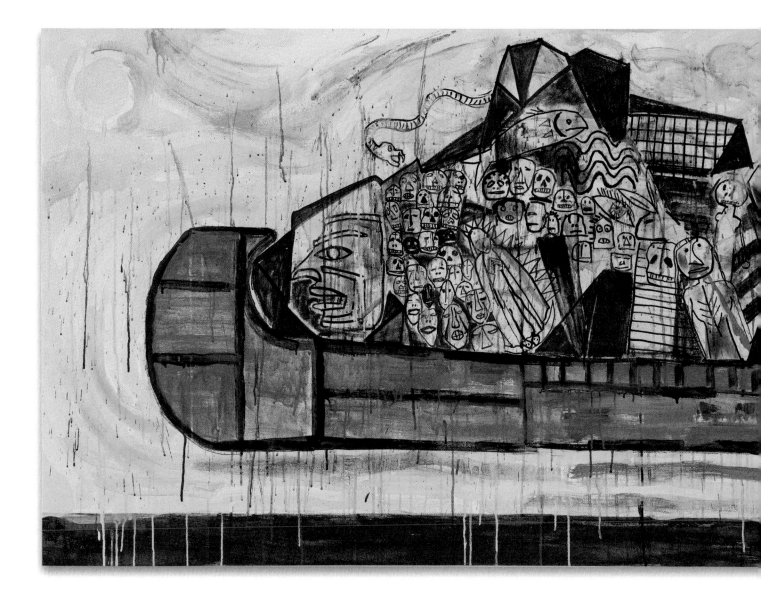

Adrift, but Not without Hope

❖ **USING ART TO ADVOCATE FOR NATIVE AMERICANS AND OTHER DISPLACED PEOPLES**

I N *TRADE CANOE: ADRIFT*, Syrian men, women, and children are crowded together in a canoe adrift on the Mediterranean Sea. The boat has stalled under several swirling, hot suns, adding to the passengers' desperation as they flee their homeland. Native American artist Jaune Quick-to-See Smith empathizes with the refugees' plight; her people have been displaced, too.

A self-described cultural arts worker and activist, Smith is a member of the Confederated Salish and Kootenai Tribes. Of Flathead Salish, Cree, and Shoshone ancestry, she is also a writer, lecturer, and organizer. Smith is known for politically charged paintings and mixed media works that address social injustice—especially issues impacting the Indigenous peoples of North America—and she vocally advocates for other Indigenous artists to be included in the American art canon.

Jaune Quick-to-See Smith's *Trade Canoe: Adrift* (2015) calls to attention the suffering of peoples forced to leave their homelands.

While a graduate student at the University of New Mexico in the 1970s, Smith founded the Grey Canyon group of Native American contemporary artists, who exhibited their work locally, nationally, and internationally. She curated a number of significant contemporary Native American art exhibitions in the 1980s and 1990s, promoting and including works by young Native American artists.

In her art, Smith confronts painful subjects with a sharp sense of humor. In 1992, while Americans planned five-hundred-year anniversary celebrations in honor of Columbus's arrival, Smith got out her paintbrushes and started her *Trade Canoe* series. In *Trade: Gifts for Trading Land with White People* (1992) and other works in this provocative series, Smith layers images, paint, and objects to suggest the complex layers of history involved in tribal land colonization, exploitation of goods, environmental destruction, climate change, and other issues.

Native American symbolism is prevalent in *Trade Canoe: Adrift*, suggesting solidarity with the plight of persecuted Syrian populations—and growing international refugee populations everywhere. The canoe has Salish design elements and holds carved wooden masks and a salmon leaping out of a stream, referencing the struggle to gain federal recognition and fishing rights for survival by the Duwamish Coast Salish. Below the stream is Nanabozho, the Cree and Ojibwe trickster rabbit who is said to have invented fishing. But amid the scene of chaos and suffering, there may yet be a glimmer of hope. Near the center of the canoe, a small, radiating heart suggests the possibility that love and compassion might still prevail. ■ —*RHT*

Museum Acronym Key

AAA	**Archives of American Art**
ACM	**Anacostia Community Museum**
CFCH	**Center for Folklife and Cultural Heritage**
CHSDM	**Cooper Hewitt, Smithsonian Design Museum**
HMSG	**Hirshhorn Museum and Sculpture Garden**
NASM	**National Air and Space Museum**
NMAH	**National Museum of American History**
NMAI	**National Museum of the American Indian**
NMAAHC	**National Museum of African American History and Culture**
NPG	**National Portrait Gallery**
NPM	**National Postal Museum**
SAAM	**Smithsonian American Art Museum**
SFW	**Smithsonian Folkways Records**
SG	**Smithsonian Gardens**
SIA	**Smithsonian Institution Archives**
SL	**Smithsonian Libraries**

2: NASM, 9A12598; 4*l*: NPM, 2005.2012.20, © United States Postal Service. All rights reserved; 4*m*: NMAH, ET.014971; 4*r*: NMAH, 1982.0288.01; 5*l*: NASM, 2009-7951, Gift of the Franklin Institute; 5*m*: NMAAHC, 2016.126; 5*r*: NPG, NPG.2016.78, © 1994, Alexis Rodriguez-Duarte, acquisition made possible through the Smithsonian Latino Initiatives Pool, administered by the Smithsonian Latino Center; 8: NPG, NPG.2004.25, © 2019 Faith Ringgold / Artists Rights Society (ARS), New York, Courtesy ACA Galleries, New York; 11: HMSG, 14.9.8, Guerilla Girls, *Dearest Art Collector (from Portfolio Compleat: 1985–2012), 1986*, offset lithograph, 21 7/8 × 16 3/4 in. (55.6 × 42.5 cm), Joseph H. Hirshhorn Purchase Fund, 2014, © *Guerrilla Girls*; 13: NMAH, 69.236.103; 14–15: CHSDM, 236409; 17*t*: SIA, 1983.0159.03; 17*b*: NPM, 2005.2012.20, © United States Postal Service. All rights reserved; 18*tl*: SFW, FW02457, © Smithsonian Folkways Recordings; 18*tr*: SFW, FW02468, © Smithsonian Folkways Recordings; 18*bl*: SFW, FW45045, © Smithsonian Folkways Recordings; 18*br*: SFW, FW40065, © Smithsonian Folkways Recordings; 20, 22 (detail): NMAI, 00/9469; 23*t*: CHSDM, 1941-69-243, bequest of Mrs. Henry E. Coe; 23*tr*: SAAM, 1999.27.82; 23*m*: NMAH, 2013.0157.036; 23*bl*: NMAAHC, 2012.40; 23*b*: NMAAHC, 2017.30.48, Collection of the Smithsonian National Museum of African American History and Culture shared with the Library of Congress; 25: NMAI, 17/4161; 26: NPG, NPG.72.65; 28: NPG, NPG.91.152, Partial gift with funding from the Smithsonian

Collections Acquisitions Program and the Governor's Mansion Foundation of Maryland; 29: NMAH, 1985.0849.01; 30: NMAH, 388220, gift of Dr. and Mrs. Arthur M. Greenwood; 31: NMAH, 64.545, gift of Alexander B. C. Mulholland; 32–33: NMAH, 2001.0253, gift of Julia Child; 34: SAAM, 2008.21.7, museum purchase made possible by the Ford Motor Company, © 1975, Martha Rosler, courtesy of the artist and Mitchell-Innes & Nash, New York; 35*l*: NMAAHC, 2014.218.1, gift of Dooky Chase's Restaurant and Chef Leah Chase; 35*r*: NPG, NPG.2011.144, © Gustave Blache III, gift of the artist in honor of Mr. Richard C. Colton Jr.; 36: SAAM, 1986.65.113, gift of Herbert Waide Hemphill Jr. and museum purchase made possible by Ralph Cross Johnson; 38: NMAI, 24/2011; 39: NMAH, 2008.0159.01; 40: NMAAHC, 2008.14, © Catlett Mora Family Trust/Licensed by VAGA at Artists Rights Society (ARS), NY; 41: NMAAHC, 2012.46.46; 42–43: NMAH, TE.T11197.000; 45: NMAAHC, 2009.47.1, gift of Candace Green; 46: NMAAHC, 2014.312.5, gift of Oprah Winfrey; 47: NMAAHC, 2012.46.11; 48: NPG, NPG.2009.32; 49: NMAH, 2013.0193.04; 50: NMAAHC, 2009.50.39, gift of Charles L. Blockson; 51: NMAAHC, 2017.30.47, Collection of the Smithsonian National Museum of African American History and Culture shared with the Library of Congress; 53: NPG, NPG.68.1; 54: NMAH, ZZ.RSN80846W40; 55*l*: NMAH, 1977.0564.01; 55*r*: NMAH, 310679.01; 56: NMAH, 323566; 57: NMAH, 2009.0212.01, Paul Neely; 58: NMAH, ET.014971; 59: NMAH, 1983.0853.01, gift of Ida M. Savoy Anderson; 60: NMAH, 335239, Phillips Brooks Keller & Mrs. Gordon Erwin; 62: NMAH, 335239, Phillips Brooks Keller & Mrs. Gordon Erwin; 63*t*: NMAH, PL.026168; 63*tm*: NPG, NPG.72.13, purchased through generous contributions to the Victor Proetz Memorial Fund; 63*bl*: NMAH, PL.242991.057; 63*br*: NPG, NPG.96.204, gift of Margaret Sanger Lampe and Nancy Sanger Pallesen, granddaughters of Margaret Sanger; 63*b*:NASM, 99-15415; 64–65: NMAH, 1983.0618.01; 66: SAAM, 1994.17; 67: NMAI, 25/2192; 68–69: NMAH, 1982.0288.01; 70: NPM, 1984.1128.333.1-21; 71: *from left to right:* NMAI, 18/8227, 24/6949, 22/1927, 24/4103, 24/6951; 72–73: AAA, (DSI-AAA)7664; 73*l*: AAA, (DSI-AAA)8588; 73*r*: AAA, (DSI-AAA)10311; 75: NPG, NPG.2009.36; 76: SAAM, 1911.2.1, gift of William T. Evans; 77: NMAAHC, 2014.37.14; 78: SL, DU627.2.L72X; 79: NPG, NPG.80.320, gift of the Bernice Pauahi Bishop Museum; 80: NMAH, 2009.0207.01, gift of Martin Louthan; 80–81: NMAH, 323503.01; 82: NMAAHC, 2011.57.14; 83: NMAAHC, TA2017.13.10.2, gift of Ray and Jean Langston in memory of Mary Church and Robert Terrell; 84: NMAH, 2010-01243; 85: NMAAHC, 2010.2.2a-d; 86–87: NMAH, 2008-5260; 87*t*: NMAH, PL.033280.A; 87*b*: NMAH, 2017.0093.01; 88: NMAH and SIA, PL.227739.1886.V03; 88*tr*: NMAH, 227739.1960.B10; 88*b*: NMAH, 2018.0242.001; 89*t*: NMAH, PL.055862; 89*m*: NMAH, 1991.0121.01, Barbara P. Bush; 89: *from left to right:* NMAH, 1982.0624.03, 1982.0624.09, 1982.0624.10, 1982.0624.11, 1982.0624.13, 1982.0624.14, 1982.0624.18, 1982.0624.19; 90: NMAH, 1998.0165.83.01, gift of the Navy Department through The National Society of the Colonial Dames of America; 91: CHSDM, 1980-32-1186; 92*l*: NMAH, 2014.0315.03, gift of Edith R. Gima; 92*r*: NMAH, 2009-24926; 93*l*: SIA, SIA2008-4909; 93*ml*:

SIA, SIA2010-1082; 93*mr*: SIA, SIA2008-3576; 93*r*: SIA, SIA2008-5689; 94*t*: NMAAHC, 2009.9.2; 94*b*: NMAAHC, 2011.59.17, gift of Linda Crichlow White in honor of her aunt, Edna Stevens McIntyre; 95: NMAAHC, 2013.153.2.1, gift of A'Lelia Bundles / Madam Walker Family Archives; 96: NPG, NPG.73.5, gift of the Girl Scouts of the United States of America; 97: NMAH, 1977.0881.01; 98: NMAH, MG.M-00545.01; 99: NMAH, 1986.0434.04; 100–101: NASM, NASM 92-13721; 101*t*: NASM, NASM 84-18035; 101*b*: NPM, 2018.2002.1; 102: NMAH Archives Center, Scurlock Studio Records 0618; 104: NMAAHC, 2014.27.2, gift of Ginette DePreist in memory of James DePreist; 105*t*: NPM, 2001.2010.47, © United States Postal Service. All rights reserved; 105*tr*: NMAH Archives Center, image #: AC0618-004-0000287, AC0618 Scurlock; 105*m*: NMAAHC, 2014.315ab; 105*bl*: NMAH, 1996.3034.11383; 105*b*: NMAH, 1983.0183.01; 107: SG, AAG.GCA, Item NY076006; 108–109: SG, AAG.GCA, Item MA353004; 110: NMAH, 1978.0845, gift of Edith M. Lawall; 111*l*: ACM, acma PH2003.7063.033, Evans-Tibbs Family Papers, gift of the Estate of Thurlow E. Tibbs Jr; 111*r*: ACM, 2002.5001.0001a-b; 112: HMSG, 89.17, Louise Bourgeois, *The Blind Leading the Blind*, 1947-1949, wood and paint, 70 3/8 x 96 7/8 x 17 3/8 in. (178.7 x 246.1 x 44.1 cm), Regents Collections Acquisition Program with Matching Funds from the Jerome L. Greene, Agnes Gund, Sydney and Frances Lewis, and Leonard C. Yaseen Purchase Fund, 1989; 113: CHSDM, 1994-55-1-ab, gift of Belle Kogan; 114–115: SIA, SIA2009-4223 and SIA2009-4227 and Chase 1847; 115*t*: NMNH, US National Herbarium Sheet 732184; 115*b*: NMNH, Chase 6730; 116: NPG, NPG.2006.70, acquired through the generosity of the Honorable Anthony Beilenson in honor of his wife Dolores; 117: SAAM, 1998.161, purchase through the Smithsonian Institution Collections Acquisition Program, © 1991, Amalia Mesa-Bains; 118–119: NASM, 2009-7951; 119: NPG, NPG.75.82, gift of Edith A. Scott; 120*t*: NASM, NASM 2011-00632; 120*bl*: NASM, NASM2005-52-01; 120*br*: NPM, 0.279483.3; 121: NPM, 0.279483.1.18.1; 122: SAAM, 1995.3.1, gift of the Georgia O'Keeffe Foundation; 123: SAAM, 1984.150, gift of John Young; 124: NASM, NASM2015-05056; 125*t*: NMAI, P07128; 125*b*: NMAI, 21/3256; 126: NMAH, EM.333610; 127: NMAH, 2006.0236.03; 128: NMAH, PL.256405.01; 129: NPG, NPG.99.41; 130: NMAAHC, 2014.63.81a-d; 131*t*: NASM, A19710163000cp05; 131*m*: NASM, A19951204000, © Disney; 131*b*: NASM, NASM 2011-2504; 132: NMAH, 1985.0851.05; 134: NMAH, AP1. L722; 135: NMAH, 1985.0481.002, gift of Sidney Glaser; 136*l*: NMAH, 2011.0164.02; 136*r*: NMAH Archives Center, Gottlieb and Bodansky Family Papers 1245; 137*l*: AAA, (DSI-AAA)6246, A watercolor titled *Tanforan*, ca. 1942-44. Bob Stocksdale and Kay Sekimachi Papers; 137*r*: AAA, (DSI-AAA)21097, United States War Relocation Authority indefinite leave card for Kay Sekimachi, August 7, 1944. Bob Stocksdale and Kay Sekimachi Papers; 138: NPG, NPG.2018.31; 139: NPG, NPG.99.45, © Nickolas Muray Photo Archives; 141: NMAH, PL.044042, The Kiplinger Washington Agency; 142*t*: NMAH, 1977.0208.01; 142*tl*: NMAH, PL.227739.1968.B30, gift of Ralph E. Becker; 142*bl*: NMAH, 2010.0184.01; 142*b*: NMAAHC, 2014.167.3, gifted with pride from Ellen Brooks; 143*l*: NMAH, 1986.0540.16; 143*tr*: NMAH, 2017.0135.02; 143*br*:

Italicized page numbers indicate images and captions.

❖ **Smithsonian Books gratefully acknowledges the Smithsonian Women's Committee and the Smithsonian American Women's History Initiative for their generous support of this publication.**

DONORS

BECAUSE OF
HER
STORY

Smithsonian

19th Amendment Society

Mary and David Boies

The Case Foundation

Dick and Betsy DeVos Family Foundation

Ford Foundation

Bill & Melinda Gates Foundation

David M. Rubenstein

Elaine P. Wynn & Family Foundation

Lead Donors

Acton Family Giving

Major Sponsors

Booz Allen Hamilton

First Century Leaders

Melissa and Trevor Fetter

Sakurako, Remy, Rose and Jess Fisher

Julie and Greg Flynn

Rick and Susan Goings Foundation

HISTORY/A+E Networks

Mrs. Kathleen K. Manatt and Michele A. Manatt

Sue Payne

Christine and William Ragland

Alison Wrigley Rusack

Deborah Sara Santana

Smithsonian Women's Committee

Written by Smithsonian Contributors as listed on page 6

Note from the Smithsonian American Women's History Initiative by John Davis and Stephanie Stebich

Foreword by Jill Lepore

Introduction by Michelle Delaney

Timelines by Jennifer Schneider

Smithsonian Editorial Committee

Chair: Michelle Delaney

Project Leaders: Nancy Bercaw, Lisa Kathleen Graddy, Matthew Shindell, Margaret Weitekamp

Members: Daina Bouquin, Ariana Curtis, Brandon Fortune, Cécile R. Ganteaume, Saisha Grayson, Sandy Guttman, Evelyn Hankins, Lynn Heidelbaugh, Pamela Henson, Catrina Hill, Melissa Ho, Meredith Holmgren, Betsy Johnson, Jennifer Jones, Kate Lemay, Katherine Ott, Harry Rubenstein, Emily D. Shapiro, Ann Shumard, Michelle Wilkinson

Project Manager: Jennifer Schneider

Published by Smithsonian Books

Director: Carolyn Gleason

Creative Director: Jody Billert

Senior Editor: Christina Wiginton

Editorial Assistants: Duke Johns and Jaime Schwender

Edited by Victoria Pope and Christine Schrum

Supplemental expert review by Bonnie J. Morris

Designed by David Griffin, D Griffin Studio, Inc.

Design assistant: Trish Dorsey

This book may be purchased for educational, business, or sales promotional use.

For information, please write: Special Markets Department, Smithsonian Books, P.O. Box 37012, MRC 513, Washington, DC 20013

Library of Congress Cataloging-in-Publication Data

Names: Pope, Victoria, and Christine Schrum, editors. | Smithsonian Institution, issuing body.

Title: Smithsonian American Women : Remarkable Objects and Stories of Strength, Ingenuity, and Vision from the National Collection / Smithsonian Institution ; edited by Victoria Pope and Christine Schrum.

Description: Washington, DC : Smithsonian Books, [2019] | Includes index.

Identifiers: LCCN 2019002217 | ISBN 9781588346650 (hardcover)

Subjects: LCSH: Women--United States--History--Exhibitions. | Women--United States--History--Sources. | Smithsonian Institution--Exhibitions.

Classification: LCC HQ1410 .S626 2019 | DDC 305.40973--dc23 LC record available at https://lccn.loc.gov/2019002217

Manufactured in the United States of America

23 22 21 20 19 5 4 3 2 1

For permission to reproduce illustrations appearing in this book, please correspond directly with the museums as listed on pages 240–241. Smithsonian Books does not retain reproduction rights for these images individually, or maintain a file of addresses for sources.